FROM THE FOREST
TO THE BATTLEFIELD

FORTY CIVILIAN CONSERVATION CORPS MEMBERS

WHO WERE AWARDED THE MEDAL OF HONOR

DURING WORLD WAR II

First Edition

ISBN-13: 978-1546906384
ISBN-10: 154690638X

DEDICATED TO

RICHARD B. CHRISINGER

(1922-2017)

CCC BOY

WORLD WAR II VETERAN

LIFETIME CONTRIBUTOR TO CCC HERITAGE

CONTENTS

PREFACE

World War II was a long and costly war. From the attack on Pearl Harbor on December 7, 1941, until the end of the war on August 15, 1945, 2,175 days elapsed. Sixteen million Americans fought this deadly war and over 400 thousand died in service to their country. Close to 700 thousand were wounded. Among these brave soldiers were former Civilian Conservation Corps (CCC) enrollees.

The CCC was one of the most popular and successful programs of President Franklin D. Roosevelt's New Deal of 1933. During the Great Depression, the CCC promoted economic relief and natural resource conservation. The CCC ended in June 1942 when funding ceased for agencies not deemed essential to the war effort. By that time over 3.5 million men had been placed in 4500 CCC camps in every state plus Alaska, Hawaii, Puerto Rico, and the Virgin Islands.

Estimates are that approximately 60 percent of the 3.5 million enrollees served in the armed forces. It was impossible to identify the specific contributions to the war effort of that staggering amount of men. But it was possible to identify CCC men in World War II who became recipients of the Medal of Honor. In this sense, the Medal of Honor men became a microcosm of *all* CCC men who served in the military.

Ultimately, forty former CCC men received this prestigious medal. After identifying these men of valor, we wrote a complete biography of each man. Our research is validated with individual CCC records from the National Archives in St. Louis, military press releases, emails and phone conversations with family members, and other sources. Our overall purpose in publishing this book is to preserve the legacy of the Civilian Conservation Corps through the stories of forty extraordinary men.

These forty CCC men stand tall among the 473 recipients of the Medal of Honor in World War II. This group includes thirty-one Army personnel, eight Marines, and one Navy diver. They hailed from twenty-three home states and served in sixty-two CCC camps in twenty-seven states. Twenty of these men died in combat.

The twenty men who survived the battlefield came home to a world vastly different from the one they left. No longer anonymous, they were recognized as American heroes and became symbols of strength and freedom. For them the war was never over. Some struggled unsuccessfully with the stress. Others compartmentalized that part of their lives and eventually found inner peace by learning to live with their pasts. Nevertheless, the remaining twenty men carried the memories of war to their graves.

All forty former CCC enrollees came from humble origins but rose to Olympian heights. For them the Medal of Honor was a lifetime commitment to uphold the dignity and standards of that award. They not only changed the landscape of America as CCC "boys" but went on to earn the nation's highest military award during the deadliest war in history. May they long be remembered!!

ACKNOWLEDGMENTS

Heartfelt thanks to Ashley Mattingly, an archivist formerly at the National Archives in St. Louis. This book would have never got off the ground without Ashley's expertise.

With deep appreciation we thank Naomi Shaw, friend and CCC advocate, who drove to the National Archives in St. Louis for us. Naomi copied the CCC record of each man and then mailed the documents to us in a neatly organized package. These records were invaluable to our research.

A huge thank you to all the family members whom we interviewed. The families' willingness to share family history with us was immensely helpful.

With sincere gratitude we thank Carolyn McKinney, niece of Alfred Wilson and author of *The Gentle Giant of the 26th Division.* Carolyn's book is truly a loving tribute to her Uncle Alfred who sacrificed his own life to save others.

We acknowledge Ed Slagle for giving us a treasure trove of CCC and Medal of Honor materials. Ed's generosity is deeply appreciated.

We are grateful to Al and Nancy Vicere, owners of the Whipple Dam store in Pennsylvania. The serenity and comfort of their Stone Cottage was perfect for long days of writing and proofreading in the heart of CCC country.

Special thanks to Laura Jowdy, archivist with the Congressional Medal of Honor Society.

We are indebted to retired English teachers, Grace Gunderman, Barbara Kimbrough, and Sylvia Nandin. Their insightful editing showed once again that writing is a team sport!

Credit is due to HomeOfHeroes.com for a photo of each recipient from the website's Medal of Honor Photo Gallery.

A big thank you to our family and friends who always listen patiently to our CCC stories. We have many to tell!

A special thanks to John Schultz who formatted the manuscript and designed the cover.

To Walter A. Bunt, Jr., a friend and fellow historian, thanks for your support.

With gratitude and appreciation, we thank the CCC Legacy of Edinburg, Virginia. We are proud to be members of this exceptional organization dedicated to promoting the heritage of the Civilian Conservation Corps.

HISTORY OF THE MEDAL OF HONOR

The Medal of Honor has been an important part of American military history since Congress and President Abraham Lincoln authorized it during the initial stages of the Civil War. At that time, there was a need for recognition of an individual's heroic deeds in a war that had become quite deadly. Subsequently, this medal filled the immediate need for recognition of a person's valiant efforts during combat. The first recipients of the medal were members of the Great Train Raid, a Union incursion into the Deep South in the spring of 1862, aimed at the disruption of the Confederate rail system. Since then, there have been approximately 3,500 Medals of Honor awarded. Since 1862 there have been about forty million men and women mobilized in the US military, but an infinitesimal few from that pool have been awarded the Medal of Honor.

The military medal and award system is a process that has slowly evolved into the Pyramid of Honor. Ranking first in prestige and honor is the Medal of Honor. The Army Distinguished Service Cross and its equivalent the Navy Cross, the Air Force Cross, and the US Coast Guard Distinguished Service Medal are second in importance. There have been about twenty thousand of these medals distributed since their inception during World War I. The Silver Star and the Bronze Star round out the third and fourth tiered military valor awards. Originated in the early 1930s, the Silver Star has been awarded to approximately 125,000 servicemen. The Bronze Star, first awarded in 1944, was originally thought of as the infantryman's badge. No record exists regarding its distribution. Both the Silver Cross and the Bronze Star can be awarded to a member of any branch of the armed services.

Significantly, only the President of the United States awards the Medal of Honor. He does this in the name of Congress for heroic deeds above and beyond the point of valor; that is, he awards only the bravest of the brave. Perhaps Paul Roper of *The Pueblo Chieftain* encapsulated its meaning best when he says, "The Medal of Honor is a small five-pointed star that hangs on a blue ribbon, but it comes at such a terrible price that it is an unquestioned tribute to the bravery of anyone who wears it."

Prior to World War I, the Medal of Honor had a less prestigious place in military honors. The Army during the Civil War presented over 1,500 medals. The 27th Regiment of Maine received the medal en masse for just renewing their enlistments in 1863. Another four hundred medals were awarded during the Indian Wars (1862-1890) even though some of the "battles" verged on massacres. Also, the medal was distributed disproportionately to the actual number of men involved in a particular fight. For example, in 1876, Custer's regiment numbered seven hundred at the Battle of Little Big Horn, yet twenty-four cavalry men received the Medal of Honor that day. Sixteen years later at the Battle of Wounded Knee, twenty soldiers from a regiment numbering six hundred became recipients of the award.

In 1916-1917 a panel acting under the aegis of the Department of the Army reexamined every Medal of Honor issued to ascertain whether the recipients had been in combat. Consequently, it disqualified 911 individuals, most of whom were members of the 27th Regiment from Maine. This was the first step regarding the overhaul of the award's process. Since then, there has been a gradual evolution of the criteria for the selection process to make it applicable to military times.

After the Civil Rights movement hit its full stride, it became embarrassing to explain why no black person received the Medal of Honor during World War II. Additionally, only a handful of Asian Americans and a few Hispanics had grudgingly gained this coveted award at the same time. Even more painfully obvious was that the distribution of the Medal of Honor did not reflect the substantial increase of minorities within the military that occurred since the Korean War. It became apparent even to a casual critic that something was badly amiss. Finally, in 1993 the Shaw Committee convened to study this matter. Its findings jolted the government into action: people of color who performed heroic deeds of valor on the battlefield had been overlooked, forgotten, or simply ignored regarding the awarding of the Medal of Honor.

Since then, Presidents Clinton, G.W. Bush, and Obama have moved to eliminate these and other omissions. As a result, over fifty men have received their long overdue Medals of Honor that otherwise had been overlooked because of their race, color, or creed. Fortunately, the momentum to remove those oversights has continued. In 2015 President Obama awarded the Medal of Honor posthumously to a Jewish soldier, Sergeant William Shemin, and a black soldier, Private Henry Jackson, both of whom had served in World War I and had met all the requirements for the Medal of Honor.

NOTES ABOUT THE MEDAL OF HONOR

One does not "win" the Medal of Honor. The individual is *awarded* the medal.

A person who receives the medal is called a *recipient.*

One cannot be considered for the Medal of Honor by simply following an order such as "Take that hill." This heroic deed must be beyond an ordinary act of bravery. For a specific act of valor to be considered, there must be two witnesses for verification, and there must be incontestable evidence.

The greatest single reason for a man receiving the Medal of Honor is smothering a grenade to save his comrades.

The oldest person to become a Medal of Honor recipient was General Douglas MacArthur. He was sixty-four years old.

The youngest Medal of Honor recipient was Willie Johnston, a Union drummer boy. He was eleven at the time and was recommended by President Lincoln. Young Willie, surrounded by fleeing Union soldiers who had thrown away their weapons, kept his cool and also his drum.

The youngest Medal of Honor recipient since the Civil War was Jack Lucas who died on Iwo Jima when he was seventeen years old.

In World War II, there were 473 recipients of the medal and 273 received their awards posthumously.

New York State has the most Medal of Honor recipients: 666.

The US Coast Guard has only one Medal of Honor recipient.

Jacob Parrott was the first of six men to receive the Medal of Honor in 1863.

Texas A and M University had seven of its former students honored as recipients of the Medal of Honor in World War II.

MEDAL OF HONOR BENEFITS AND PRIVILEGES

After World War II, the US government extended job offers to all Medal of Honor recipients through the rapidly expanding Veterans Administration. Many recipients availed themselves of these positions.

The Department of Veterans Affairs provides a $1,198 monthly pension.

The recipient's children automatically become eligible for entry to one of the service academies if they qualify physically and academically.

The recipients are eligible for a government health care program.

If the recipient is a twenty-year veteran, his pension is increased by another 10 percent.

All recipients can fly free on military planes if seats are available.

All recipients receive invitations to the presidential inaugurations and to the inaugural balls.

As a matter of respect and courtesy, service members regardless of their rank are traditionally encouraged to salute Medal of Honor recipients.

Each recipient receives a Medal of Honor flag.

FROM WHENCE THEY CAME

During the 1930s the world was in trouble. A massive depression had struck the industrialized nations of the West. Political unrest abounded with dictators like Hitler, Mussolini, and Stalin in positions of absolute power. Hitler had begun his march to conquer Europe. By 1938 Japan occupied much of China. The world saw a glimpse of the horror to come when Japanese troops stormed Nanking, the longtime capital of China, killing more than 42,000 civilians.

The United States struggled with economic and social chaos. One in four people was unemployed and more were losing their jobs daily. Soup lines became common. Many cities saw gangs roaming the streets and striking fear into the population. Farmers burned crops and poured milk into the streets while people living in shacks or cardboard boxes were starving. Political and industrial leaders feared a revolution as Fascism and Communism gained converts daily.

A revolution did occur as feared, but it occurred at the ballot box rather than with bullets. The presidential election of 1932 was proof that the Constitution still worked. The electorate overwhelmingly elected Franklin Delano Roosevelt (FDR) with hope in his New Deal.

FDR was inaugurated on March 4, 1933, and acted quickly. First, he came up with a plan for the failing banks. Next, he addressed the staggering unemployment rate (54 percent) for young men between the ages of seventeen and twenty-five. On March 21, 1933, the newly elected president proposed to the 73rd Congress the creation of a peacetime army of young men who would battle erosion and destruction of our natural resources. Ten days later, the Emergency Conservation Work Act had passed in both houses and was on the President's desk for his signature. Executive Order 6101, dated April 5, 1933, authorized the program, and Robert Fechner was appointed the first director. The Civilian Conservation Corps was born! On April 7 Henry Rich of Alexandria, Virginia, became the first enrollee. Ten days later, the first camp, Camp Roosevelt, was established in Luray, Virginia.

The CCC's organizational structure flowed from Washington to individual states and then to county and community levels. The Department of Labor was responsible for selection and enrollment through local relief offices. The Departments of Agriculture and Interior were responsible for organizing work in every state across the nation. The Department of War, specifically the Army, had the large task of operating the camps as well as providing transportation, food, clothing, equipment, recreation, and religious services for the enrollees.

The US Army had experienced severe cutbacks due to the Great Depression; therefore, the CCC was a "shot in the arm" with thousands of reserve officers being recalled to fill the organizational demands of this new organization. Many the generals from World War II had been involved with the CCC. General George Marshall, the nation's chief of staff during the war and later Secretary of State said, "I found the CCC the most instructive service I have ever had and the most interesting."

Mobilization from April to June 1933 was phenomenal. Colonel Duncan K. Major of the War Department was a key architect in the plan. In a report to Roosevelt on July 1, 1933, Colonel Major stated that the full quota of 274,375 men was garrisoned in 1,468 camps. With justifiable pride, Major disclosed that in so doing, "All American war and peacetime records have been shattered." Colonel Major acknowledged, "Few military campaigns have equaled such a performance." To the Army, the CCC offered a real logistical opportunity.

The Army did not reinvent the wheel when structuring the CCC. Previously, the Army had divided the country into nine districts and then into sub-districts. This structure also applied to the CCC. A chain of command existed. Each district had a commanding officer, usually a general or a colonel. He was assisted by a military staff of officers and up to fifteen civilian technical advisers. Each sub-district had its own headquarters, officers, and technical staff. Also, each camp had a commanding officer, at least two junior officers, civilian technical personnel, and leaders.

A typical enrollee was eighteen years old, unmarried, unemployed, and came from a family on relief. Each enrollee had to pass a physical exam and was required to serve a six-month period with the option of serving up to two years. The enrollee was paid thirty dollars a month with twenty-five dollars being sent directly to the family. This allotment saved many families from starvation and homelessness.

The camps were in isolated, almost primal areas. Frequently, the nearest town was twenty miles away. Spike camps could be as far as fifty miles from the base camp. Initially, the enrollees lived in tents with a primitive wood floor. Few, if any, amenities existed. Some of the tent canvas had deteriorated in storage, and leaky roofs were common. When permanent structures were completed, two hundred men lived in four barracks with fifty men in each. Ancillary buildings such as mess halls/kitchens, infirmaries, lavatories/showers, classrooms, recreation halls, offices, tool shops, and garages supported the camp.

The Quartermaster Corps supplied the camps with everything from toothbrushes to trucks. Initially olive drab uniforms left over from the Great War were issued. The CCC boys joked that their uniforms and boots came in two sizes: "too big" and "too small!" Work uniforms were blue denim work pants and shirt plus a cloth "Daisy Mae" hat. In 1939 a spruce green uniform became standard issue. Just as in the military, the enrollees wore badges, stripes, and skill badges.

The CCC was a civilian agency with a paramilitary structure. There were no weapons training, drills, guardhouses, or MPs. The men did not salute officers, but they did address them as "Sir." The Army, however, ran the camps on a tight military schedule. The bugle sounded at 6:00 A.M. followed by a flag raising ceremony and breakfast. After breakfast, the enrollees policed the grounds and barracks before inspection and roll call. Work began by 8:00 A.M. The men usually had a bag lunch in the field at noon. Quitting time was at 4:00 P.M. and the men returned to camp. There was some time to clean up and relax before retreat, a flag lowering ceremony. At 6:00 P.M. dinner was served family style with the men in dress uniform. Classes and recreation were offered in the evening. The PX was open for evening snacks. Lights out was at 10:00 P.M.

CCC Director, Robert Fechner, described camp food as "wholesome, palatable, and of the variety that sticks to the ribs." Initially, the Quartermaster Corps was not prepared for the voracious appetites of the enrollees, and rations were increased by 5 percent. Many of the enrollees arrived at the camps undernourished. Hard labor in the forests made them ravenous. The vast majority said, "I never saw so much food in my life!" On his first day, one rookie enrollee was shoveling food into his mouth as if he'd never eat again. One of his barrack's companions said, "Slow down! Save room for dessert." The rookie replied, "What's dessert?" While the quartermaster personnel were pushed to the limit in arranging for the purchase and distribution of unprecedented amounts of food, local vendors and farmers appreciated the business. On the average the CCC pumped $5000.00 a month into the host town's economy.

The Forest Service, National Park Service, Soil Conservation Service, Bureau of Reclamation, Bureau of Land Management, and state parks provided work projects. Local Experienced Men (LEMs) with specific skills supervised the work along with CCC senior and assistant leaders. Teamwork and following orders were basic principles in the field. Each man was expected to complete his assignment; "gold bricking" was not tolerated. The men were not bound by the Army's Code of Military Justice, but they were disciplined. An enrollee could be dismissed for refusal to work, drinking, theft, or fighting. Weapons and personal vehicles in camp were forbidden.

In June 1940 FDR declared a limited national emergency and encouraged the CCC to begin military training. Enrollees were excused from five hours of conservation work per week for defense training in the classroom. Drills were conducted with enrollees in simple military uniforms. By December 1941 the CCC had established eighty camps at Army, Navy, and Marine reservations across the United States. CCC men helped build barracks, air fields, target ranges, parachute landing sites, recreational centers, and other facilities. In military hospitals and reception centers, the men served as cooks, bakers, grounds keepers, bookkeepers, clerks, and maintenance workers. In January 1942 the CCC initiated a "Victory War Program." By May that year, twelve thousand enrollees from 175 camps were placed at military forts and reservations. With war clouds hovering over the nation and the future of the program in jeopardy, all CCC labor became war related. Roosevelt's "Tree Army" was preparing for war!

The CCC was shut down on June 30, 1942. The war had raged for 205 days since Pearl Harbor. Many former CCC enrollees were already fighting overseas. The draft had been instituted in 1940 and policy allowed CCC alumni to become corporals and sergeants due to their CCC experience. The strength of any army depended upon the leadership of these non-commissioned officers.

Wherever the flag waved, the CCC alumni were there, whether it was Bataan, Corregidor, or during the countless island-hopping campaigns throughout the Pacific. They fought in the air over Japan and Europe while other enrollees stormed the beaches at Anzio, Salerno, and Normandy. They froze through Europe's coldest winter at Bastogne and crossed the Rhine en route to Berlin. They rejoiced at the end of the war!

No doubt, all were in full agreement with General Mark Clark, commander of the Fifth Army and later President of the Citadel, the Military College of South Carolina, who said, "To my way of thinking, the CCC became a potent factor in enabling us to win World War II. Though we did not realize it at the time, we were training non-commissioned officers."

RICHARD B. ANDERSON

BIRTH DATE: June 26, 1921

BIRTH PLACE: Tacoma, Washington

DEATH: February 1, 1944. KIA.

MEDAL OF HONOR ACTION: Roi Island, part of the Marshall Islands. February 1, 1944.

RANK: Private First Class

UNIT: Company E, 2nd Battalion, 23rd Regiment, 4th Marine Division

YEARS OF SERVICE: July 6, 1942 - February 1, 1944

AWARDS: Medal of Honor, Purple Heart, Asiatic-Pacific Medal, World War II Victory Medal

CCC: F-9, Missoula, Montana. July 1937.

RICHARD B. ANDERSON

Richard's family was comfortably middle class, a rarity during the Great Depression. His father, Oscar Anderson, was born in Wisconsin, migrating to Idaho and later to Washington. The Andersons were married in Idaho where their first child was born. Oscar spent one year in college and became an accountant. He then managed a shingle factory. The couple owned a home worth $5000.00. The 1940 census records showed that Oscar enjoyed full employment in 1939. Richard's mother, Hazel, who spoke French fluently, was a salesperson. They had three children: Mary (1920), Richard (1922), and Robert (1924).

Friends described Richard as a handsome young man who had brown eyes and mahogany brown hair and was of moderate height and weight. Anderson was a popular young man and an above average student who graduated from high school in 1937 at Sequim, Washington. After his graduation, he worked in his father's shingle factory.

Although his family's economic status did not warrant his entry into the Civilian Conservation Corps, Richard somehow enrolled after high school graduation. This was a poor choice. After a week at conditioning camp at F-19 at Quilcene, Washington, he moved to F-9 in Missoula, Montana, where his duty was picking weeds. Apparently, that job was not to his liking, for he deserted. Richard gave no reason for his rapid departure. Returning home, he worked in a shipyard prior to enlistment in the US Marine Corps in 1942.

Richard's stateside experience in the Marines fared considerably better than his brief stay in the CCC. After receiving his basic training at the Marine Recruit Center at San Diego, California, he went into infantry training at Camp Eliott, San Diego. He earned his first stripe there, and then, like many Marines before him, he had his arm tattooed: *Death Before Dishonor.* On February 1, 1944, he hit the beaches of Roi Island.

AN ACCOUNT OF ANDERSON'S BRAVERY AS WITNESSED BY PRIVATE HARRY PIERCE

Somewhere around 1500 hours (3 P.M.). I had advanced about 2/3 of the way across Roi Island (500 yards) and found myself alone in a large shell crater. I was receiving small arms fire from enemy snipers in front of me about 300 yards away.... I was shortly joined by Lt. Joseph Salome and Sergeant Joseph Kennedy and the three of us, side-by-side, peered from the shell crater. The incoming fire lessened and I was aware of a new Marine who had entered the crater. Taking a second look, I discovered it was PFC Anderson, a mortar man. Why he was so far forward without his mortar crew only God knows. I always thought that he came forward to observe before going back to direct mortar fire. He was a damn good mortar man and could "lay his eggs in the basket" without even using the base plate of the launcher...I saw Richard remove his pack, lay his rifle down, and remove a canister of grenades. I saw him take the top off the canister and I looked away. The next thing I knew I heard a pop and as I looked at him, I was aware of a live grenade in his hand...The canister had a live grenade in it or the pin sheared, and the handle blew off but Anderson had a hot grenade in his hand. Anderson's actions at this point were nothing but heroic. He threw it backward over his shoulder much like you would do with a hot potato but it rolled back to him. At this point he pulled it to his groin and said, "Oh my God." He curled around it as the grenade exploded. His actions shielded the three of us from certain death.

A POSTSCRIPT

Private Pierce survived the war; Kennedy and Salome did not. Lieutenant Salome died at Saipan, and Sergeant Kennedy died on Iwo Jima.

MEDAL OF HONOR CITATION

For conspicuous gallantry and intrepidity at the risk of his life above and beyond the call of duty while serving with the Fourth Marine Division during action against enemy Japanese forces on Roi Island, Kwajalein Atoll, Marshall Islands, February 1, 1944. Entering a shell crater occupied by three other Marines, Private First Class Anderson was preparing to throw a grenade at an enemy position when it slipped from his hands and rolled toward the men at the bottom of the hole. With insufficient time to retrieve the armed weapon and throw it, Private First Class Anderson fearlessly chose to sacrifice himself and save his companions by hurling his body upon the grenade and taking the full impact of the explosion. His personal valor and exceptional spirit of loyalty in the face of almost certain death were in keeping with the highest traditions of the US Naval Service. He gallantly gave his life for his country.

MEDAL OF HONOR PRESENTATION

Rear Admiral S.F. Taffinder, Commandant, 13th Naval District, presented Anderson's Medal of Honor posthumously to his parents, Oscar and Hazel Anderson, at ceremonies held in Seattle, Washington, in 1944.

HONORS

In 1945, the United States Navy launched a destroyer, the USS Richard B. Anderson. His mother, Mrs. Oscar Johnson, commissioned the ship, while his brother, Motor Machinist Mate Robert L. Anderson, became a plank holder (original crew member of the ship). The ship had a rich naval heritage that included four battle stars in the Korean War and eleven battle stars in the Viet Nam War. It remained in service until 1977. The vessel achieved cinematic stardom when at the end of the *Caine Mutiny*, a popular film in 1954, it doubled for the fictional USS Caine, as it sailed under the Golden Gate Bridge.

From the Forest to the Battlefield

Thirty-five miles south of Baghdad, Iraq, the Marine Corps named a major military installation Camp Anderson in honor of three Marine Medal of Honor recipients: Richard B. Anderson (World War II), Richard A. Anderson (Viet Nam), and James Anderson (Viet Nam).

The Port Angeles Federal Building was renamed the Richard B. Anderson Federal Building in 2008.

A memorial to PFC Richard B. Anderson is located at a small park near the county courthouse at Port Angeles, Washington.

PFC Anderson's memory was honored at a dedication ceremony that took place at his grave site on May 14, 1997. Lieutenant Colonel Kelly Kvigne, Inspector-Instructor, 4th Landing Support Battalion, was guest speaker.

THE SEARCH FOR ANDERSON'S BURIAL SITE

Anderson suffered from the cruel vicissitudes of fame. Although newspapers marked his passing, he quickly slipped through the cracks of history. This hero suffered more indignities when his remains were reinterred at the New Tacoma Cemetery, Tacoma, Washington. Cemetery officials lost track of his burial site, and no Medal of Honor emblem had been placed on the stone! As a result, Anderson's body remained there unrecognized for fifty years. Indeed, he had become a forgotten hero.

THE END OF THE STORY

According to Terry Roth of Lynwood, Washington, the recently established Port Angeles Marine Corps League was looking for an appropriate local Marine Corps hero whom the group could honor. Someone mentioned Anderson's name. It took months before the group located Anderson's grave. It was only then that Richard B. Anderson received the honors due him as the area's only Medal of Honor recipient.

By this time, (2001) Anderson's mother and father had died and his brother, Robert, had moved out of state. Only Richard's sister, Margaret Anderson Roderick, remained in the state. After the grave had been restored along with appropriate military honors, Ms. Roderick gave Roth her brother's memorabilia, including his Medal of Honor. She said, "I don't want my brother to be forgotten, and I don't want his things to be left on a dusty shelf in the back room of a museum to be forgotten."

BURIAL SITE

Richard B. Anderson's remains rest at the New Tacoma Cemetery in Tacoma, Washington.

DARRELL S. COLE

BIRTH DATE: July 20, 1920

BIRTH PLACE: Park Hills, Missouri

DEATH: February 19, 1945. KIA.

MEDAL OF HONOR ACTION: Iwo Jima. February 19, 1945.

RANK: Sergeant

UNIT: Company B, 1st Battalion, 23rd Marines

YEARS OF SERVICE: August 25, 1941 - February 19, 1945

AWARDS: Medal of Honor, Bronze Star, Purple Heart (2), Others

CCC: F-13, Berryman, Missouri. Asst. Forestry Leader, Asst. Educational Adviser, Asst. Forest Service Clerk. October 1939 - December 1940.

DARRELL S. COLE

Darrell Cole was born July 20, 1920. His parents were Samuel Randall Cole and Mary Magdelina (Williams) Cole. He was one of twelve children, five of whom died in infancy. Growing up in Esther, Missouri, he was a member of the First Baptist Church. In 1938 he graduated fifth out of thirty-three students from Esther High School where the class motto was: "Out of school life into life's school."

His father was disabled when Darrell was in eighth grade. He told his son that if he wanted to continue his education, he would have to get a job. Darrell became the school janitor. As a result, he usually arrived at school a few hours before his peers and left after 6:00 P.M. But, this did not stop him from having a well-rounded high school life.

> In high school I was on the track team (Mile), Vice President of the Dramatic Club, Editor-in-Chief of the High School annual, in band, Boy's Glee Club, Mixed Chorus, Boy's Quartet, the Pep Squad, French Horn Trio, and was in the NYA. Graduated out of 12th grade in three years at age seventeen.

Darrell Cole was a good-natured kid with a ready smile. Tall, with blue eyes and a fair complexion, he stood six feet two inches and weighed 175 pounds. A high school graduate, a member of the church choir, and superintendent of his Sunday school, Cole had the necessary attributes of an all-American boy in the 1930s. At least, he did on the surface.

The Great Depression squeezed the life out of everyone and everything whether it was in the city or rural Missouri where Darrell lived. In that chaotic world, the American dream - work hard and you shall succeed - was not applicable. Undaunted, he continued his quest for this dream, searching for a place in society where he might belong. Unfortunately, Cole's work experiences never provided the stability and order that he sought until Cole enlisted in the Marines four months before Pearl Harbor.

This was his self-description prior to the Marine Corps:

> I was a footloose vagabond before entering the Marine Corps. I have tried my hand at nearly everything and have been successful at nothing simply because it never held my interest enough for me to continue it.

While undergoing R & R after Guadalcanal, he wrote a short autobiography that provided some insights into this young man. After those hellish five months on that killing field, this seasoned combat veteran recognized his own mortality. Or perhaps, it was a way of setting things straight to restore a modicum of order to his life. Nonetheless, Cole's writing showed a bright, articulate young person who was a master of understatement.

> At three, I burned down a barn with my bro, Stanley... I ran away when I was ten...I organized a

rebellion in my CCC camp...I have been in nearly all states of the Union by riding freights...I'm becoming used to wine, women, and song. The night clubs got most of my money. Wasn't getting anywhere so I enlisted...The Marines sent me to Parris Island...I was forced to go into music school. I joined to fight but I was put to playing the bugle.

Darrell Cole had seen hell close at the tender age of twenty-two. Except for his barbs hurled at the US Army, he showed little rancor. His presentation was matter of fact and quite orderly. As a writer, he set the tone, allowing the reader to experience the gut-wrenching time that was Guadalcanal. This young man, barely out of high school, wrote about standard scenarios that since then have been written for war movies *ad infinitum*.

TO THE PACIFIC:

We weighed anchor, sailed under the Oakland Bay Bridge out past and around Alcatraz Island into the sea. All in all, a small convoy of thirteen ships. We only had one tin can (destroyer) as an escort. We watched land recede far behind us until it was out of sight. We were sure that it was the last we would see of the US...We hit rough water and sailors as well as Marines were green in the face, hanging over the side puking...I never felt particularly well...but I never heaved yet because of sea sickness...On board, two decks down, our hold was rather small...Some bunks were five on top...Everyone wore Kapok life preservers. Slept on them...We had general quarters daily, gun watches, and the rest of the time we seemed to be standing in long lines for chow...Couldn't go top-side. Couldn't do nothing but sit on the steel deck and read. Sit not lay down. There wasn't enough room. Then every fifteen minutes the swab jockeys came by swabbing down the decks with hoses. Such was the life on any transport. The guys would sing, shoot craps, play poker, black-jack, cribbage - anything to occupy time and mind.

THE NIGHT BEFORE THE INVASION:

Sharpened our bayonets, cleaned our rifles all day long, packed and repacked our combat packs so as to have the right things, or just the right amount. Our knives were like razors. Everyone wrote their last letters home and gave them to sailors to take back for us...Finally the night before, Colonel Cates, our Battalion Commander, made a speech on the loud speaker of the ship...Lots of bullshit about how we were picked to start the first American offensive, that Marines were picked to do it...etc...etc... and so on. Then we sang the Marine Hymn which did settle our nerves.

AWAY ALL BOATS:

I saw smoke billowing high in the air. Dive bombers were bombing in one continual roar. I caught all this in one glance when I went over the side. We looked like rats pouring out of a hole. Our faces were black from cork. Each man had a belt full of ammunition and two bandoliers more around his shoulders. You could see a lot of them nervous, some were praying, others were shaking hands with their buddies. We rendezvoused with other boats already in a circle and then took for shore at top speed...We ducked our heads and waited.

A FOOT SOLDIER'S VIEW OF WAR:

> We had every type of warfare known on Guadalcanal, including tanks, flamethrowers, submarine shelling, also Jap battleships blasting our positions, bombing constantly during the day and night... We had to fight snipers everywhere. There was Jap land based artillery as well as strafing from their zero planes. It's no fun lying in your foxhole watching those bastards drop eggs on us and you can't do a thing about it...One day alone we lost eleven guys from my company...Our patrols would find native women tied to trees, hands and feet tied...breasts and tongues cut off...their bodies looked like pin cushions where they had been bayoneted many times. We found a few of our men that way also. Thus, no prisoners were taken afterward.

CCC EXPERIENCE

Shortly after graduation, Cole joined the Civilian Conservation Corps. He was stationed at Camp F-13 at Berryman, Missouri. His room, board, clothing, and medical care were provided by the government. In turn he had to work eight hours a day, five days a week, in a state forest.

The average education level in the CCC was the eighth grade. It was quite common to find a much lower education level in many camps. In addition, most camps had enrollees who were illiterate. Since Darrell had a high school diploma, he had a significant advantage over his peers. He had another advantage: Cole was a "take-charge" young man whose leadership skills blossomed in the Civilian Conservation Corps.

> I joined the CCC for fourteen months and served as an Assistant Educational Adviser, a Forest Service clerk, drove caterpillars, and operated a jack-hammer. Did timber survey work, planted pine trees, studied map reading, and led a revolt in camp. I took a forestry course under a Forest Service foreman. Learned photography and developed, enlarged, and printed for the camp. I was rated Assistant Leader. Got an honorable discharge to accept outside employment.

In some camps throughout the country, it was not unusual for overly ambitious company commanders to save a buck to curry favor with their superiors. The easiest way to do this was to cut corners with the food budget. Generally, it did not take long for the enrollees to complain bitterly about the quality and quantity of food. A most common form of protest was a sit-down strike in the mess hall. No doubt, they turned to Darrell Cole to be their spokesman. Since his CCC record was exemplary, it appears as if the "food revolt" was justified. There is nothing in his record to indicate otherwise.

When an enrollee first entered a camp, his job selection was usually at Level One...grunt work. But once he became known by the staff, the enrollee advanced to more skillful positions. Witness Darrell Cole's work assignments: He was assigned to Timber Survey because he knew math, took excellent notes, and recognized different types of trees. He was not wary of challenging work like manning a jack-hammer. To become Forest Service Clerk, he had to know how to type and keep records. He reached his high point in the CCC when he became Assistant Educational Adviser, a responsible position that required trust and rapport with his fellow enrollees.

The Educational Adviser was usually a teacher from a nearby town. It was his job to survey the educational needs of the CCC company and then address those needs through the creation of a wide and varied curriculum. The courses included truck mechanics, typing, reading and writing, building ham radios, and creating a camp radio station.

The tough sell was getting as many enrollees as possible to take evening courses. To make it more difficult, going to school in the evening was not mandatory. This was the crux of the Assistant Educational Adviser's job. He had to sell evening classes to the enrollees. Within a short time, Darrell was promoted to Assistant Leader.

BETWEEN THE CCC AND WORLD WAR II

After being honorably discharged from the CCC in 1939, Darrell continued his quest for a better life. Ultimately, his travels led him to Detroit, Michigan, where thousands of young Americans hoped to start life anew. Al Stark, a columnist for the *Detroit News*, said of these new arrivals:

> Wave after wave of young men, rawboned, and funny talking, came to Detroit from Tennessee and Kentucky and points west to get their name on a time card...They took rooms near the factories, they drank beer at hillbilly bars, their eyes lit up when they talked of home.

Young Darrell Cole's odyssey to Detroit was a bit more circuitous.

> Worked for Kansas City Brokers where I sold household items door to door...everything from fly spray to cosmetics. Drove tractors one summer long. All night work. Hitch-hiked and rode freights a lot. Went to Detroit and worked as a truck driver, became a store room clerk, worked at the Fordson Hotel in Dearborn as a bell-boy and trouble shooter, then as cork operator at Wolverine Manufacturing and Fabrication Company.

As Darrell settled into city life, his short autobiography shows that he enjoyed the many attractions of a big city. He liked to dance to his favorite tunes of the day. His list was the standard songs from the popular radio show, *Your Hit Parade*. They ranged from *Moonlight Becomes You* to *Stardust*, from *Sentimental Over You, Beer Barrel Polka,* and *White Cliffs of Dover* to *Smoke Rings* and *Sugar Blues.* His musings also contained names and pictures of young ladies of his age. One was Margaret Willott who sang in his church choir in Detroit. They married on Christmas Eve 1943, in San Diego, California, prior to Darrell's shipping out to the South Pacific for his second tour of overseas duty.

Darrell Cole joined the United States Marines on August 25, 1941, and was assigned to Parris Island, South Carolina. After completing basic training, he attended Field Music School. Not happy with this assignment, he complained that he signed up to fight, not to blow a bugle. Citing his proficiency with the French horn and recognizing a severe shortage of buglers, the Marine Corps prevailed. He accepted the decision but groused, "There is a right way and the Marine Corps way." After qualifying as a bugler, Cole transferred to New River, North Carolina, where he became part of the Fleet Marine Force. He trained diligently and began to mature as a Marine. He wrote, "As the Marine Corps on a whole, I am pretty proud of it. I think no other service equals it."

By early May 1942, his unit was rife with speculation. A big move was imminent. But no one knew where. Everyone, however, was sure it was not going to be Europe as their training exercises in the Caribbean dictated otherwise.

> At last the great day came (June 8) ...After boarding our Pullman, we stowed away our gear and leaned out the window for a last look....The band was playing. Just as the train whistled one long blast, they broke into the Marine Hymn until we gathered speed and left them behind. Officers and men alike were waving and hollering at the tops of their voices... After tons of scuttlebutt, calculations, hard training, landing maneuvers, after drawing equipment, we were ready to shove off!...Was on Train B for the cross-country trip of over 4,000 miles due to zigzagging of the troop train. San Francisco was our point of embarkation...supposed to be a secret. My lieutenant wrote the name on paper and "accidentally" dropped it in front of us. San Francisco it was!

After a short stay in San Francisco, the men transferred to the USS George F. Elliott bound for the South Pacific. Twenty days later the thirteen-ship convoy reached New Zealand. On June 22, 1942, the ships were on the move again; this time to the Fiji Islands, a prelude to the Guadalcanal invasion. They left Fiji on August 1, and six days later, August 7, Darrell Cole's outfit hit the beaches. The first offensive land action by the Allies had begun.

The Battle of Guadalcanal was a six month long, bitter, and bloody conflict that took place simultaneously on the sea, air, and land. Six major naval engagements occurred from August until late November 1942 before the US Navy finally gained supremacy. Constant air raids based from nearby Japanese held fortifications were lethal. Finally, there were bloody conflicts in the jungle and near daily attacks on Henderson Field, a small air strip won by the US in the very first days of the invasion. Reinforcements from both sides poured in as the significance of this island became clear. Japanese victory meant total domination of the entire Pacific. On the other hand, Allied victory would doom Japanese efforts in New Guinea, would secure Australia, and would cut off the Japanese supply lines.

For the Marines at Guadalcanal, many constants remained: mud, rain, the jungle, regular naval and air bombardment from the Japanese, and infantry attacks day and night.

> There followed days and days of lying in the foxholes, watching Jap bombers come over and bomb us. We never could leave the foxhole for fear of the bombing attacks. Early on we did not have

enough planes to keep up with them...It wasn't until the first Grumman planes arrived (at Henderson Field) until the 20th...One day I had a 500-pound bomb hit in the back of my foxhole, and two anti-personnel bombs hit 65 feet away. It caved in the dirt on my legs and arms. I got out OK. Picked up a piece of shrapnel the size of my head out of the hole.

Guadalcanal was a fetid, insect-ridden island with excessive rain, up to ten inches in a storm. The swamps near the coast were almost impassable, while the rain forest was impenetrable except for combat troops who cut, hacked, and clawed their way to take the war to the enemy. Dysentery was common. Also, malaria began to take its toll. Within weeks, men were stricken with dengue fever, jungle rot, and typhus, all common to the jungle environment. To make matters worse, malnutrition became prevalent.

> For one month and a half, we ate Jap rice with the husks on it, and it was full of little white worms. Japs had the rice in small sacks and it was easy for the worms to get in. We couldn't throw them out. We got one lump in the morning and one in the evening. Then we got coffee at first and later corn beef, coffee and rice for a long time. We smoked Jap cigarettes, ate Jap cookies, and ate Jap candy.

As casualties mounted daily, Cole became quite realistic.

> I write my letters or postcards mostly when I hear an air raid is on its way. I laid the letters about fifty feet away so if I got killed maybe they still wouldn't be damaged any and someone would send them on.

At the same time, he put on a happy face when writing home: "I used to write that I was well and in good health and was eating three squares a day."

By late October and into November, the two navies squared off for the final battles for control of the island. Although both sides lost heavily, the United States won through attrition. The Tokyo Express, the nightly run of ships from Raboul and Truk, had been slowed considerably. The Japanese Army suffered from malnutrition, disease, and daily combat losses while their Air Force had ceased to be a factor. Unbeknownst to the Allies, the Japanese high command had decided to abandon the island. At about the same time, the United States Army XIV Corps assumed operational control. The First Marine Division had been relieved for recuperation. Darrell Cole was unhappy to see that General MacArthur's boys were in charge.

> I don't have much to say about them They were really a mess...Scared to death because we were going to leave...They came into combat with bathrobes, good clothes, cots to sleep in and right across from them there we were with clothes almost torn off, had to sleep on the ground, no blankets, hardly no chow, nothing at all...They (the army troops) lived like kings, us like rats. One month there and they cried for relief. We had been there for four months and no relief...You couldn't tell them anything at all. Lots of men died on that account...They have more weapons and better equipment, everything! Yet one battalion of Marines can take sticks and kill more Japs

than an Army regiment.

His final account of that deadly island was chilling.

> I don't believe there is a man who can tell 1/10th of what happened there. Something was happening. Happening every minute. And no one will ever know the thoughts and ideas that a man gets in a hell like Guadalcanal. A place where you were starved for food and water. Mosquitoes and flies by the millions, hot in the day, cold as hell at night. No blankets to keep warm...Continual rain, have to carry a rifle at all times and meals two times a day...shelled and bombed at night, bombed during the day...Always waiting for an attack by the Japs...Everyone's skin and bones with low resistance. A small cut turns into a running sore overnight.

Darrell Cole left Guadalcanal on December 22, 1942, after spending 136 consecutive days in combat.

The battle continued for six more weeks as the Japanese fought bitterly. By early February, the Japanese Navy successfully evacuated nearly five thousand men, leaving behind thirty thousand dead. Their Navy and Air Force suffered terrible losses with thirty-six ships sunk and nearly nine hundred planes lost.

The US losses were also staggering: seven thousand killed, seven hundred planes lost, and twenty-nine ships sunk. Losses were so horrific that they remained a military secret long after the battle had ended.

In the meantime, Darrell moved to Australia and New Zealand with time for shore leave in Melbourne. His malaria, however, worsened and necessitated his being sent back to the States.

He arrived in San Francisco on January 31, 1943. Immediately, he rudely met the harsh realities of war on the home front: "After all that, get in the states and have some guy ask you if you knew there was a war on, all because I asked for two packs of gum not knowing anything about rationing and other things."

It was during this time that Private First Class Darrell Cole asked for a change of his military occupational specialty (MOS), that is, to be relieved of his official bugler status and to be assigned to a weapons company. He argued that on Guadalcanal when his company's machine gunners were wounded, he manned a machine gun and did well.

He came home with the bugle.

He remained stateside the rest of the year. After recovering from his bout of malaria, Darrell left Camp Elliott at San Diego, California, transferring to New River, North Carolina, for additional training. While at New River, Cole was again refused a change in his MOS. From there, he moved with his unit, the First Battalion, 23rd Regiment, the Fourth Marine Division, to Camp Pendleton, California. Their next destination was the Kwajalein Atoll in the Marshall Islands. Eighteen days out of California, Cole's battalion hit the beaches on two tiny islands adjacent to the prime objective, Roi-Namour. Although many Light Vehicle Transports (LVTs) floundered on coral shoals, the smaller islands were secured in less than twelve hours.

From mid-June to August 1, 1944, the US Marines invaded Saipan and Tinian, Japanese strongholds in the Mariana Islands. Strategically, both islands had landing strips long enough to handle the B-29, a long-range bomber capable of hitting the Japanese homeland. The Japanese fought to the last man on Saipan, where its entire garrison of thirty thousand men died either in combat or by suicide, but not before extracting a huge price from the Marines: fourteen thousand casualties. After Saipan was secured, the Marines stormed the beaches of Tinian. The subsequent five-day battle cost the Japanese another nine thousand men. As a portent of things to come, two Japanese strategies became evident: their use of fortified caves as a prime defense, and even more alarming, their determination to fight to the last man.

Darrell Cole participated in both invasions. At Saipan he replaced his squad leader who was killed. Although wounded, Cole successfully led his machine gun section against the enemy. Subsequently, he received the Bronze Star, a Purple Heart, and was promoted to Sergeant.

After the Mariana Campaign, Sergeant Cole again petitioned for a change in his MOS. He argued that his experience and his leadership proficiency warranted the change. This time, he stowed away his bugle for good.

Iwo Jima, considered part of the Japanese homeland, became a priority for American planners in the latter half of 1944. The Navy hoped to establish a fleet port and the US Army wanted to use the island as a staging area for the eventual invasion of Japan. Not overlooked were Iwo Jima's two air strips which could be used for fighter and bomber bases against the Japanese homeland. While these objectives were still theory, there arose an immediate objective for securing the island.

In November 1944, the B-29s had begun pounding Japan. Over the next few months, plane losses increased because severely damaged planes had a difficult time making it back to Tinian, a trip of 1300 miles from their target. Iwo Jima, strategically located between Tokyo and Tinian, became a logical choice as a haven for emergency landings.

Unfortunately, the Japanese recognized Iwo Jima's strategic location as well. As a result, they carved a labyrinth of interconnected tunnels and fortifications into the cliffs and the mountain, thereby allowing for a deadly, overlapping field of fire. In addition, the garrison of twenty thousand men knew that they were doomed even though their code of the warrior remained unquestioned. The US Marines hit Iwo Jima on February 19, 1945, after two months of aerial bombing and intense shelling by American ships.

Cole's unit, the First Battalion, 23rd Marine Regiment, led the first assault wave. Relatively unopposed, they still had difficulty moving inland because of the loose volcanic soil. As the beach continued to swell with men and material, the Japanese finally opened fire according to their well -calculated plan. There were so many men on the beach that the Japanese could hardly miss. When the Marines scrambled to dig foxholes, the volcanic ash simply caved in. They had no choice but to move ahead or die.

The First Battalion, 23rd Regiment's primary objective was to secure the Motoyama Airstrip, but he did not see this happen. Darrell Cole died, a valiant warrior, still seeking to restore order in his tiny portion of his world. America lost yet another hero that day.

The Battle for Iwo Jima lasted from February 19 to March 26, 1945. US causalities numbered 26,000 while the Japanese lost almost every defender. Subsequently, there were twenty-seven recipients of the Medal of Honor: twenty-two Marines and five men from the US Navy. The battle will be known forever as the place where "Uncommon valor was commonplace."

MEDAL OF HONOR CITATION

For conspicuous gallantry and intrepidity at the risk of his life above and beyond the call of duty while serving as Leader of a Machine-gun Section of Company B, First Battalion, Twenty-Third Marines, Fourth Marine Division, in action against enemy Japanese forces during the assault on Iwo Jima in the Volcano Islands, 19 February 1945. Assailed by a tremendous volume of small-arms, mortar and artillery fire as he advanced with one squad of his section in the initial assault wave, Sergeant Cole boldly led his men up the sloping beach toward Airfield Number One despite the blanketing curtain of flying shrapnel and personally destroying with hand grenades two hostile emplacements which menaced the progress of his unit, continued to move forward until a merciless barrage of fire emanating from three Japanese pillboxes halted the advance. Instantly placing his one remaining machine gun in action, he delivered a shattering fusillade and succeeded in silencing the nearest and most threatening emplacement before his weapon jammed and the enemy, reopening fire with knee mortars and grenades, pinned down his unit for the second time. Shrewdly gauging the tactical situation and evolving a daring plan of counterattack, Sergeant Cole, armed solely with a pistol and one grenade, coolly advanced alone to the hostile pillboxes. Hurling his one grenade at the enemy in sudden, swift attack, he quickly withdrew, returned to his own lines for additional grenades and again advanced, attacked, and withdrew. With enemy guns still active, he ran the gauntlet of slashing fire a third time to complete the total destruction of the Japanese strong point and the annihilation of the defending garrison in this final assault. Although instantly killed by an enemy grenade as he returned to his squad, Sergeant Cole had eliminated a formidable Japanese position, thereby enabling his company to storm the remaining fortifications, continue the advance and seize the objective. By his dauntless initiative, unfaltering courage and indomitable determination during a critical period of action, Sergeant Cole served as an inspiration to his comrades, and his stouthearted leadership in the face of almost certain death sustained and enhanced the highest traditions of the United States Naval Service. He gallantly gave his life for his country.

MEDAL OF HONOR PRESENTATION

His widow, Margaret Williot Cole, received her husband's Medal of Honor at the Naval Armory in Detroit, Michigan, on April 17, 1947. The presenter was Lt. Colonel W.F. Whitaker.

HONORS

On July 20, 1985, Cole's sixty-fifth birthday, a bust of Sergeant Cole was unveiled at Mineral Area College, Missouri.

A flagpole at the Memorial Complex in Flat River was dedicated to Cole (Then Flat River, now Park Hills, Missouri).

That same year the American Legion Post at Leadington, Missouri, changed its name to the Coleman-Frazier-Cole Post.

In December 1986, the Darrell S. Cole scholarship was established at Mineral Area College.

In 1986 the Marine Corps dedicated Cole Hall at Quantico, Virginia.

The USS Cole, DDG-67, named after Darrell S. Cole, was launched February 10, 1995, at Pascagoula, Mississippi, and commissioned in 1996. On October 12, 2000, she put into Aden, a port of Yemen, for routine refueling where she became a target of a terrorist bombing that killed seventeen and wounded thirty crew members. Although suffering severe damages, The USS Cole was redeployed in less than two years. In the interim, she had been updated with the latest weapons. In 2017 she returned to Yemen as part of her overall mission.

BURIAL SITE

Initially, Sergeant Darrell S. Cole had been interred on Iwo Jima. In December 1945, his remains were shipped home and buried December 30, 1945, in the Parkview Cemetery at Farmington, Missouri.

HENRY GURKE

BIRTH DATE: November 6, 1922

BIRTH PLACE: Neche, North Dakota

DEATH: November 9, 1943. KIA.

MEDAL OF HONOR ACTION: Bougainville. November 9, 1943.

RANK: Private First Class

UNIT: Company M, 3rd Raider Battalion, 2nd Raider Regiment

YEARS OF SERVICE: April 15, 1942 - November 9, 1943

AWARDS: Medal of Honor, Purple Heart

CCC: SP-5, Larimore, North Dakota. July - October 1941.

HENRY GURKE

Henry Gurke, a son of Julius and Hulda Gurke, grew up in Neche, North Dakota, a rural community of fewer than five hundred people, a few miles from Gretna, Manitoba, Canada. He was baptized in St. Olaf's Lutheran Church. In high school Henry sang in the school chorus, excelled in basketball, and maintained good grades. Unable to find a job after graduation, he and his brother, Tom, joined the Civilian Conservation Corps in 1941.

CCC EXPERIENCE

According to his aunt, Purdy Horgan:

> Henry and Tom were very happy to come home that first weekend. ... Perhaps the chance to exploit their bravado in the presence of the more timid souls who had yet to test the waters of the outside world. Homesickness took a back seat. The second weekend seemed more prosaic. New friends, new activities and other interests dulled the attraction of home which of course was less than a 100 miles. Now only the holidays mattered. Their trips home dwindled.

When Henry Gurke began his CCC service, he found new challenges almost daily. Certainly, his life was vastly different and more structured than at home. Making new friends from diverse areas, he thrived in the new environment. It took only a few months before he advanced to Assistant Leader which brought an increase in pay as well as an increase in responsibilities.

Gurke was quick to learn and possessed an ability to work with anybody, thereby allowing him to maintain his leadership position. Every day he led a squad of ten men into wide and varied assignments. Work had already begun on the park custodian's house. Tree planting, reclamation, and road work were high on the camp's priority list. The stream of assignments was endless.

The camp had a full complement of night school classes for the young men. The curriculum ranged widely from basic reading and writing to academic and technical studies. Additionally, the camp initiated correspondence courses with the University of North Dakota enabling Henry to sign up for a metallurgy course.

His aunt wrote, "Although, the boisterous, rowdy barrack's life appealed to Henry, he had tired of planting trees, dismantling old telephone lines, and building things. He left the CCC with an honorable discharge." Gurke returned to Neche, North Dakota, where he worked as a truck driver for the next few months.

Gurke enlisted in the Marine Corps in 1942 and received his basic training at San Diego before shipping overseas. The next six months of his itinerary read like a trip to exotic places: British Samoa, Pago Pago, and, eventually, Espiritu Santo, where he landed in January 1943. Transferred to Company M, 3rd Raider

From the Forest to the Battlefield

Battalion, 2nd Raider Regiment, 1st Marine Amphibious Corps in June, Gurke, then a PFC, moved to New Caledonia. Three days after celebrating his twenty-first birthday, he died in combat at Bougainville.

In a letter written to Robert Lorenz, Corporal Orville Fisher provided this account of Gurke's death on Bougainville.

> On November 9, 1943, our company was on a road block on the Piva Trail about two miles inland from our beachhead on Bougainville. We were attacked by a re-enforced battalion or a regiment of Japs. They dug in within five yards of our road block and were throwing high explosive grenades. We were all in two-man foxholes. Gurke had a Thompson sub machine gun and the other man named Probst had a Browning automatic rifle. Gurke told his buddy to keep his more effective weapon firing while he would take care of the grenades that were being thrown. He had thrown out several that were on a short 2 or 3 second fuse, when one came in that he could not find. So immediately he smothered the grenade with his body at the cost of his life. Probst did continue the fire and was awarded the Silver Star...Gurke was my best friend. We had known each other two years, very important years in my life.

MEDAL OF HONOR CITATION

For extraordinary heroism and courage above and beyond the call of duty while serving with the Third Marine Raider Battalion during action against the enemy Japanese Forces in the Solomon Islands area on November 9, 1943. While his platoon was engaged in the defense of a vital road block near Empress Augusta Bay on Bougainville Island, Private First Class Gurke, in company with another Marine, was delivering a fierce stream of fire against the main vanguard of the Japanese. Concluding from the increasing ferocity of grenade barrages that the enemy was determined to annihilate their shallow, two–man foxhole, he resorted to a bold and desperate measure for holding out despite the torrential hail of shells. When a Japanese grenade dropped squarely into the foxhole, Private First Class Gurke, mindful that his companion manned an automatic weapon of superior fire power and therefore could provide more effective resistance, thrust him roughly aside and flushing his own body over the missile to smother the explosion. With unswerving devotion to duty and superb valor, Private First Class Gurke sacrificed himself in order that his comrade might live to carry on the fight. He gallantly gave his life in the service of his country.

TWO LETTERS WRITTEN BY FRIENDS OF HENRY GURKE

Both letters were written to Mrs. Clayton (Elsie) Geiger, Henry Gurke's sister. These letters clearly came from the young men's hearts. The first was written by PFC Donald G. Probst whose life had been saved by Gurke's selfless actions.

> I was very glad to hear from you. I had wanted to write to you and express my feelings, but I didn't have your address. Also I have not been able to write for some time. I know you understand

why. Gurke, as he was known to us, gave the most that any man could to his country. I am eternally in his debt. He saved me more than once that day from grenades. He was recommended for the Congressional Medal of Honor and whether he is awarded it posthumously or not, we that are left in the old third platoon sincerely believe even <u>that</u> is not worthy of his supreme sacrifice. The night before he died he told me that he was going to NZ (New Zealand) for liberty. In closing I can only say that anything I could do or say wouldn't replace him, but I realize the sacrifice he made and that he has found his place in heaven.

The second letter was written by Corporal Orville L. Fisher, another buddy of Gurke's.

The Congressional Medal of Honor, as you probably know, is the highest award that can be given to anyone. We hope that it would go through for your sake and ours and the recognition it gives to Henry's memory. Therefore, I want you to talk to your mother and persuade her to accept enough money from me so she can get to Washington. Please make her understand that this is not a gift because I want one thing in return, a picture of her with the medal. Write me when she can go and I want an estimate of the expenses. I will get the money to her within three days after I get your letter. Please persuade her to do this because it will make her very proud and me very happy. I am in the hospital now recovering from malaria. If you lose my address and want to get in touch with me, just write to my parents, Mr. and Mrs. Roy Fisher, Murdock, Kansas. Guess that is all I can think of to write about. PS The money will not be hard to get as I have sent quite a bit home since I've been gone and I can think of nothing I would rather spend it for.

The Medal of Honor was presented to Henry Gurke's mother by the Assistant Secretary of the Navy on May 31, 1944. Henry's sister was also in attendance.

PFC Probst and Corporal Fisher made the financial arrangements for Gurke's mother and sister to go to Washington. Each man had won the Silver Star for his actions on the same day Henry Gurke, their close friend, died. The two men survived the war.

THE USS GURKE

In 1945 the USS Gurke was launched at the Todd-Pacific shipyards in Tacoma, Washington. Henry Gurke's aunt, Mrs. (Rhoda) Gurke was Matron of Honor while Mrs. Julius (Hulda) Gurke, Henry's mother, christened the ship. According to R.H Calkins, editor of the *Marine News*, "Mrs. Gurke was weeping quietly as she watched the new destroyer move swiftly down the ways as if hurrying off to avenge the death of her gallant son in the Pacific Theater of War."

Captain Wallin, a US Navy representative, said before the launching:

The men and women of this shipyard are doing their part to carry the war against the Japanese. Henry Gurke did his part and made the supreme sacrifice. His loyalty and devotion to duty is an urge for us to show a similar loyalty and devotion to work which is necessary to carry the fight to the finish. Henry Gurke did what he was called upon to do with the utmost loyalty and devotion.

From the Forest to the Battlefield

The USS Gurke was a destroyer whose mission was to provide anti-submarine and anti-surface defense for other ships. It was one of 103 Gearing Class destroyers built during the war.

In 1943 the *Stars and Stripes* ran a short article about PFC Henry Gurke. It proclaimed in bold type, "Sacrifice of a Life for a Pal Wins the Congressional Medal of Honor." Still another service newspaper began its story about Gurke with the oft quoted saw, "No greater love hath a man have...."

BURIAL SITE

Henry Gurke is buried in Union Cemetery at Neche, North Dakota.

LUTHER SKAGGS JR.

BIRTH DATE: March 3, 1923

BIRTH PLACE: Henderson, Kentucky

DEATH: April 6, 1976

MEDAL OF HONOR ACTION: Guam. July 21 - 22, 1944.

RANK: Private First Class

UNIT: 3rd Battalion, 3rd Marines

YEARS OF SERVICE: October 6, 1942 - April 4, 1946

AWARDS: Medal of Honor, Purple Heart

CCC: SP-9, Henderson, Kentucky. October 1939 - March 1940.

LUTHER SKAGGS JR.

Luther Skaggs Sr. and Ida Dalton were married on July 28, 1909. They had six boys and one girl. Their fourth born son, Luther Jr., was born on March 3, 1923, in Henderson, Kentucky. Neither Luther Sr. nor his wife had advanced beyond eighth grade. He worked sporadically during the 1930s. Ida worked as a housekeeper. Young Luther completed sixth grade at Central Street School in Henderson before dropping out.

By the time the boy had become a teenager, Henderson's population was nearly twelve thousand people. Its claim to fame is an association with the artist and naturalist, John James Audubon. In 1810 the twenty-five year old Audubon and his business partner operated a general merchandise store in Henderson. Audubon did very well in his new enterprise for a few years, but eventually lean economic times forced him to return to Louisville.

By 1939 Luther Sr. was unable to find employment. Due to his family's economic plight, Luther Jr. worked as a general laborer for Pricer Wood Products, a furniture manufacturer, in Detroit, Michigan. That job lasted only during the summer of 1939. As a result he enrolled in the CCC on October 19, 1939. His reason was simple: to help his family.

CCC EXPERIENCE

Luther was assigned to Camp Cromwell, SP-9, Company 1540. The camp, just three miles north of Henderson, was one of three state park CCC projects in Kentucky. His monthly allotment was sent to his mother. Luther was only seventeen years old at the time of his enrollment even though CCC regulations required an enrollee to be eighteen. Luther magically became a year older by indicating he was born in 1922 rather than 1923. This form of deception by applicants was very common in the CCC because these young men and their families had fallen upon such desperate times.

Luther Skaggs Jr. received all satisfactory and good ratings for his work at Camp Cromwell. He took classes in painting and carpentry and his personnel record noted an outstanding rating for camp maintenance and repair. Upon his honorable discharge on March 25, 1940, James D. Berry, Project Superintendent, wrote, "Luther Skaggs, Jr. while working under the supervision of the Technical Service performed his duties in an excellent manner."

Camp Cromwell was an excellent camp. Established on October 4, 1934, it would later become John James Audubon State Park. The camp was named in honor of the director of Kentucky state parks, Emma Guy Cromwell.

From the Forest to the Battlefield

The CCC boys built two lakes, developed trails, gardens, and roads, constructed cabins and picnic shelters, and built a museum in honor of John James Audubon. Alfred Cornebise, CCC historian, notes that the librarian in Henderson wrote an editorial about Camp Cromwell. Her words of praise appeared in the camp newspaper, *The Cromwell Cardinal*. The librarian wrote, "Rarely does a detachment of men, stationed near a town, make the good impression on the community that the CCC camp has made on Henderson. This most satisfactory condition is due, of course, not only to the boys but to the institution of the camp, to its discipline, its educational system, its general conditions."

After his stint in the CCC, Luther worked at various jobs in Henderson. Howard Sapp, the Western Union manager in Henderson, remembered Luther as a reliable telegraph messenger. His last known civilian job before enlisting in the Marines was with the Rural Electrification Administration. After the war John Hardin, the manager of the R.E.A. Office in Henderson, said, "He was a tough little guy, all right. He was always looking for the hardest job-always!"

On October 6, 1942, Luther enlisted in the Marines. His basic training was at Parris Island, South Carolina, and Camp Lejeune, North Carolina. From there he moved to Camp Elliott near San Diego, California. Two days before his twentieth birthday, he received his orders for overseas deployment to the Pacific on March 1, 1943.

On July 21, 1944, The Second Battle of Guam was about to begin. Guam, a former American territory, and the largest island in the Marianas group had been captured by the Japanese just a few days after their successful attack on Pearl Harbor. The Japanese commander, General Takashina, had carved out a command post in a sandstone cliff overlooking the beachhead. From this strategic vantage point, he watched the 3rd Marine Division head for shore. The landing began under cover of a beautiful blue sky, but soon all the beaches had turned into dust, smoke, and fire.

At 0808 an air observer shouted into his microphone: "First wave on the beach." A bit later another announcer proclaimed, "Troops ashore on all beaches." Luther found himself on the Asan-Adelup Beachhead amid heavy enemy fire.

When a section leader was killed by mortar fire, Luther took command and led the unit through heavy fire to a position where the Marines could cover the assault on a strategic cliff. Through the night they defended this position while under enemy attack. Luther was critically wounded when a Japanese grenade lodged in his foxhole. The explosion shattered his left leg below the knee. Quickly Luther applied his belt as a tourniquet, slowing the bleeding. He fought another eight hours using his rifle and hand grenades. Fortunately, mud from the Japanese grenades caked the stump of his leg which stopped the bleeding. Later, he crawled to the rear unassisted and continued to fight on until the Japanese were annihilated. Luther was referred to as a "tough little guy" by his buddies. They didn't know that he had been hit until the battle was over. He was modest about his heroic action. He simply said, "Someone had to do it. It just happened to be me."

Luther lost his left leg as a result of his wounds. After he returned stateside for medical treatment, Colonel Lawrence Forsyth, the executive officer of Fort Knox, said, "Luther realized to call for a medical corpsman would reveal the position of his unit so he calmly applied a tourniquet to his shattered leg and fought on. " This "tough little guy" was awarded the Medal of Honor by President Truman on June 15, 1945, at a ceremony at the White House.

MEDAL OF HONOR CITATION

For conspicuous gallantry and intrepidity at the risk of his life above and beyond the call of duty while serving as Squad Leader with a Mortar Section of a Rifle Company in the Third Battalion, Third Marines, Third Marine Division, during action against enemy Japanese forces on the Asan-Adelup Beachhead, Guam, Marianas Islands, on 21–22 July 1944. When the section leader became a casualty under a heavy mortar barrage shortly after landing, Private First Class Skaggs promptly assumed command and led the section through intense fire for a distance of 200 yards to a position from which to deliver effective coverage of the assault on a strategic cliff. Valiantly defending this vital position against strong enemy counterattacks during the night, Private First Class Skaggs was critically wounded when a Japanese grenade lodged in his foxhole and exploded, shattering the lower part of one leg. Quick to act, he applied an improvised tourniquet and, while propped up in his foxhole, gallantly returned the enemy's fire with his rifle and hand grenades for a period of eight hours, later crawling unassisted to the rear to continue to fight until the Japanese had been annihilated. Uncomplaining and calm throughout this critical period, Private First Class Skaggs served as a heroic example of courage and fortitude to other wounded men and, by his courageous leadership and inspiring devotion to duty, upheld the highest traditions for the United States Naval Service.

DAY OF CELEBRATION

On June 26, 1945, the town of Henderson, Kentucky, welcomed PFC Luther Skaggs Jr. home from the war. Luther had a ten-day leave before returning to a Navy hospital in Philadelphia. Merchants closed their stores, and Mayor Clore proclaimed "Luther Skaggs Day." Thousands lined a parade route to greet and applaud their hero. It was the longest parade that Henderson, Kentucky, had ever witnessed. Countless bands, floats, soldiers, and armored equipment from Fort Knox, Kentucky, passed by. Skaggs sat in the back of an open car and waved to the crowd. A program and reception was held in Henderson's Central Park. Skaggs said, "It's great to be decorated by the President of the United States. It's great to meet high officials in Washington and it's great to be on a national radio program, but none of these things mean as much to me as this reception." After several speakers praised Luther, the Jean Campbell Accordion Band played a medley of war songs. When they played the Marine Hymn, Luther grinned appreciatively. Just before the program ended, Henry A. Taylor, War Bond Chairman for Henderson County, handed Luther a "wad" of folded money and announced, "We understand that the government will furnish you with an artificial leg, but we also understand that a better one can be bought. We have raised this fund for that purpose." Luther graciously accepted the monetary gift, and then cleverly said, "I have a lot of buddies who won't be home until this war is over. You can help get it over by buying war bonds." He then went home to rest in the afternoon. A banquet was held that evening with Major D. Banks as master of ceremonies and the keynote speaker. During the banquet, Skaggs was given a wrist watch, a picture of President Truman putting the Medal of Honor around his neck, and other gifts.

LIFE AFTER WORLD WAR II

Luther Skaggs was promoted to corporal and honorably discharged from the Marines Corps on April 4, 1946. He relocated to the Bethesda, Maryland, area and worked as a budget analyst in the Department of Defense at the Pentagon. Later Luther was a Veterans Administration employee until his retirement. Luther met Irma, a nurse, while in Maryland. They never married, but together moved to Sarasota, Florida, in 1974.

FAMILY MEMORIES

Jean Skaggs, Luther's sister-in-law, remembers him as a "gentleman" who was handsome, had an infectious grin, and exuded a strong personality. In fact she called him "Mr. Personality" and offered that he was a good dancer, too. Richard, Jean's husband and Luther's younger brother, remembers that Luther advised him not to join the Marines. Despite those words of caution, Luther's great-niece, Jennifer, and great-nephew, Michael, enlisted in the United States Marine Corps. Jennifer became a Staff Sergeant. She remembers touring the National Museum of the Marine Corps and was shown a wall of fame with Luther's photo on display. The Sergeant Major asked, "Do any of you know any of these men?" He was astounded when Jennifer replied, "Yes! That's my great -uncle!" Her brother Michael had a similar experience when graduating from boot camp at Parris Island. The Skaggs family is a proud Marine Corps family! Jean vows that the honor and integrity of Luther's Medal of Honor will be passed on to future generations.

Julie Skaggs, Richard and Jean's daughter, remembers visiting her Uncle Luther when she was a child. "He never talked about the war or what he did," she said. Julie fondly remembers giggling when Luther would remove his leg (prosthesis) and go in the swimming pool! Luther always lamented he never had an education beyond sixth grade. He told Julie when she was a teenager, "Be sure to get an education."

CONGRESSIONAL MEDAL OF HONOR SOCIETY

On August 5, 1958, President Eisenhower had signed legislation chartering the Congressional Medal of Honor Society. The major purpose of the organization was to protect, uphold, and preserve the dignity and honor of the Medal of Honor. It also offers a bond of friendship and comradeship to all holders of this prestigious medal.

Luther became the first enlisted man to become president of the Congressional Medal of Honor Society, an honor shared with three generals. On November 11, 1963, Luther attended a Veterans Day ceremony at Arlington National Cemetery with President John F. Kennedy and several military dignitaries. Eleven days later President Kennedy was assassinated in Dallas, Texas. Kennedy's death was a severe blow to Luther, as he had been heavily involved in the Kennedy-Johnson campaign in 1960.

Only two enlisted men have headed up the Congressional Medal of Honor Society. Sergeant Major Gary L. Littrell served two consecutive terms as president. Littrell was awarded the Medal of Honor for heroic actions in Viet Nam in April 1970. He was born in Henderson, Kentucky, just three months after Luther lost his leg in Guam. What an honor for Henderson, Kentucky, to be the hometown of two presidents of this exclusive society!

HONORS

Green highway signs were erected on the U.S. 41-Bypass on August 6, 2014, declaring the roadway to be named in honor of Henderson County's two Medal of Honor recipients: Luther Skaggs Jr. and Gary Lee Littrell.

On the second floor of the Henderson County Courthouse, the uniforms of Skaggs and Littrell are on display. Visitors can watch a video recording there of Skaggs talking about his experiences.

Luther's name, as well as the names of all veterans from Henderson county, was inscribed on the Henderson War Memorial. That memorial was dedicated on Memorial Day 1999.

On March 15, 2012, Governor Steve Beshner unveiled a bronze plaque listing the names of Kentucky's sixty Medal of Honor recipients including PFC Luther Skaggs Jr. The plaque hangs in the Capitol Rotunda opposite a statue of Abraham Lincoln who worked with Congress to create the Medal of Honor in 1862.

BURIAL SITE

Luther Skaggs, Jr. died of lung cancer in Sarasota, Florida, on April 6, 1976, at age fifty-three. He was buried with full military honors in Section 46 of Arlington National Cemetery, Arlington, Virginia.

TONY STEIN

BIRTH DATE: September 30, 1921

BIRTH PLACE: Dayton, Ohio

DEATH: March 1, 1945. KIA.

MEDAL OF HONOR ACTION: Iwo Jima. March 1, 1945.

RANK: Corporal

UNIT: Company A, 1st Battalion, 28th Marines, 5th Marine Division

YEARS OF SERVICE: September 22, 1942 - March 1, 1945

AWARDS: Medal of Honor, Purple Heart

CCC: BR-88, Redmond, Oregon. October 1939 - March 1940.

TONY STEIN

Steve and Rose Stein were immigrants from Austria-Hungary who came to America in 1909 and settled in Dayton, Ohio. Steve Stein was born in 1888, while Rose, his wife, was two years younger. Poorly educated, collectively they had less than seven years of formal education. The 1920 census showed that Rose spoke only German. Steve worked in Dayton as a molder at a Dayton foundry while Rose remained at home with their children. Of the couple's three children, Tony, the middle child, was born on September 30, 1921. He had two sisters: Theresa and Mary Louise.

Tony grew up on the streets of North Dayton. He was a tough, streetwise kid who excelled in athletics, especially boxing. Quite likely his physical size hurried along his maturation. He was only five feet four inches tall and weighed 110 pounds soaking wet. Very quickly, his nickname became "Tough Tony" because of his pugnaciousness.

His uncle Tony proudly admitted, "That kid don't mess around."

Charlene Rubush, a relative of Tony Stein, recalled how Tony's uncle egged him on to fight anyone the kid took a dislike to." She added, "Young Tony was the kind of guy that liked to have a lot of action going around him and he was smart and handsome."

Elinor Sluzas, who had a restaurant in North Dayton, remembered Tony as he grew up in the neighborhood. "Tony was a raw-boned, rugged kid who put his heart and soul into everything he did...He was a child of destiny who became a leader of men. Like all the kids at Old North Dayton, he loved softball, boxing, and golf...He became a Golden Gloves champion and set pins in the neighborhood."

James "Pee-Wee" Martin, a fellow World War II hero and a classmate of Stein, remembered him clearly when interviewed by a Dayton, Ohio, newspaper in 2017:

> Tony was a good guy and known to be on the rough side. We grew up together in Old North Dayton...We were typical Depression Era kids...Tony had a habit of speaking "Truth to power" and that included some of our teachers. Tony felt the same as I do, 'When your country needs you, you go and do your best.'

Tony went to Kiser High School, where he received average grades. He dropped out of school, in tenth grade because, "All the action was elsewhere." Later, he joined the CCC to help his widowed mother.

CCC EXPERIENCE

Every CCC enrollee's silent prayer was an assignment in California so he could soak his feet in the Pacific Ocean. Of course, this rarely happened since need dictated assignments, usually in their home states.

Stein's posting did not hit the Golden Gate Jackpot. Instead, he garnered second prize: six months in Oregon, two hundred miles from the Pacific.

He served at BR-88 from October 1939 to March 1940 near Redmond, Oregon, in the center of the state. It was a reclamation camp where Tony worked at stream improvement work, helped maintain a fish hatchery, and constructed primitive camping sites. His was a hands-on job. Tony admitted that Oregon was a far cry from the streets of North Dayton where he had grown up.

His CCC stint was routine because most CCC work relied on brawn not brains. His work was rated satisfactory, and his educational adviser judged him as having good character. Tony enrolled in a cooking class, and he continued to box, a very popular camp activity. His allotment went to his mother, Rose Parks, who had remarried. Tony received an honorable discharge from the CCC in March 1940.

When he returned to Dayton, Tony went to work with Delco Products, a division of General Motors. There he worked as a tool and die maker until his enlistment in the US Marine Corps in September 1942.

After completing basic training at Parris Island, Tony applied to the Paramarines, an elite Marine parachute outfit that had a 50 percent dropout rate. But "Tough Tony" made it. After rigorous training, he received his coveted Paramarine patch. Tony shipped out to the South Pacific with the 3rd Marine Division where he saw action at Bougainville and Vella Lavella in 1943 and 1944.

ALLIED STRATEGY: BOUGAINVILLE AND VELLA LAVELLA

The strategy was to cut off any Japanese advance southwest to the Solomon Islands and to neutralize the huge Japanese strongholds at Raboul and Truk Island. These two giant installations had contributed greatly to the near defeat of the American forces at Guadalcanal as the Japanese Navy supplied their troops there with impunity for most of the six-month struggle. Additionally, there had been a real threat of a Japanese invasion of Australia in 1942. But General Douglas MacArthur negated that danger by taking the fight to the Japanese in New Guinea, thereby putting Raboul and Truk on constant alert.

Bougainville was important to the Allied cause because of its port facilities and existing air bases that the Japanese had built in 1942. Vella Lavella, considerably smaller than Bougainville, had an excellent four-thousand-foot runway, sufficient to support bombers capable of hitting Raboul and Truk.

After combat in Vella Lavella, Tony went home to Dayton where he married his sweetheart, Joan Stominger. They enjoyed a three-day honeymoon before he returned to the South Pacific.

In the meantime, the Paramarines had been dissolved, and Tony became part of the 5th Marine Division. Many of Tony's buddies from jump school also soldiered with the 5th Marines. In fact, five former members of this elite group became recipients of the Medal of Honor at Iwo Jima.

From the Forest to the Battlefield

Corporal Stein always seemed to do things in a big and unconventional way, no matter whether it might be to come up with a new weapon or to get a large tattoo. *On the Axis History Forum,* a blogger posted, "Stein had a full arm tattoo of some kind of cat, maybe a panther. Back in those days, people just didn't go out and get big tattoos on their arms like that but Tony didn't think twice."

TONY STEIN AND HIS "STINGER"

Tony Stein stormed the volcanic sands during the Iwo Jima invasion on February 19, 1945, with his weapon of choice: a modified 30 caliber machine gun, a killer of Japanese pillboxes. Called the "Stinger," this gun was not standard Marine issue. But after tests before the Iwo Jima invasion, the Marine Corps approved the weapon, and Stein became one of six Marines who carried it into battle.

The weapon represented Marine ingenuity born out of combat needs. Actual field experiences showed the need for a lighter and more user- friendly machine gun. The traditional Browning M1919 machine gun, excellent as a defensive weapon, was considered cumbersome and heavy as an assault weapon.

Stein, a tool and die maker and a combat savvy Marine, envisioned a potent field weapon available only in salvage depots. With the advice of a Marine armorer, he commandeered a mounted, rear-turret 30 caliber machine gun from a wrecked Douglas Dauntless dive bomber. One source claimed that he broke the weapon down and carried it with him in his pack, thereby giving him additional time to think through this project.

Tony knew that this gun was lighter than the traditional Browning machine gun and could fire an incredible 1,300 rounds a minute, twice the capability of the traditional M1919. Cannibalizing the sights and the bipod from a Browning automatic rifle, he employed his machinist's know-how and attached these pieces onto the machine gun. Then came a stroke of genius! He added an M1 rifle stock, thereby allowing the gunner to engage the weapon while lying in a prone position. From an infantryman's view, the addition of the stock was significant. Since the weapon weighed only thirty pounds, a Marine "grunt" could fire the piece while on the move, thus creating an incredible assault capability. For someone on the receiving end of this weapon, this weapon was nothing less than "shock and awe." Another source called Tony Stein "a bullet-spewing Frankenstein."

Mission: History provided a graphic account of Stein's first hours on the beach:

> When the 28th hit Green Beach at Iwo Jima, the landing spot closest to Mount Suribachi, the 1st Battalion was to drive straight across the island with the 2nd Battalion following part of the way and then turning toward the volcano. It wasn't long before A company's commander, Aaron Wilkins, was the only company commander left in his battalion. When A company moved out Tony Stein was in the lead, and he headed straight for a Jap pillbox. With his stinger he suppressed the Jap fire and a demolition team blew up the emplacement. That worked so well,

they did it all morning. In the first hour of the advance Stein personally killed 20 Japs, then he ran out of ammo. It was exceedingly difficult to run or even walk on this sandy volcanic ash of Iwo, so Stein took off his shoes. Then he took off his helmet. He grabbed a wounded Marine and hustled him off to the beach. Then he grabbed as many ammo boxes as he could carry and ran back to his outfit. He made that trip eight times that day, each time getting a wounded man to safety. His stinger was shot out of his hands twice but at the end of the day he was still shooting Japs with it...On Wednesday evening D+2, Tony got hit in the shoulder and was told to hustle himself to the beach for evacuation. The wound was a "million dollar" injury. He was, however, back in the line by Saturday.

On D Day+10, the 28th was on the other end of the island, the "fat" part. The 1st and 2nd Battalions were faced with an eighty-foot cliff leading into a ravine full of enemy riflemen in tunnels and caves. The only way to the other side was to go around on the shoulders which were certain to be covered by every sort of fire the Japanese had. Additionally, the place was crawling with snipers. Captain Wilkins of Able Company called for volunteers, and Tony Stein responded. Wilkins led a twenty-man patrol to the shoulder to clear out the snipers. Only seven Marines returned. Neither Wilkins nor Stein was among them.

Tony Stein was awarded the Medal of Honor for his conspicuous gallantry on D-Day. His heroics on D Day+10 made the medal posthumous.

Terence Kyle, a blogger on *The Drawn Cutlass,* related that his uncle, Kent Stenger, was part of that ill-fated patrol and was with Tony when he died. This is an excerpt from his uncle's journal:

> The next morning we moved up over a bank in line with the skirmishes without opposition, and started to advance over one of the few long, level areas we had experienced on the island. When we got to the middle of the area we were hit from all directions. Pete Hansen went down on my left, Tony Stein on my right. Earl Dent dragged Ben to a shell hole for cover, a corpsman had Pete, and I had Tony Stein. He was alive but not for long. He had a hole in his back larger than my fist. He died in my arms.

MEDAL OF HONOR CITATION

For conspicuous gallantry and intrepidity at the risk of his life above and beyond the call of duty while serving with Company A, 1st Battalion, 28th Marines, 5th Marine Division, in action against enemy Japanese forces on Iwo Jima, in the Volcano Islands, 19 February 1945. The first man of his unit to be on station after hitting the beach in the initial assault, Cpl. Stein, armed with a personally improvised aircraft-type weapon, provided rapid covering fire as the remainder of his platoon attempted to move into position. When his comrades were stalled by a concentrated machinegun and mortar barrage, he gallantly stood upright and exposed himself to the enemy's view, thereby drawing the hostile fire to his own person and enabling him to observe the location of the furiously blazing hostile guns. Determined to neutralize the strategically placed weapons, he boldly charged the enemy pillboxes 1 by 1 and succeeded in killing 20 of the enemy during the furious single-handed assault. Cool and courageous under the merciless hail of exploding shells and bullets which fell on all sides, he continued to deliver the fire of his skillfully improvised weapon at a tremendous rate of speed which rapidly exhausted his ammunition. Undaunted, he removed his helmet and shoes to expedite his movements and ran back to the beach for additional ammunition, making a total of 8 trips under intense fire and carrying or assisting a wounded man back each time. Despite the unrelenting savagery and confusion of battle, he rendered prompt assistance to his platoon whenever the unit was in position, directing the fire of a half-track against a stubborn pillbox until he had effected the ultimate destruction of the Japanese fortification. Later in the day, although his weapon was twice shot from his hands, he personally covered the withdrawal of his platoon to the company position. Stouthearted and indomitable, Cpl. Stein, by his aggressive initiative sound judgment, and unwavering devotion to duty in the face of terrific odds, contributed materially to the fulfillment of his mission, and his outstanding valor throughout the bitter hours of conflict sustains and enhances the highest traditions of the US Naval Service.

MEDAL OF HONOR PRESENTATION

Stein's posthumous Medal of Honor presentation occurred February 19, 1946, in the office of the Ohio governor, Frank Lausche. Mrs. Joan Stein received the medal for her husband.

HONORS

The American Legion Tony Stein Post 619 in Dayton, Ohio, was established shortly after the war.

A two-block street in Dayton was named Tony Stein Way.

A bridge formally called the Keowee Bridge over the Mad River located in North Dayton was renamed Tony Stein Bridge. Ronald Bookly, President of the Kiser High School Alumnae Association, said at the dedication, "This memorial bridge should not be thought of as a war memorial but rather a memorial to the sacrifice of a North Dayton citizen." It is ironic that the bridge is close to the place where Tony saved a boy from drowning.

A Knox Class frigate, USS Stein FF 1965, was put into service by the United States Navy in 1972. It served the fleet admirably until 1992 when it was retired from service.

Tony Stein was inducted into The Dayton Walk of Fame on July 11, 2012. Retired Marine Master Sergeant Jim Snyder read Stein's Medal of Honor citation at the induction.

The residents of North Dayton, Ohio, celebrated Heritage Day on August 8, 2014, at Eintracht Park. The festival honored Tony Stein, Dayton's only Medal of Honor recipient.

From the Forest to the Battlefield

The Parris Island Historical and Museum Society's Living History Detachment features a profile of Tony Stein as well as his singular weapon, the Stinger.

THE TONY STEIN WORKOUT

The US Marine Corps instituted a Stein Workout based on Stein's heroic dashes on the first day's battle at Iwo Jima. This became part of the physical training schedule for Marine recruits in the 1950s.

Ingredients: A twenty-five-yard PT site; eight Marines to be carried individually by an "active" ninth Marine, who represents Stein; a thirty-pound kettle bell represents the Stinger, fully loaded; and sixteen thirty-pound ammunition cans to be carried two at a time by the "active" Marine on each trip to the front.

A Marine must do eight replications representing the number of times Stein raced from the front line to the rear line.

After the ammunition cans have been placed on one side of PT site, the "active" Marine must sprint to the front; do ten kettle swings (representing the Stinger being fired) before picking up a "wounded" Marine. Then the "active" Marine must run to the other end of the PT site while carrying his comrade via the fireman's carry. On his return trip, the Marine must carry two thirty-pound ammo boxes. At this point he will do ten kettle bell swings before picking up a "wounded" Marine and returning him to the starting line.

BURIAL SITE

Originally, Stein was interred at the 5th Division Cemetery on Iwo Jima. His remains, however, were repatriated and reinterred at the Calvary Cemetery in Kettering, Montgomery County, Ohio. A full military service and a Mass was held at Our Lady of the Rosary Catholic Church in Dayton, Ohio.

WILSON D. WATSON

BIRTH DATE: February 16, 1922

BIRTH PLACE: Tuscumbia, Alabama

DEATH: December 19, 1994

MEDAL OF HONOR ACTION: Iwo Jima. February 26 - 27, 1945.

RANK: Private

UNIT: 2nd Battalion, 9th Marines, 3rd Marine Division

YEARS OF SERVICE: August 6, 1942 - 1946 (USMC) September 30, 1946 - 1966 (Army Air Force and the US Army as a Mess Hall Cook).

AWARDS: Medal of Honor, Purple Heart

CCC: F-190, Lowell, ID. SP-2, Two Harbors, Minnesota. July - August 1941. F-10, Tote, Minnesota. July - October 1941. F-5, Grand Marais, Minnesota. November 1, 1941. Never reported to F-5.

WILSON D. WATSON

Wilson's parents were Charles G. Watson (1898-1980) and Ada Belle Posey Watson (1899-1989) both of whom were natives of Alabama. Their abject poverty had already doomed this couple. They were poorly educated and neither was twenty when they married. Ultimately the couple had had twelve children before they reached their mid-forties. The family lived in a rented farm house where Charles Watson labored as a sharecropper. Barely able to sustain his family, he moved them to Earle, Arkansas, only to find sharecropping there was a dead end too. His annual income for 1939 was $100.00.

Wilson quit school after sixth grade because he said, "I had to work." As a teenager, he stood five foot seven inches tall and weighed 130 pounds. His blue eyes had a sadness in them that belied his handsome features. Watson worked sporadically at a sawmill until the owner moved the mill out of state. Possessing an innate ability at mechanics, Watson enjoyed tinkering with trucks. When he enrolled in the CCC, he began a rather bizarre adventure.

Upon examination of the lives of these Medal of Honor recipients prior to their becoming CCC enrollees, one thing stands out: nearly all their families were mired in poverty. Had it not been for the CCC, these folks would not have survived. One has to look only at the dreary family statistics of these recipients. Hope had disappeared from their vocabulary as the misery of the Great Depression strangled them. Family structure disintegrated, and many young men drifted into oblivion. The CCC offered a respite from this bleak cycle of hopelessness. Significantly, the monthly allotment that each family received was manna from heaven, temporarily averting a life-threatening crisis, either physically or psychologically.

For the individual enrollee, the CCC provided a window to the outside world that hitherto had been unattainable and created a glimmer of hope for each enrollee who now actually had a job. The work was long and hard, but the CCC brought together men from all parts of the country who lived and worked together. Additionally, CCC service benefited the men by improving self-esteem, self-discipline, and providing a sense of purpose.

At the height of the Great Depression, few men had ever seen a dollar bill, yet the enrollee received food, clothing, housing, medical care, education, and a wage of five dollars a month for their personal use. They were living "high off the hog!" More importantly, the CCC helped develop an individual's work ethic which had a profound impact later when they entered the service or defense plants. Most men had unremarkable CCC experiences. A few bridled from the experience and deserted. But significantly, it marked the first time these young men were introduced to military discipline, a trait badly needed in the forthcoming war.

Wilson Watson was a typical CCC enrollee. Dirt poor with no hope of rising above sharecropping status,

CCC membership altered his life. He had traveled as far away as Idaho, served with men from California, and interacted with enrollees who had vastly different backgrounds. His CCC service became a cultural leap into a rapidly expanding modern world.

CCC EXPERIENCE

Enrolled initially in October 1940, Wilson served until March 1941 at F-190 at Lowell, Idaho, where he cut clearings and trimmed brush along newly constructed forest trails. His superiors rated his work as satisfactory. He took classes in first aid, arithmetic, grammar, and spelling and received above average grades. After six months Wilson received an honorable discharge.

Then he enlisted again. He spent his first six weeks at Camp SP-2, at Two Harbors, Minnesota, working on trails and building camp sites. Six weeks later, he transferred to Camp F-10 at Tofte, Minnesota, where he drove a truck. When he was reassigned to Camp F-5 at Grand Marais, Minnesota, he had lost his truck driver position. Consequently, he never reported to camp, leading to his subsequent dismissal.

MILITARY EXPERIENCE

Watson's proclivity of not adhering to rules continued through his military career, thereby causing several demotions from PFC to buck private, particularly in his hitch in the Marine Corps. Even when he enlisted in the Army, after his service in World War II, Wilson Watson marched to a different drummer.

Watson began his military career when he enlisted at Little Rock, Arkansas, on August 6, 1942. There is no doubt that his was an unusual career. As he said much later, "I started my service in the Marines, then the Air Force and ended up in the Army."

He received his basic training at Marine Corps Recruit Depot in San Diego, California, and served as an Automatic Rifleman in Company Y for Yankee, 2nd Battalion, 9th Marine Infantry Regiment, 3rd Division. The unit deployed to New Zealand from January to March 1943 with additional training at Guadalcanal for another six months. Watson saw his first combat at Bougainville in late September 1943.

A few days prior to the invasion of Bougainville, he wrote to his friend, Tom Sellers, from Earle, Arkansas. "How is farming this time? From what I hear it is not so hot...Well, I think, I could stand a little more tractor driving now for if I was ever tired of anything, this is it." Apparently thinking ahead to combat, he wrote: "I know what those bombs are like and guess you know I don't like them one damn bit."

The following summer he saw more hard fighting during the liberation of Guam. The fighting was severe on both islands. His division suffered 30 percent causalities.

But the worst was yet to come.

From the Forest to the Battlefield

The conflict on Iwo Jima had been waging for six days before Watson and his comrades came ashore. While the Japanese rained down fire, his outfit dug in for the night. The next morning, they hit the line, facing one desperate situation after another leading eventually to Watson's heroism. During those two days, he single-handedly killed over sixty enemy soldiers while sustaining seven serious wounds. Finally, a bullet to his neck forced him from the field. The legend of the One-Man Regiment was born.

Later when asked what had happened, he said, "I was running on adrenaline. The only thing on my mind was that we had to knock out those machine gun nests or they were surely going to kill us." His buddies had to remind him of his wounds. Watson said, "They told me to lay down until they could get a medic." When he looked down at himself he saw blood spurting from all over his body. "I hadn't felt a thing up to that point," he admitted.

MEDAL OF HONOR CITATION

For conspicuous gallantry and intrepidity at the risk of his life above and beyond the call of duty as Automatic Rifleman serving with the Second Battalion, Ninth Marines, Third Marine Division, during action against enemy Japanese forces on Iwo Jima, Volcano Islands, 26 and 27 February 1945. With his squad abruptly halted by intense fire from enemy fortifications in the high rocky ridges and crags commanding the line of advance, Private Watson boldly rushed one pillbox and fired into the embrasure with his weapon, keeping the enemy pinned down single-handedly until he was in a position to hurl in a grenade and then running to the rear of the emplacement to destroy the retreating Japanese and enable his platoon to take its objective. Again pinned down at the foot of a small hill, he dauntlessly scaled the jagged incline under fierce mortar and machine-gun barrages and with his assistant automatic rifleman charged the crest of the hill, firing from his hip. Fighting furiously against Japanese troops attacking with grenades and knee-mortars from the reverse slope, he stood fearlessly erect in his exposed position to cover the hostile entrenchments and held the hill under savage fire for fifteen minutes, killing sixty Japanese before his ammunition was exhausted and his platoon was able to join him. His courageous initiative and valiant fighting spirit against devastating odds were directly responsible for the continued advance of his platoon and his inspiring leadership throughout this bitterly fought action reflects the highest credit upon Private Watson and the United States Naval Service.

MEDAL OF HONOR PRESENTATION

President Harry Truman presented the Medal of Honor to Watson at the White House on October 5, 1945. None of his family attended because they received the invitation too late.

LIFE AFTER WORLD WAR II

Upon returning home immediately after the war, Watson was feted in his hometown of Earle, Arkansas. A newspaper headline read, "Killer Of 60 Japs Welcomed Home." His brother Paul said, "They even brought in the Clydesdale horses from St. Louis." The appreciative townspeople gave him a 12-gauge shotgun. Later, he lost it in a card game.

Kenneth Watson, a younger brother, remembered Wilson as one who liked the outdoors and was an avid hunter and fisherman. Kenneth visited his brother frequently at Fort Rucker and fondly remembered their fishing trips at a nearby lake. "We'd take a taxi cab to the lake for thirty-five cents, enough to get us to the lake and back."

Watson had married in the early 1950s. He and his wife, Patricia, had three children: a son, Ricky, and two daughters, Darlene and Betty. After his retirement from the Army in 1966, he was employed as a forester.

A STARK REMEMBRANCE OF A HERO

Carl Hurst of Marble Hill, Missouri, oversaw the mess hall storeroom at Fort Rucker, Alabama, where Watson served during 1961-1962. Hurst remembered that Watson was a private even though he was forty:

> Watson was not a large man, rather skinny and a heavy drinker which gave him a ruddy face. He did the cake baking and when the occasion called for it, he could roll up a cone of wax paper, fill it with frosting, and create a work of art. He was quiet and unassuming and something of a loner. He did not fit the image of a hero. On payday he would disappear for three or four days. It was kind of a joke in the company. They would say, "Well Watson's gone again but he'll come back when he runs out of money." He made private first class once but was busted the next day for being AWOL.
>
> When a buddy told me that Watson had a Medal of Honor. I said, "Oh! You've got to be kidding. He wouldn't hurt a flea." One day I was poking around the post library and came across a book on the Medal of Honor. Sure enough Watson was in there...Shortly after that I asked him, "Watson, someone told me you have the Medal of Honor." He responded matter-of-factly, "Yeah, I have one." I said, "You're a hero." He said, "No I'm not a hero. That's just what I had to do."

While in his office, Hurst received a startling phone call from the Commanding Officer of Fort Benning, Georgia, who needed to talk to Watson. After the call was completed, Hurst wanted to know what it was about. Watson said, "The General is going to a Medal of Honor Convention at Seattle, Washington, and he wanted to know if I wanted to ride up with him." Hurst responded, "Watson, I've been in the Army long enough to know that generals don't hang around with privates." Watson replied, "Oh, this is different. If you are a Congressional Medal of Honor winner, there is no rank."

Hurst was astounded for he knew Watson as someone who drank heavily, decorated cakes, and was frequently AWOL. To Hurst, Watson was a "professional private," that is, someone who just floated through the military system in a haze, producing nothing and waiting for a discharge.

Watson's brother, Paul, tried to explain his brother's action to Mark Randall, a reporter from *The Evening Times* in Marion, Arkansas. Paul said, "My brother was a man of action with little regard for authority...who realized that decorating cakes was a far cry from his Marine combat days." As a result, Paul Watson thought a combination of boredom and drinking triggered his brother's disregard for military rules.

WILSON WATSON AND JOHN WAYNE

In 1949 Republic Movie Studio produced *The Sands of Iwo Jima*, a film starring John Wayne. Since the war was fresh in the minds of Americans, and in an effort to capitalize on the movie, the studio brought in many of the heroic Marines who had participated in that battle. The men were given official titles: military advisors. Actually, their involvement was a massive publicity stunt, recognized by all.

According to mythic lore, Wayne heard how Watson had charged a crest of a hill at Iwo Jima while firing his weapon from his hip. Wayne was keen on that image and incorporated Watson's technique into the film, thereby creating an iconic picture of the warrior: John Wayne.

TO THINE OWN SELF BE TRUE

Wilson Watson was his own man. He was an independent individual who chafed under authority. Initially, this trait was manifested during his second stint in the CCC. He lost his truck driving position over a simple reassignment. Unhappy, he went AWOL and returned home. Life in the Marine Corps wasn't much different. He remained a perpetual private, running afoul of the system in a myriad of ways.

After three major island campaigns from 1943-1945 where his outfit took huge losses, Watson still remained a private. In 1946 he joined the Air Force, but it was a poor fit. By this time he had begun drinking more heavily; most likely brought on by his horrific experiences in the Pacific. Watson was not unusual. Many soldiers languished in this role. These men were assigned to the mess hall or to a headquarters company where they could do the least harm to themselves and to the Army.

In October 16, 1962, Wilson Watson took off again. He got into his car and drove home from Fort Rucker, Alabama. He remained AWOL for 121 days. On February 14, 1963, the Crittenden County police arrested him in Marked Tree, Arkansas, less than twenty miles from Earle, Arkansas. He had been living at home in a small town of less than 2,500 people. Well known to all, he certainly was not hiding out.

No one knows who told the police, prompting Watson's arrest. He ended up in the county jail where his jailer was Robert Warren, a long-time friend. According to Warren, Watson told him, "I just got tired of it all... The Army messed up my records...I wanted to get out. So I got teed off. I got in my car and drove off." The Army authorities took Watson back to Fort Sill, Oklahoma, where ordinarily he would have faced charges of desertion.

Article Fifteen of the Uniform Code Of Military Justice states that a person who has been AWOL for fewer than 180 days and is returned to the military by law officials is subject to a court martial. The defendant, however, could avert a trial if he decides to leave the service with less than an honorable discharge. Watson's desertion should have ended this way, but it did not. He may have had less than a seventh-grade education but he had accrued twenty years in the service. In short Wilson knew how to play the military game.

Paul Watson told newspaper reporter, Mark Randall, that his brother played his trump card. He called his wife from jail and told her to leak his arrest to the press. He said, "The Army don't want that kind of embarrassment." His story was picked up nationally in newspapers and became a huge public relations problem. It soon became obvious that the Army was much more embarrassed than Watson.

It is unclear what happened at Fort Sill. James Hallas reported that Watson was there for "rest and consultation." Later, Watson transferred to Walter Reed Hospital where "things were sorted out" physically and financially. From there he returned to Fort Rucker and completed his enlistment. The "professional private" retired as a Specialist 5, equivalent to a sergeant.

Watson did not consider himself a war hero. He did not brag about the Medal of Honor. He said, "There were probably a hundred men on that day who deserved it more than me, but the right people didn't see them." He was unimpressed with the prestige attached to the Medal of Honor, nor was he willing to live with the ideals that the Medal of Honor represents.

Watson suffered a heart attack in the early 1990s. His health had gradually deteriorated, exacerbated by his having twenty-seven pieces of a mortar shell still in his body. He died December 19, 1994, at age seventy-two. He was survived by his wife, three children, eight brothers and one sister, ten grandchildren, and three great-grandchildren.

BURIAL SITE

Watson's final resting place is at the Russell Cemetery at Russellville, Arkansas. Ironically his grave marker reads Medal of Honor. World War II. US Army. Korean War. There is no mention of his service in the Marine Corps.

HERSHEL W. WILLIAMS

BIRTH DATE: October 2, 1923

BIRTH PLACE: Fairmont, West Virginia

DEATH:

MEDAL OF HONOR ACTION: Iwo Jima. February 23, 1945.

RANK: Demolition Sergeant

UNIT: 1st Battalion, 21st Marines, 3rd Marine Division

YEARS OF SERVICE: May 26, 1943- 1945. 1948 - 1949. 1954 - 1969.

AWARDS: Medal of Honor, Purple Heart, Others

CCC: S-75, Morgantown, West Virginia. September - November 8, 1941. BR-80, Augusta, Montana. November 15 - November 30, 1942. G-127, Whitehall, Montana. December 1941 -April 1942.

From the Forest to the Battlefield

HERSHEL W. WILLIAMS

Lloyd Williams and Lurena Williams were Hershel's parents. They lived a hardscrabble life in the hills near Fairmont, West Virginia, where Lloyd had a small dairy farm. The couple had eleven children, six of whom died in the influenza epidemic of 1919. Lloyd passed away in 1934 and left his wife with a rocky soil farm and five children: four boys and one girl.

Woody, as Hershel became known, was eleven when his dad died. According to records he went to school at Quiet Dell in Marion County, West Virginia, where he rode to school frequently on a milk truck. He quit school in ninth grade because it was too difficult to get to the school. In addition he could not afford to buy the nice clothes that the other boys in school wore.

He wore the badge of poverty, symbolic of Appalachia-- not of his own doing, but by circumstance. Geographically and economically isolated, he labored on, trying to make it from one day to the next while holding to the core values inculcated by his impoverished mother. For Hershel life was a personal and a public struggle. Ordinary perks like a good education or a decent job were but elusive dreams.

Woody's brother, William Gerald Williams, had joined the CCC in 1936. When his brother came home to visit, Hershel listened to the stories of the CCC and enjoyed hearing about the guys his brother had met. "I seldom saw a dollar bill during those rough Depression days back in Quiet Dell, West Virginia. When my brother showed us the dollar bill that he had earned, I said that I wanted to join the CCC, too."

CCC EXPERIENCE

Hershel Williams enrolled in the CCC with S-75, Company 3527, near Morgantown, West Virginia, on September 15, 1941. He left that camp for duty in Montana on November 8, 1941. At S-75 he worked as a laborer, running the gamut from tree planting to pounding rocks for road building. His work was evaluated as being very satisfactory by his superiors, although he lost one day's pay on September 17 for not making roll call. From November 15, 1941, to the end of that month, he was stationed at Camp BR-80, Augusta, Montana. Then, from December 1, 1941, to April 30, 1942, he served at G-127 at Whitehall, Montana. At the former camp he was a laborer, but at Camp G-127 he became a certified truck driver. During that time, he attended four classes, receiving satisfactory or very satisfactory ratings. His educational adviser commented that Hershel read widely. Woody was discharged April 30, 1942, when his six-month hitch had expired.

In 2014 Richard Bailey, a CCC historian from West Virginia, interviewed Woody about his CCC experiences. Here are some of the observations Williams had about CCC life:

> Initially I went to a Morgantown CCC camp at Coopers Rock State Park. We stayed at camp all the time and if anyone went out he was on his own. I was sixteen and I didn't quite know where we

were. We worked on rock fences at Coopers Rock to keep people from falling off the cliff there. When they put me to work with a jack hammer, they put me over the mountain about a thousand feet up. It was dangerous. While there I met a kid from Steubenville, Ohio, and we ended up in Montana together. We drove trucks out there. The CCC crews built miles and miles of fences. The pine posts were eight feet long and they had to be cut, sharpened, and then creosoted. After that they were driven into the ground while other men would string five strands of wire. Miles and miles of these fences. I drove a truck that carried the posts and wire to wherever they were needed. I had to drive from Whitehall to Missoula, Montana...two trips a day. It was a flatbed '37 Chevy truck. What was fun? Some of us would go into Missoula and sit around the general store and wait for our Saturday night entertainment. We'd watch the fierce fights between the sheep herders and the cowboys. They did not get along at all. Absolutely no women. Never saw one. At the White Hall camp there were West Virginians, New Yorkers, and guys from Pennsylvania. They thought we talked funny. We did not have gangs but all us state guys hung together. Civilians ran the work crews, the Army ran the camps. Our leader was a forester. He was a civilian and always rode on the passenger side of the truck whenever we went out to work. He always went home at night. I sent my Mom the CCC allotment. Being a widow running a farm alone, the money was priceless. The mess sergeant was a drinker and every once in a while there would be a problem. A fellow from Shinniston, West Virginia, a big man, I forget his name, gave us a signal about the food and then we'd walk out because the food was bad. It was a strike. Several guys picked up pineapples on the way out. The pay? It was a lot of money. We did not think about being poor. Everyone was in the same boat. I never saw a Christmas tree. On December 8, 1942, everyone was called out of the barracks and we were shocked to find out that Pearl Harbor had been bombed. We were told we could go directly into the Army or we could request our release from the CCC so we could join whichever of the services we wished. I was seventeen. As a kid, I knew several young men in the community who went to serve in the Marine Corps. When they came home, I remember being impressed with their Marine dress blues. I said if I ever went to the military, that would be who I joined up with.

When Williams returned from the CCC, he worked at several jobs. He drove a truck and even a taxi. As a cab driver, he delivered messages from the War Department to the front door of the next of kin, telling them of the loss of a loved one. Those awful moments were seared in his mind. The military seemed to be at least a temporary fix, especially after Pearl Harbor. So, this young man went to war where he accomplished prodigious deeds.

ENTRY INTO THE MARINES

Everyone around Williams thought poorly of the Army. Woody declared, "The Army was not well thought of...You went to the Army if you were in trouble with the law or too lazy to work." But he admired the two guys in town who had joined the Marines, especially their dress blues. "We'd follow them around and think about the twenty-one dollars a month they made plus a warm bed and the clothing."

Joining the Marines posed a logistical difficulty, however. He said, "Everyone wanted to sign up so there was a waiting time of two months." The first-time Williams tried to enlist, the Corps turned him down. He was two inches too short at five foot six inches tall. He waited until May 1943 and reapplied. By this time, the Marines had waived the height requirement. Williams got his ticket to the Marine Corps.

After boot camp at Camp Pendleton near San Diego, California, he went to Jacques Farm on Camp Pendleton to train with a tank unit. Six weeks later, he moved on to infantry training and then received additional training at Camp Elliott, California, where he became a member of a tank battalion. From there he became part of a replacement battalion. That assignment led to his being shipped out in December 1943, to New Caledonia. His next stop was Guadalcanal. There, he became a flamethrower operator and received training in explosives. A friend told him, "You put that pack on and if you get hit, you're going to explode." (Later on at Iwo Jima, he would become one of the few battalion flamethrower operators who survived.) In July and August 1944, he saw combat in Guam.

THE HELL THAT WAS IWO JIMA

Iwo Jima is one of three volcanic islands nearly eight hundred miles south of Tokyo and was considered part of the governing unit of that city. Translated, Iwo Jima means Sulphur island. Nothing more than a volcanic speck shaped like a pork chop, it was a tiny island of only eight square miles. Japan owned the island and intended to keep it at all costs. The Americans coveted it as a staging base for the invasion of Japan, as well its becoming a safe landing site for crippled B-29s.

The Japanese had been fortifying the island with an elaborate cave and tunnel system for nearly two years. When completed, the system was a near-impenetrable fortress designed to throw the enemy back into the sea. Pillboxes pockmarked the entire area. Every vertical landmass had tunnels and dugouts. Mount Suribachi had been honeycombed with an elaborate maze of tunnels. These enabled men to move from one position to another without exposing themselves to American fire.

General Tadamitchi Kuribayshi knew that Iwo Jima was to be a fight to the death. There were to be no foolish suicide charges. Instead, the Americans would have to root out the Japanese defenders. Even though his soldiers knew of their fate, he imposed his iron will upon the twenty-thousand-man garrison.

On February 19, 1945, the largest armada of American ships ever assembled in the Pacific Theater of War moved on to its objective. Eighty thousand men in landing crafts circled the area waiting for the sign to move to the beach. Most of the Marines were considerably younger than Williams who was twenty-one. Almost one of every four Marines became a statistic in the next brutal six weeks.

The first wave of Marines came in without much opposition. A false hope arose that the intense two-month plastering the Japanese had taken had reduced their ability to defend the island. Then, one hour later, when Marines continued to stack up on the beach, all hell broke loose. General Kuribayshi's well-planned defense went into full gear.

Iwo Jima was not one specific battle. Countless smaller fire fights were going on everywhere. When a slight lull existed in one spot, furious battles took place elsewhere. The volcanic soil bogged down foot traffic much like a runner trying to get traction in a granary. Tanks were helpless. Landing crafts that were lined up waiting for landfall were shot out of the water. A rain of metal poured down. The Japanese lobbed in mortar shells that looked like flying barrels. When they exploded, the shrapnel was deadly. Advances, if any, were measured in yards. There was no haven. In the evening men hunkered down in shell holes, as it was futile to dig a foxhole because the volcanic sand immediately refilled the hole. The Japanese constantly attempted to infiltrate the American lines during the night.

Combat on Iwo Jima was reduced to the lowest of common denominators. There was no grand strategy. Each dugout, every tunnel, and each pillbox became a vicious little war. Then, after neutralizing one obstacle, the Marines moved to take out another.

On February 23, 1945, the day that Joseph Rosenthal took his iconic picture of the flag raising on Mount Suribachi, Woody Williams engaged the Japanese in a four-hour fire fight. His weapons were a flamethrower and satchel charges.

MEDAL OF HONOR CITATION

For conspicuous gallantry and intrepidity at the risk of his life above and beyond the call of duty as Demolition Sergeant serving with the First Battalion, Twenty-First Marines, Third Marine Division, in action against enemy Japanese forces on Iwo Jima, Volcano Island 23 February 1945. Quick to volunteer his services when our tanks were maneuvering vainly to open a lane for the infantry through the network of reinforced concrete pillboxes, buried mines and black, volcanic sands, Corporal Williams daringly went forward alone to attempt the reduction of devastating machine-gun fire from the unyielding positions. Covered only by four riflemen, he fought desperately for four hours under terrific enemy small-arms fire and repeatedly returned to his own lines to prepare demolition charges and obtain serviced flame throwers, struggling back, frequently to the rear of hostile emplacements, to wipe out one position after another. On one occasion he daringly mounted a pillbox to insert the nozzle of his flame thrower through the air vent, kill the occupants and silence the gun; on another he grimly charged enemy riflemen who attempted to stop him with bayonets and destroyed them with a burst of flame from his weapon. His unyielding determination and extraordinary heroism in the face of ruthless enemy resistance were directly instrumental in neutralizing one of the most fanatically defended Japanese strong points encountered by his regiment and aided in enabling his company to reach its objective. Corporal Williams' aggressive fighting spirit and valiant devotion to duty throughout this fiercely contested action sustain and enhance the highest traditions of the United States Naval Service.

MEDAL OF HONOR PRESENTATION

President Harry S. Truman presented the Medal of Honor to Hershel Williams on the White House lawn on October 13, 1945. Woody had been called back to the United States for the presentation and admitted that he had never heard of the medal. Williams said, "I was a bashful, shy country boy. I never thought I'd see the president. I was frightened to death. I was shaking when the president put the ribbon around my neck...President Truman told me, 'I'd rather have this medal than be president.'"

Shortly after President Truman presented the Medal of Honor to Woody, Marine Commandant Alexander Vandergrift told Williams, "This medal does not belong to you. It belongs to the Marines who never made it home. Don't do anything to tarnish it." These words became the mantra that has guided Williams since that time. He said, "I could not have received it without the assistance of other Marines. So when I wear this medal, I don't wear it for what I did. I wear it in honor of the two Marines--I don't know their names-- who gave their lives protecting me. It really belongs to them; I am just a caretaker of it."

Immediately after the Medal of Honor presentation, Williams married his childhood sweetheart, Ruby Meredith, who was his tower of strength. From this union came two children, Travie Mae and Tracey Jean, five grandsons, and two great- grandchildren. Ruby passed away in 2007.

The consequences of war are horrendous. War sucks the blood from a generation who otherwise would have been doing a myriad of things characteristic of young people. It robs humanity by taking the best and the finest, scarring their souls and debilitating their physical well-being. It lays waste to countries and people. War is a gigantic brutality...an assault upon civilization.

Yet from the near-Armageddon found on every battleground, humanity somehow prevails. Amid slaughter, hope appears. Generals garner the credit while grunts suffer the casualties, but they too prevail. In battle after battle, anonymous men, plucked from obscurity, secured the day so the world could be saved, at least temporarily, from yet another scourge.

Woody grappled with his personal demons brought on by the nightmares of combat. Williams returned as a hero, but like so many returning veterans, suffered pain and anguish while adjusting to a peaceful environment. Woody experienced a religious awakening in the mid-1960s that set him on a course of change. He immediately became the Chaplain of the Congressional Medal of Honor Society.

He talked widely and often, crisscrossing the nation, and spoke not of war, but for the dignity and worth of the individual. Slowly, he embarked on a path hitherto undreamed of. Maturing in mind and spirit, he told a Marine class:

> I have the hope that someone in this world will be smart enough to say we can figure how to get along with each other without having to kill each other. Somehow our country and the other

countries have got to find a peaceful way of solving our problems. It's just crazy to train people to kill other people. I still have hope. I'll never lose it.

IWO JIMA: SEVENTY YEARS LATER

In March 2015 Japanese and American veterans gathered on the volcanic sands of Iwo Jima to commemorate the seventieth anniversary of that struggle. On the heights of Mount Suribachi, the symbol of this awful battle, representatives of both nations spoke. More than thirty veterans from the United States participated in a very emotionally charged day. The only surviving Medal of Honor recipient of the Battle of Iwo Jima, Hershel Williams, attended. His feelings toward his Japanese counterparts had not changed. "They were just doing their jobs," he said. "We tried to kill them before they could kill us. But that's war."

GOLD STAR FAMILY MEMORIALS

Williams founded the Hershel Woody Williams Medal of Honor Foundation. This foundation encourages the establishment of permanent Gold Star family memorial monuments in communities throughout the United States. During World War II, parents with a family member in the service flew a small blue star flag in their window. If that person died in the service, the blue flag was replaced by a gold. Thus, the term Gold Star Mothers came into being. "I have been told that wounds heal with time but some scars don't go away. They are there for a lifetime."

Seeking to create these memorials is Hershel Williams's effort to ease the grief of those left behind. He envisions a monument in every state that will stand in mute testimony of a family's wartime losses. Kicking off the project, he gave a personal contribution of $5000.00. The project had the backing of the Obama administration as well as Marine Corps organizations throughout the nation. By early 2017, thirteen monuments had been completed while twenty-nine monuments are in the planning stages nation-wide from Riverside, California, to Fall River, Massachusetts.

Williams is in constant demand to appear before public groups whether it's an affair of state or a speaking engagement before a grade school assembly. He is grateful for his chance to serve and credits his strong Christian beliefs for his successes in life. "I think I am speeding up," he said. "I've had such a blessed life."

HONORS

Williams has received the West Virginia Distinguished Service Medal and the Daughters of the American Revolution Medal of Honor.

The National Guard Armory in Fairmont, West Virginia, is named after Woody as is the former Barboursville Bridge and the Memorial Field House in Huntington, West Virginia.

From the Forest to the Battlefield

Williams is the Chaplain Emeritus of the Congressional Medal of Honor Society.

In 1967 the Veterans Association presented the Viet Nam Service Medal to Williams for his service as a civilian counselor to the armed services.

In 1969 Williams retired after seventeen years with a final rank as Chief Warrant Officer.

The West Virginia State Civilian Conservation Corps Museum inducted Hershel Williams into its CCC Hall of Fame on October 19, 2013.

In 2013 the United States Postal Service issued a Medal of Honor stamp containing the images of twelve recipients of the Medal of Honor on a postage sheet. Williams is one of the honorees.

Williams was honored at the Military Bowl that was held at the Navy-Marine Corps Stadium at Annapolis, Maryland, on December 29, 2013.

Williams received the 2014 Founder's Award from the Pritzker Museum and Library in Chicago.

On January 14, 2016, the United States Navy named an Expeditionary Sea Base (ESB) ship, USNS Hershel "Woody" Williams.

FRANK P. WITEK

BIRTH DATE: December 10, 1921

BIRTH PLACE: Derby, Connecticut

DEATH: August 3, 1944. KIA.

MEDAL OF HONOR ACTION: Guam. August 3, 1944.

RANK: Private First Class

UNIT: 1st Battalion, 9th Marines, 3rd Marine Division

YEARS OF SERVICE: January 20, 1942 - August 3, 1944

AWARDS: Medal of Honor, Purple Heart

CCC: Camp McCoy, Wisconsin. Camp G-144, Shoshone, Idaho. January - June 1940.

FRANK P. WITEK

John Witek (1868-1935) and his wife Nora (1892-1958) were born in Austria. They married there in 1908 and then emigrated to the United States the following year before settling in Derby, Connecticut. John had no formal education while his young wife, Nora, had but two years of school. Initially, neither could speak English; Polish was their native tongue. John's health deteriorated slowly, and eventually he was unable to work. The couple had six children, four boys and two girls. Frank, the fifth child, was born in 1921. The family lived in a rented home. Nora worked sporadically in a silk mill, a factory that made silk garments. Her income was at the poverty level. After moving to Chicago, Nora continued to work in various factories to eke out a living. By that time, she had become a widow with three children to support.

Frank was only nine when his family relocated to the Windy City. There he went to Crain Technical School, completing ninth grade before dropping out. Possessed of a stocky physique, he weighed 140 pounds, stood five foot eight inches tall, and had a demeanor that made him look more mature than his age. Eventually he worked for Standard Transformers Company as well as a metal plating company. Prior to entry into the military, Frank had become a carpenter working on bridge construction. During 1939 he worked for thirty-six weeks at a wage of nearly $800.00.

When he was laid off, Witek joined the CCC on January 4, 1940, serving the required hitch of six months. His duty took him to Camp McCoy, Wisconsin, and ultimately to Camp G-144, near Shoshone, Idaho. A member of the "pick and shovel" brigade, Witek also acquired some forest fire fighting experience. His CCC tour of duty was unremarkable. Using the educational opportunities offered at the camp, Frank enrolled in three classes: carpentry, operation of heavy machinery, and range improvements. His instructors rated him satisfactory in every class while Frank's educational adviser judged him to be cooperative and courteous at all times. When his enrollment had expired, he opted not to reenlist. Frank received an honorable discharge and returned to Chicago.

MILITARY EXPERIENCE

Witek enlisted in the US Marine Corps shortly after Pearl Harbor. For the next six months, he trained at Camp Elliott and at Camp Pendleton in California. After almost a year in the States, he shipped out for New Zealand, a staging/training area for future combat operations. Later, he participated in the Bougainville Campaign, seeing action during three major battles there. Guadalcanal was his next stop where he enjoyed rest and recuperation before the imminent invasion of Guam.

Guam is part of the Marianas Islands. From a strategic point of view, it was of major importance to the Allied conquest of Japan. In addition to Tinian and Saipan, these three islands had airfields capable of handling the super fortress, the B-29, a long-range bomber destined to bomb the Japanese homeland.

From the Forest to the Battlefield

Additionally, retaking Guam was high priority. It had been an American possession since the Treaty of Paris, which concluded the Spanish American War in 1898. As a result, Guam loomed large, as it would become the first American land regained from the Japanese who had taken the island immediately after Pearl Harbor.

The Japanese, however, had well over ten thousand troops lying in wait. By the summer of 1944, the Japanese strategy had become painfully evident: to inflict major casualties on the enemy invading forces. The fate of the Nippon foot soldiers had already been sealed. Their fate had been sealed as their Navy had lost control of the sea. Escape was impossible. Even though death was inevitable, their mantra was to kill at least ten Americans prior to each Japanese soldier's glorious death for the Emperor. Guam, Tinian, and Saipan consequently were destined to become killing fields awash with Japanese and American blood.

The Battle for Guam, an island thirty miles long and ten miles wide, lasted from July 21, 1944, to August 10, 1944. Although the outcome was never in doubt, the enemy defense remained stubborn and bitter. The American forces slowly pushed the Japanese toward Mt. Santa Rosa, an 850-foot peak, the final bastion of Japanese strength. The Japanese had honey-combed the area with trails and road blocks. Here, particularly heavy fighting occurred on August 2 -3, 1944. Witek's role was that of a BAR (Browning automatic rifle) man, as well as being a forward scout. He died on Mt. Santa Rosa on August 3, 1944.

MEDAL OF HONOR CITATION

For conspicuous gallantry and intrepidity at the risk of his life above and beyond the call of duty while serving with the First Battalion, Ninth Marines, Third Marine Division, during the Battle of Finegayan at Guam, Marianas, on 3 August 1944. When his rifle platoon was halted by heavy surprise fire from well camouflaged enemy positions, Private First Class Witek daringly remained standing to fire a full magazine from his automatic point-blank range into a depression housing Japanese troops, killing eight of the enemy and enabling the greater part of his platoon to take cover. During his platoon's withdrawal for consolidation of lines, he remained to safeguard a severely wounded comrade, courageously returning the enemy's fire until the arrival of stretcher bearers and then covering the evacuation by sustained fire as he moved backward toward his own lines. With his platoon again pinned down by a hostile machine-gun, Private First Class Witek, on his own initiative, moved forward boldly ahead of the reinforcing tanks and infantry, alternately throwing hand grenades and firing as he advanced to within five to ten yards of the enemy position, destroying the hostile machinegun emplacement and an additional eight Japanese before he, himself, was struck down by an enemy rifleman. His valiant and inspiring action effectively reduced the enemy's firepower, thereby enabling his platoon to attain its objective, and reflects the highest credit upon Private First Class Witek and the United States Naval Service. He gallantly gave his life for his country.

MEDAL OF HONOR PRESENTATION

On May 20, 1945, fifty thousand people honored Frank Witek at a huge gathering at Soldiers Field in Chicago, Illinois. The Marine Corps Commandant, General Alexander Vandergrift, presented Witek's Medal of Honor posthumously to Mrs. Nora Witek, his mother.

HONORS

Frank Witek was honored in 1945 when his regiment named a baseball field for him on the Island of Guam. According to his comrades, this field commemorated "...a fearless fighter and the kind of fellow you were thankful to have on your side."

In 2013 a Connecticut TV station honored Frank P. Witek by featuring him in a program called "Looking Up a View of the Valley."

On the island of Guam, the Marine Corps established Camp Frank Witek. Although the camp has been gone for years, the natives still refer to it as "Camp Witek."

Derby, Connecticut, is proud to call Frank Witek one of its own. As a result, the town established the 140-acre Frank Witek Memorial Park in his honor.

In 1946 the United States Navy named a Gearing Class destroyer the USS Witek. It was christened by his mother, Mrs. Nora Witek. The ship served the country for twenty-two years before being decommissioned.

The Frank Witek Memorial stands in Derby, Connecticut.

The Polish Legion of American Veterans honored him in its publication.

The Quad Cities' (Davenport and Bettendorf, Iowa, and Rock Island and Moline, Illinois) Marine Corps League, in cooperation with the VFW Chapter in Derby, Connecticut, places a wreath on Witek's grave every Memorial Day.

DEPARTMENT OF THE ABSURD

The Department of Police in Derby, Connecticut, reported on November 10, 2011, that someone had stolen three brass plaques from the Witek Memorial. The two largest plaques stolen weighed one hundred pounds each and had an estimated value of $10,000 each. The plaques had been forcibly removed from the stone monument by culprits who used heavy-duty crowbars. This act was among a spate of thefts of monuments containing brass plaques in the Derby area. Leonard Witek, the recipient's cousin asked, "Didn't you read what it was for? What the honor is? A person got killed for this and you're taking it away?" The police contacted area scrap metal dealers within a wide radius of Darby, asking them for their help but to no avail.

The following year the plaques were replaced and a rededication ceremony was held.

A faux pas occurred early on regarding Witek's portrait which hangs at the Rock Island, Illinois, Arsenal. In 2001 Major General Ben Blaz noticed that the painting was inaccurate. Witek's image was adorned in an army uniform while wearing the Navy Cross and a Purple Heart. Blaz requested and received an accurate portrait soon after.

BURIAL SITE

Initially Witek's body was buried on Guam. Five years later his remains were reinterred at the Rock Island National Cemetery in Rock Island, Illinois, in 1949.

OWEN F. P. HAMMERBERG

BIRTH DATE: May 31, 1920

BIRTH PLACE: Daggett, Michigan

DEATH: February 17, 1945. KIA.

MEDAL OF HONOR ACTION: West Loch, Pearl Harbor. February 17, 1945.

RANK: Boatswain's Mate Second Class/Diver

UNIT: United States Navy

YEARS OF SERVICE: July 16, 1941 - February 17, 1945

AWARDS: Medal of Honor, Others

CCC: SP-14, Skokie Valley, Glenview, Illinois. July -September 1938.

OWEN F. P. HAMMERBERG

Owen Francis Patrick Hammerberg was born on May 31, 1920, on a farm east of Daggett, Michigan. The boy with twenty-eight letters in his name would grow up to receive the last noncombat Medal of Honor. Owen's parents, Jonas Hammerberg and Elizabeth Leaveck, were both born in Sweden. They were married in Daggett, Michigan, in 1916. By 1924 they had four sons: Edward, Robert, Owen, and Harold. When Owen was a child, his family moved many times. They lived in Daggett, Kipling, Gladstone, Menominee, and Stephenson, all in the Upper Peninsula of Michigan. Owen attended elementary school in Gladstone and some high school at Stephenson where he played football for the Stephenson Eagles.

Owen was ten years old when Jonas and Elizabeth Hammerberg divorced in 1930. In December 1933, Owen's mother married Albert Anderson and the family moved to Flint, Michigan. This had to be quite an adjustment for the entire family after living in the small towns of Michigan's Upper Peninsula. Flint was dominated by an automobile culture. The Hammerberg family was living in Flint at the time of the Sit-Down Strike of 1936 - 1937. Governor Frank Murphy settled the strike, but the United Auto Workers triumphed over General Motors and the era of the United Auto Workers had begun. Owen attended Flint Junior Technical High School, but dropped out in 1937. He rode trains and hitchhiked out West where he temporarily worked on a ranch.

CCC EXPERIENCE

On July 21, 1938, Owen enrolled in the Civilian Conservation Corps and was assigned to Camp Skokie Valley, SP-14, Company 639, Glenview, Illinois. Camp Skokie Valley started out as a tent camp on July 27, 1933. Eventually the camp grew to house ten companies of two hundred men each, as well as consisting of 115 buildings including mess halls, kitchens, barracks, canteens, classrooms, barber shop, and a chapel. Alfred Cornebise, a CCC historian, describes the camp as "a mammoth camp serving ten companies." The camp mission was to build Skokie Lagoons Park by draining swamp land and creating a recreation area.

The twenty-five dollar allotment he earned was sent to his mother, Elizabeth Anderson, in Flint. Owen was then five foot six inches tall and weighed 138 pounds. He was missing six teeth. His records also indicated that he had scarlet fever as a child. On his enrollment record, he indicated that he had previously been employed as a truck driver for two weeks at McDonald's Dairy in Flint. Owen planned to be a truck driver or a tool and die maker after completing his CCC service. Unfortunately, the CCC was not a successful experience for the eighteen-year old Owen. He received satisfactory marks as a laborer, but then he went AWOL on September 6, 1938, after only forty-eight days of service. Owen never returned to Camp Skokie Valley, and on September 13, 1938, Owen Hammerberg was officially honorably discharged. Initially the company commander wrote "desertion" on his record. Perhaps with a change of heart, he then crossed out "desertion" and wrote "honorably discharged for the convenience of the government."

Desertion was a recurrent problem in the CCC camps. By April 1937, 18 percent of all enrollees were dishonorably discharged for desertion. By December 1938 that figure was over 20 percent. CCC officials ordered a complete study of the problem. In general, the results of the study concluded that the major reasons were homesickness and an inability to adjust to the strict structure and discipline of CCC camp life. Other reasons included unrealized expectations, weak leadership in some camps, and increased employment opportunities in the last years of the CCC. With one in five enrollees leaving the CCC nationally, Owen Hammerberg was not alone.

ANCHORS AWAY

Owen enlisted in the Navy on July 16, 1941, at age twenty-one. His boot training was at Great Lakes, Illinois, and he was assigned to the USS Idaho from November 1941 to June 1942. After more training Owen was assigned to a submarine chaser, the USS Advent, until January 1944. While he was aboard the Advent, a cable became snagged on a mine, a situation that threatened to blow up the entire ship. Hammerberg dove into the water and untangled the cable while his shipmates shot at sharks in the water. In recognition of his bravery, Owen was recommended for a Bronze Star, but he never received it. Next, Owen attended a Deep Sea Diving School in Washington, DC, and graduated in August of 1944. He reported to the South Pacific Fleet in October 1944 and was assigned to a salvage unit.

Back on May 21, 1944, on a Sunday afternoon, five Navy LST (Landing Ship Tank) ships were being loaded at West Loch, Pearl Harbor, for Operation Forager, an invasion in the Mariana Islands. A fire broke out due to a detonated mortar round on one ship and spread to the other four vessels. Many intense explosions followed and two hundred men were thrown into the water in minutes. All five vessels broke from their moorings and threatened other Navy ships in the harbor. Rather than risk a deadly explosion, officials made the decision to blow up and sink the five tankers. This accident cost 123 lives and wounded almost four hundred more men. The incident became known as the West Loch Disaster, the second largest disaster in Pearl Harbor after the bombing of the harbor on December 7, 1941. The tragic death of Owen Francis Patrick Hammerberg was linked to the West Loch Disaster 272 days later.

In February 1945, the Navy decided to clear the channel of the sunken LST ships in West Loch. Hammerberg was assigned to one of five teams to do the job. Each team was responsible for raising one ship. The promised reward was leave time for all team members once their assigned ship was raised. Owen's team quickly raised the ship out of forty feet of water and twenty feet of mud and were granted immediate leave.

Another diving team ran into trouble when two divers became trapped in a web of cable and steel. The only way to reach the men was to blow a tunnel through the mud using a jet compressor. A special diving team from New York refused to go down. Hearing the broadcast, twenty-three-year-old Owen Hammerberg returned to the diving barge in a speed boat and donned his diving gear. Owen found the first diver, George Fuller, trapped by a steel plate in the dark, muddy water. Working for five hours, he freed Fuller and put life and air lines on his helmet so he could be raised to the surface. Fuller shook Owen's hand as he departed. Despite extreme fatigue, Hammerberg moved further into the hulk and found Earl Brown trapped in a cave. Using an air phone, Owen reported that a sizable chunk of steel was sliding toward him in the mud. Owen refused to leave his mate and lay crosswise over Brown's body protecting him from further injury. The intense pressure from the huge steel plate was on Hammerberg. Rescue attempts were laborious and slow. Derricks and pumps were used to remove tons of mud, but debris was constantly plugging the pumps. Throughout the rescue operation, Owen's friends offered comfort and encouragement by air phone until Owen succumbed to his injuries eighteen hours later. Seventy-three hours later a Filipino father-son diving team finally freed Hammerberg's body as well as Earl Brown who was still alive.

MEDAL OF HONOR CITATION

For conspicuous gallantry and intrepidity at the risk of his life above and beyond the call of duty as a diver engaged in rescue operations at West Loch, Pearl Harbor, 17 February 1945. Aware of the danger when 2 fellow divers were hopelessly trapped in a cave-in of steel wreckage while tunneling with jet nozzles under an LST sunk in 40 feet of water and 20 feet of mud. Hammerberg unhesitatingly went overboard in a valiant attempt to effect their rescue despite the certain hazard of additional cave-ins and the risk of fouling his lifeline on jagged pieces of steel imbedded in the shifting mud. Washing a passage through the original excavation, he reached the first of the trapped men, freed him from the wreckage and, working desperately in pitch-black darkness, finally effected his release from fouled lines, thereby enabling him to reach the surface. Wearied but undaunted after several hours of arduous labor, Hammerberg resolved to continue his struggle to wash through the oozing submarine, subterranean mud in a determined effort to save the second diver. Venturing still farther under the buried hulk, he held tenaciously to his purpose, reaching a place immediately above the other man just as another cave-in occurred and a heavy piece of steel pinned him crosswise over his shipmate in a position which protected the man beneath from further injury while placing the full brunt of terrific pressure on himself. Although he succumbed in agony 18 hours after he had gone to the aid of his fellow divers, Hammerberg, by his cool judgment, unfaltering professional skill and consistent disregard of all personal danger in the face of tremendous odds, had contributed effectively to the saving of his 2 comrades. His heroic spirit of self-sacrifice throughout enhanced and sustained the highest traditions of the U.S. Naval Service. He gallantly gave his life in the service of his country.

MEDAL OF HONOR PRESENTATION

Boatswain's Mate Second Class Owen Hammerberg died on February 17, 1945. He was awarded the Medal of Honor posthumously later that month at Grosse Ile Naval Air Station in southeast Michigan. The medal was presented to his mother. Since the end of World War I, the Navy had two versions of the Medal of Honor: noncombat and combat. In 1963 the Navy rescinded its policy of awarding the Medal of Honor for noncombat actions. Owen Hammerberg received the last noncombat Medal of Honor. In addition to the Medal of Honor, Hammerberg was awarded the American Defense Service Medal, Fleet Clasp, American Campaign Medal, Asiatic Campaign Medal, and the World War II Victory Medal.

HONORS

Owen's Medal of Honor, uniform, and other Navy career artifacts are on display at Michigan's Military and Space Heroes Museum in Frankenmuth, Michigan.

The United States Navy named the USS Hammerberg (DS 1015) in honor of Owen. The new destroyer escort was launched on August 20, 1954. Owen's mother christened the new ship with his family present.

Hammerberg Road is located at Exit 135 on I-69 in Flint, Michigan. This last exit is known as the Pearl Harbor Memorial Highway.

Hammerberg Memorial Playground is located at Chicago and Wyoming Avenues in Detroit, Michigan.

A memorial plaque in honor of Owen Hammerberg was erected at Veterans Park in Stephenson, Michigan, by VFW Post 5966.

BURIAL SITE

Owen Francis Patrick Hammerberg was buried on February 27, 1945, at Halawa Naval Cemetery on Oahu. Lieutenant W. A. Czajowski, Padre at Aiea Barracks, officiated. The Salvage Base contributed $266.00 to a flower fund. Ninety dollars was spent for the flowers and the remaining $176.00 was sent to Owen's mother. After the war the government moved Owen's body to his final resting place at Holy Sepulchre Cemetery in Southfield, Michigan. Before the burial, Owen's parents and three thousand mourners gathered before his flag-draped coffin in front of City Hall in Detroit. A wreath was placed on his coffin and thirty seconds of silence was observed throughout the city. A brief ceremony followed. Rev. Father Bernard Kearns, Naval Chaplin for the Detroit area, said, "May the soul of this young man and all the young men who gave their lives, rest in peace."

HERBERT H. BURR

BIRTH DATE: September 13, 1920

BIRTH PLACE: St. Joseph, Missouri

DEATH: February 8, 1990

MEDAL OF HONOR ACTION: Dorrmoschel, Germany. March 19, 1945.

RANK: Staff Sergeant

UNIT: Company C, 41st Tank Battalion, 11th Armored Division

YEARS OF SERVICE: 1941-1966

AWARDS: Medal of Honor, Distinguished Service Cross

CCC: SCS-28, Bedford, Iowa. September 1939.

HERBERT H. BURR

Herbert Burr's parents were Maurice C. Burr and Edna Thompson Burr. Maurice was originally from New York while Edna was born in Iowa. The couple met in Missouri where they married in 1902. They had eight children: six boys and two girls. Herbert, the eighth child, was born on September 13, 1920. Maurice was a painter who worked first for the Hunt Construction Company. Later, he moved his family to Kansas City, Missouri, where he became a self-employed private contractor. Business was never good, but in 1940 it reached rock-bottom for Maurice. He declared no income that year. The financial plight of the family prompted his youngest son, Herbert, to join the Civilian Conservation Corps.

Herbert Burr was five foot eight inches tall and weighed only 124 pounds. He had dark black hair and hazel eyes. According to many, he was quite handsome. In fact, later when he grew a mustache, he looked remarkably like Robert Taylor, a popular MGM movie star. He completed eighth grade before opting to help his father paint houses. He worked a few months at Bon Ton Cleaners in St. Joseph, Missouri. Then he tried his hand as a pastry cook, making donuts. This last job was not financially rewarding, as his income in 1939 was a mere $125.00.

CCC EXPERIENCE

Herbert enrolled in the CCC in 1939. Initially sent to Fort Leavenworth, he received his conditioning there before receiving a permanent assignment to Camp SCS-28, a soil conservation camp, near Bedford, Iowa. He worked as part of the pick and shovel crew, not an unusual position for a rookie. After less than one month, he became homesick and went AWOL. This breach of conduct led to his dismissal on desertion charges.

When Burr returned home, he faced unemployment again. As a result, he joined the Army at Kansas City, Missouri. Burr completed his basic training at Fort Knox, Kentucky, and soon became a member of the 41st Tank Battalion, 11th Armored Division. The battalion participated in the massive Louisiana-Texas maneuvers. Later, the unit moved to California to participate in desert training. There they were introduced to the Sherman tank.

THE M-4 SHERMAN TANK

The M-4 Sherman tank was a workhorse for the Allies during World War II. Mass produced in the United States, nearly fifty thousand rolled off the assembly lines from 1942 to 1945. Used in both the Pacific and European Theaters of War, the Sherman tank became an integral part of the Allied success from North Africa to Normandy and ultimately to Berlin. This tank was fast, capable of thirty miles per hour, very maneuverable, light enough for travel over conventional bridges, and had an excellent range. Powered by gasoline, the tank possessed a formidable weapons platform.

From the Forest to the Battlefield

The Sherman tank was primarily an ultimate breakout weapon. It turned the tide against General Rommel and his vaunted Africa Corps in the North African Campaign, but it was just as valuable as an infantry support weapon. To an American foot soldier, there was nothing more beautiful than a Sherman tank leading an assault. Armed with a 75mm cannon, two .30 caliber machine guns (one in front and another parallel with the cannon), and a turret-mounted .50 caliber machine gun, it can cut a lethal swath through an enemy troop concentration. In fact, as the war progressed, the relationship between the tank and the infantryman became symbiotic. By 1944 almost every infantry division had at least one tank battalion (about sixty tanks) as part of its regular compliment.

In the North African Campaign, the Sherman tank was equal to or better than the German medium tanks. As a result, the Americans were content with the M-4 Sherman. At the same time, however, the Germans invested heavily in larger Panther and Tiger tanks equipped with awesome cannons that had superior range in addition to a greater firing force. These were used mostly on the Russian Front but when pressed into service in France during 1944, they soon became the scourges of the M-4.

The 75mm cannon on the Sherman tank had a range of about six hundred yards, weighed twenty tons less than the larger German tanks, and had less armor protection than its adversaries. The Tiger tank had a 88mm cannon deadly at 1,200 yards. Frequently, direct hits by the Sherman's cannon bounced off the Tiger and the Panther. Direct hits on the Sherman caused it to blow up prompting the British to compare it to a Ronson cigarette lighter slogan: With every strike, it lights up.

A one-on-one matchup between a M-4 and a Tiger was a grave mismatch; consequently, conventional strategy always tried to pit four Shermans against one Tiger. In this instance the Tiger tank was usually killed along with a concurrent loss of two or three Sherman tanks. Remarkably, these losses were acceptable. The Americans could simply replace destroyed tanks easily. The Germans could not.

OVER SIX MONTHS OF BLOODY COMBAT

The 41st Tank Battalion, Burr's unit, had been stateside for two years when it shipped out to England. By December 20, 1944, it landed at Cherbourg, France. The stay at Cherbourg was very short as the Germans had broken through the Ardennes section in Belgium creating a bulge in the American line almost seventy miles deep and fifty miles wide. The fate of the entire Allied offensive hung on the beleaguered men at Bastogne, Belgium. The battalion, attached to General Patton's Third Army, participated in a historic eight-day march to help relieve the battered American army in the Belgium salient. By December 30, 1944, two weeks into the German breakthrough, Burr's outfit had successfully attacked enemy positions near Lavaselle, its first combat assignment. For the next two weeks the unit fought sporadically, coming under frequent heavy German artillery assaults. Attempting to close the noose on the Germans in the Bastogne area, the battalion moved against Noville, Belgium, less than ten miles northwest of Bastogne. Here Herbert "Doc" Burr earned the Distinguished Service Cross.

His citation read

> During the attack north of Noville, Belgium, Pfc. Burr's tank was hit by anti-tank fire. The tank commander and the gunner were killed and the loader was seriously wounded. The tank caught on fire and began to burn. The bow-gunner, Pfc. Burr, had seen the flash of the anti-tank. He remained in the tank and continued to fire his 30-caliber machine gun. Through his action, the enemy was pinned down and could not return fire. His ammunition expended, Burr discovered that his crew-member, Davis Kasavan, the loader, was still alive. Despite the fire in the turret, he managed to remove the wounded loader from the tank and assisted him to a medical aid station. Pfc. Burr then returned and discovered that his burning, knocked-out tank had not exploded. He immediately went toward it, creeping, crawling, and camouflaging himself with enough snow until he got to it. Upon reaching the tank, he found the engine still running. Even though the tank was on fire and might explode at any moment, he entered the tank and extinguished the fire. Still under enemy fire, he drove the damaged tank to safety.

By the end of January, the Germans were retreating toward their homeland, but fighting furiously and exacting heavy Allied losses. Shortly, the battalion moved against the Siegfried Line. After the infantry had breached these fortifications, the 41st Tank Battalion participated in the capture of a number of German cities. By the middle of March 1945, the unit was poised to cross the Moselle River, where Burr again exhibited incredible bravery while under heavy fire from the Germans.

First Lieutenant James Wilson described Burr's actions:

> We were moving up to the edge of town when a bazooka shell, fired out the window, pierced the turret of the tank in which he was serving as a bow-gunner. There were explosions in the tank and it stopped apparently disabled, but Private Burr started it up and moved it on its mission to investigate the streets ahead. Other members of the crew had bailed out because of the fire and the explosions. The platoon sergeant was lying wounded inside the tank. Without support of tank weapons, he moved into heavy enemy fire and charged head on into a German anti-tank gun set up in the street. The German troops manning the gun were too surprised by the furious charge to fire, and the tank crashed and overran the weapon. After viewing the road conditions ahead, he sideswiped a big truck and returned to the waiting company to make his report. All this under heavy fire.

One of the crew members, Technician Fourth Class Melvin S. Azbell, told of being inside the tank when a bazooka shell struck:

> We were deafened and stunned below Private Burr's gun position. There were explosions from our ammunition and the tank was filled with smoke. We bailed out and we were counting to be sure all had made it. Burr realized the sergeant was inside and he went down through the smashed turret. Apparently, the fire had not spread because he started the tank and dashed toward the enemy lines, contacted the enemy gun, completed his observation, and returned toward our lines. The sergeant was badly wounded and he called for medical aid. The enemy laid

down heavy fire on his position, but when medical aid men could not find the tank, he went through heavy fire to contact them, and then led them back to his wounded sergeant.

The battalion continued to fight its way through Germany into Austria when the war in Europe ended, on May 8, 1945. The battalion initially had seven hundred men. It suffered 40 percent casualties: forty-nine men killed and 252 men wounded in less than six months of combat.

MEDAL OF HONOR CITATION

He displayed conspicuous gallantry during action when the tank in which he was bow gunner was hit by an enemy rocket, which severely wounded the platoon sergeant and forced the remainder of the crew to abandon the vehicle. Deafened, but otherwise unhurt, S/Sgt. Burr immediately climbed into the driver's seat and entered the town to reconnoiter road conditions. As he rounded a turn, he encountered an 88mm anti-tank gun at pointblank range. Realizing that he had no crew, no one to man the tank's guns, he heroically chose to disregard his personal safety in a direct charge on the German weapon. At a considerable speed he headed straight for the loaded gun which was fully manned by enemy troops who had only to pull the lanyard to send a shell into his vehicle. So unexpected and daring was his assault that he drove his tank completely over the gun, demolishing it and causing its crew to flee in confusion. He then skillfully sideswiped a heavy truck, overturned it, and wheeled his lumbering vehicle toward American lines. Medical personnel had been summoned to treat the wounded sergeant but could not locate him. The valiant soldier ran through a hail of sniper fire to direct them to his stricken comrade. The bold, fearless determination of S/Sgt. Burr, his skill and courageous devotion to duty, resulted in the completion of his mission in the face of seemingly impossible odds.

MEDAL OF HONOR PRESENTATION

On August 23, 1945, in the East Room of the White House, President Harry Truman presented the Medal of Honor to Sergeant Burr. He was one of twenty-eight recipients who received the Medal of Honor that day.

The medals were given out alphabetically, and the citations were read by Major General Edward F. Witsell. White House officials searched frantically for Burr who had become confused in the White House maze and somehow went through a rear door. Fortunately, Burr discovered his mistake and returned in time for his ceremony. He was especially happy that a fellow Missourian placed the Medal around his neck.

After the ceremony, President Truman said, "The twenty-eight men who represent a cross section of America are men who loved peace but were able to adjust themselves to war."

Some years later after Burr had received his Medal of Honor, Edward Murphy, President of the Mesa,

Arizona, Medal of Honor Society, said, "Herb Burr is the only person to receive the Medal of Honor for reckless driving!"

LIFE AFTER WORLD WAR II

Burr remained in the Army until his retirement in 1966. Then he became a painter for the General Services Administration in the Kansas City area. He retired in 1986 and moved to Urbana, Missouri.

HONORS

The Kansas City Junior Chamber of Commerce feted Burr on September 7, 1945. At that dinner, the JCs bestowed upon him a life-time membership as well as giving him $3000.00 toward a house for his family.

General Jonathan Wainwright, the hero of Bataan and Corregidor, and Sergeant Herbert Burr led the Kansas City, Missouri, Victory Parade on November 5, 1945. Prior to the parade, the two men were honored guests at a dinner hosted by the city.

Sergeant Burr turned the first spade of dirt for a 498- bed Veterans Hospital in Kansas City, Missouri, in 1949.

In October of 1987, the Galmey, Missouri, VFW Post 9368 honored Burr with a plaque to acknowledge his designation as a Medal of Honor recipient.

BURIAL SITE

Herbert H. Burr died on February 8, 1990. He was predeceased by his wife, Lillian. He was survived by three sons, one daughter, a brother, two sisters, and twelve grandchildren.

One friend said, "The only award higher than the Medal of Honor is when the Lord will say, 'Well done, my good and faithful servant, enter into the kingdom of heaven.'" According to another friend, "It was a quiet funeral for a quiet man." Prior to the closing of the casket, a funeral attendant removed the Medal of Honor from Burr's neck and presented the medal to Burr's oldest son, Jack Burr.

Herbert Burr is buried in the Garden of Valor at the Mount Washington Cemetery at Independence, Missouri. Burr rests between two other Medal of Honor recipients, Charles R. Long, killed during the Korean War, and Thomas Toohey, a Civil War veteran.

JAMES L. HARRIS

BIRTH DATE: June 27, 1916

BIRTH PLACE: Hillsboro, Texas

DEATH: October 7, 1944. KIA.

MEDAL OF HONOR ACTION: Vagney, France. October 7, 1944.

RANK: Second Lieutenant

UNIT: 756th Tank Battalion

YEARS OF SERVICE: March 1941 - October 7, 1944

AWARDS: Medal of Honor, Bronze Star, Purple Heart

CCC: F-28, High Rolls, New Mexico. April - May 1935. F-49, South Fork, Colorado. May 1935 - April 1936. F-55, Beulah, Colorado. April 1936-March 1937. F-59, San Isabel, Colorado. April -September 1937.

From the Forest to the Battlefield

JAMES L. HARRIS

Albert Lee Harris (1888-1968) and his wife Bessie (1887-1972) were the parents of six children, three boys and three girls. James was their third child. Lee was a native Texan; his wife had been born in Mississippi. Each had a grammar school education and grew up as sharecroppers. Albert paid six dollars a month to rent his farm. His income was $200.00 for 1930. By 1940 it was zero dollars, even though he worked forty-six weeks that year.

James Harris was born June 27, 1916. He attended school in Bynum, Texas, where he dropped out in tenth grade. Harris was a tough, wiry, young man but was five foot eight inches tall and weighed only 120 pounds. Loyal and industrious, he worked side-by-side with his father, eldest brother, W.C., and his kid brother, Ben. For two winters he worked at construction jobs. To further help his family, he enlisted in the Civilian Conservation Corps and designated his father to receive his monthly allotment.

CCC EXPERIENCE

His enlistment in the CCC signaled the beginning of a two-year odyssey in New Mexico and Colorado. His first assignment was Camp F-28 at High Rolls, New Mexico. From there he was transferred to Camp F-49 at South Fork, Colorado, where he remained for eleven months. He then moved on to Camp F-55 near Bealuh, Colorado, where he worked for a full year from April 1936 -1937. His last CCC stint was at Camp F-59 near San Isabel, Colorado, where he remained another six months before being honorably discharged in 1937.

In the first three camps, Harris worked on road and trail construction, a very difficult occupation. He also cleared and built right of ways for the forest roads. Occasionally, he fought brush fires in addition to hunting for missing persons. At Camp F-59, he became a parts manager, working mostly with the motor pool. His superiors judged his work as excellent.

Everyone called him Red. Throughout his tours of duty, he attended evening classes. He became certified in Red Cross Training which provided an opportunity for him to escape some of the tough labor on the road construction crews. He also availed himself of reading, leadership, and first aid classes. He received straight A's.

After being honorably discharged, Harris returned home and continued to work the family farm. He also worked in construction in the off season. This led to a construction job at Corpus Christi, Texas, where he worked at the naval base.

On March 20, 1941, Harris was drafted, entering service in the United States Army at Fort Sam Houston. He received his basic training at Fort Knox, Kentucky, before being assigned to the 756th Tank Battalion.

From the Forest to the Battlefield

The 756th trained at a number of military locations: Fort Lewis, Washington (1941); Fort Ord, California (1942); and Camp Pickett, Virginia (1942). The next stop was North Africa in November 1942. By early January of the next year, the battalion saw its first combat against the Germans. That same year Harris became a sergeant and a tank commander of a Sherman tank.

MORE ABOUT THE M-4 SHERMAN TANK

The M-4 Sherman tank usually had a five-man crew, consisting of the commander, the driver, the assistant driver/bow gunner, the gunner, and the loader. The commander, usually a sergeant, frequently rode topside and issued driving and firing directions. The driver steered the tank, using lateral sticks instead of a steering wheel. The gunner operated the large cannon with the help of the loader. The assistant driver or bow gunner operated another .30 caliber machine gun. Each man knew how to do the other man's job.

Nearly 1,400 American tanks were either destroyed or knocked out in the Allied drive to Berlin. The average combat life of a tank crew was six weeks. Some likened the interior of a tank to a coffin. When buttoned down, the outside is visible only through a periscope or narrow slits. The radio, located on the rear of the tank served as the umbilical cord to those outside the tank. Near deafening noise and the claustrophobic environment were the norm. Throw into this mix a running battle that required absolute coordination of the crew amid the smell of cordite, the sound of small arms fire pinging against the armor, the howl of the engine, and a distinct possibility of imminent death. This kind of combat produced a special warrior, perhaps even more so than a submariner.

A FURIOUS PATH OF ACTION

Harris's battalion saw considerable action near Paestrum, Italy. From that time forward, the battalion moved doggedly north. His battalion participated in the bloody crossing of the Rapido River. The Italian winter was a significant factor during the heavy fighting with Harris's unit suffering severe losses of men and material. On March 26, 1944, James L. Harris received his battlefield commission near Cassino. His Company Commander, Captain Roy B. Sears said, "He was a staff sergeant doing a lieutenant's job." Sears had effusive praise for Harris:

> James Harris was a quiet, unassuming, well-disciplined soldier and officer...We liked each other the first time we met (he as a draftee and I as a lieutenant). He was my personal tank driver as a private and later when I became "A" Company Commander I promoted him to Staff Sergeant, second in command of five tanks and twenty-four men...It was my personal pleasure to pin the gold bars on his shoulders. His men respected him...and above all trusted his judgment.

Harris was wounded at Cassino and received the Purple Heart. Shortly after, he also received the Bronze Star for his bravery during a two-week period of daily combat between February 4 and February 19, 1944.

From the Forest to the Battlefield

His wounds required a brief hospital stay where he encountered his brother Ben who was in the Fifth Army. Turning down a thirty -day recuperation leave, Red returned to his battalion, because there were rumors of another big operation coming up. He did not want to leave his men. His outfit distinguished itself in the Anzio breakthrough in late May 1944. Finally, the 756th Battalion was relieved a week after the fall of Rome, June 5, 1944.

This time, the rumors were true. His battalion was scheduled to participate in the landings in Southern France on August 15, 1944, near St. Tropez, as part of Operation Dragoon. The path to Germany was north through the Rhone River Valley. This proved to be an almost daily fight, and the Germans made the Americans pay dearly for every captured mile. As a result, the 756th Tank Battalion fought continuously until V-E Day, May 8, 1945.

On October 7, 1944, near Vagvey, France, the Germans, under cover of darkness, moved against an American Infantry position protected by a tank and two platoons of soldiers. After a German hand grenade attack upon the American outpost, the enemy pulled back under cover of dense fog, hoping to gain an element of surprise. Harris, using his instinct and experience gleaned from a year of combat, warily moved his vehicle forward in expectation of a trap. Harris ordered his tank to halt, and then emerged from the vehicle to personally reconnoiter. Armed only with a pistol, he moved slowly through the darkness.

Technical Sergeant Gerald Hennings provided this account of what happened after Harris moved forward:

> Suddenly the machine gun in the Kraut tank opened up at ten yards, the first burst catching Harris squarely in the chest and stomach, knocking him to the ground. Machine gun fire was lashing down the road, belly high. We were in a spot, with walls on either side of the road, there was no room to maneuver. Lieutenant Harris did not forget his mission. Despite the painful wounds he crawled thirty yards through a hail of fire to his tank. Although intense fire was ricocheting off the tank, he attempted to climb to the turret. Finding that he was too weak to make it he fell to the ground beside the tank, shouted a fire order to the gunner, and told the driver to maneuver the tank into a covered archway. As our tank started backing up, its 75mm gun barked twice. While backing away, its machine guns started blasting the enemy infantry. The German tank responded instantly firing three rapid shots, then pulled back. The M-4 burst into flames. Our tank exploded and huge pieces of armored plate flew through the air, one of them severing Lieutenant Harris' leg at the hip. Lieutenant Harris beckoned to me when I got to where he was lying in the road. He told me to get another man to safety before he was hit the second time. I started to move Lieutenant Harris but he said, "Forget about me. I'm done for. Take care of that other man."

While dying, Harris still brandished his pistol toward the retreating Germans who had heard American tanks moving toward them. He died before receiving any medical attention.

MEDAL OF HONOR CITATION

For conspicuous gallantry and intrepidity at risk of life above and beyond the call of duty on 7 October 1944, in Vagney, France. At 9 p.m. an enemy raiding party, comprising a tank and 2 platoons of infantry, infiltrated through the lines under cover of mist and darkness and attacked an infantry battalion command post with hand grenades, retiring a short distance to an ambush position on hearing the approach of the M-4 tank commanded by 2d Lt. Harris. Realizing the need for bold aggressive action, 2d Lt. Harris ordered his tank to halt while he proceeded on foot, fully 10 yards ahead of his 6-man patrol and armed only with a service pistol, to probe the darkness for the enemy. Although struck down and mortally wounded by machine gun bullets which penetrated his stomach he crawled back to his tank, leaving a trail of blood behind him. Too weak to climb inside it, he issued fire orders while lying on the road between the two contending armored vehicles. Wounded a second time, he stood the enemy off until friendly tanks came to his aid. This action caused the enemy to withdraw, thereby saving an entire battalion command from being captured or killed. Suffering a second wound that had severed his leg at his hip, 2d Lt. Harris refused aid until after a wounded member of his crew had been carried to safety. He died before he could be given medical attention.

MEDAL OF HONOR PRESENTATION

Brigadier General A.O. Gorder awarded the Medal of Honor to James L. Harris posthumously on April 23, 1945, at Fort Hood, Texas. Albert Lee Harris accepted his son's medal. Three platoons of forty-eight men made up the honor guard.

HONORS

The citizens of Vagney, France, installed a commemorative plaque within the city square honoring Harris.

In September 2013 the citizens of Hillsboro, Texas, erected a dedication marker that honors their native son, James L. Harris.

At Brownsville/McAllen, Texas, a Veterans War Memorial was erected honoring the eighty-three Texans who became Medal of Honor recipients. Harris is on the list.

On March 28, 1958, Army officials at Fort Knox, Kentucky, named Building # 2363-C Harris Hall.

At Fort Sam Houston, Texas, a 340-room housing unit was named Harris Heights. A brick marker with a bronze plaque identified the housing unit as honoring. Harris.

BURIAL SITE
Originally buried in France, James L. Harris's remains were reinterred at Ridge Park Cemetery in Hillsboro, Texas, in 1951.

GERALD L. ENDL

BIRTH DATE: August 20, 1915

BIRTH PLACE: Fort Atkinson, Wisconsin

DEATH: July 11, 1944. KIA.

MEDAL OF HONOR ACTION: Anamo, New Guinea. July 11, 1944.

RANK: Staff Sergeant

UNIT: Company C, 128th Infantry Regiment, 32th Infantry Division

YEARS OF SERVICE: April 1941 - July 11, 1944

AWARDS: Medal of Honor, Purple Heart

CCC: F-21, Townsend, Wisconsin. August 1934 - March 1935.

GERALD L. ENDL

Ferdinand (Fred) Endl (1885-1956) and his wife Ellen Walther Endl (1890-1965) were lifelong residents of Wisconsin. Each had an eighth-grade education. They married when Fred was twenty-two, and Ellen was eighteen. This union resulted in three children: two girls and one boy. Gerald was the youngest child. Fred worked in the farm supply business in the 1920s and 1930s but became a farm hand later. Ellen stayed at home when the children were young, but during the 1930s she worked in a meat processing plant. The Endls owned a modest home valued at $4500.00. Contrary to the situation in those times, Ellen Endl always had a larger income than her husband. In 1939 Fred worked only eight weeks, earning a mere fifty dollars in that year. On the other hand, his wife worked thirty-six weeks making $750.00.

Both of Gerald's sisters left home before they were twenty. Gerald, nicknamed "Sparrow," remained at home with his parents helping them financially whenever he could. Following his high school graduation, he enrolled in the Civilian Conservation Corps assigning his monthly allotment to his mother.

Wisconsin had sixteen recipients of the Medal of Honor during World War II. Five recipients survived the war while eleven others received their medals posthumously. Naturally, the best-known recipient was General Douglas MacArthur who entered the United States military at Ashland, Wisconsin. Major Richard Bong, an American flying ace with fifty kills, also had significant name recognition as the nation followed his air exploits in the South Pacific for three years. Of the sixteen Wisconsin recipients, only Gerald Endl had been an enrollee in the Civilian Conservation Corps.

CCC EXPERIENCE

After two week at Fort Sheridan, Illinois, Gerald transferred to F-30, Camp Boot Lake, located in the Nicolet National Forest near Townsend, Wisconsin, ninety miles north of Green Bay. There he served from August 1934 to March 1935. In addition to planting trees and road building, he participated in building several campgrounds in the immediate area.

Gerald's tour of duty in the CCC was unremarkable. He took a first aid class as well as a forestry class in tree identification. He received average ratings from his camp superiors. His educational adviser judged him as a well-adjusted young man with a good sense of humor. Like most CCC enrollees, Endl left camp showing a significant weight gain. He was honorably discharged in August 1935.

When he returned home from CCC service, Endl worked a number of odd jobs. For a few years, he served as a messenger for Western Union. Eventually he learned the machinist trade, an occupation that provided him with a steady job at about $1400.00 annually.

From the Forest to the Battlefield

The year 1941 was a busy year for Endl. He married his sweetheart Anna "Rhee" Goethe from neighboring Janesville, quit his job as a machinist, and joined the Army.

MILITARY EXPERIENCE

Endl became a member of the 32nd Infantry Division, the Red Arrow Division, that had been formed in Wisconsin. The division soon moved to Louisiana for well over a year and participated in the Louisiana War Games. Moving again, the division trained in California for desert warfare before traveling east for embarkation to Europe.

The year 1942 was a very dark time in our military history. The war in the Pacific had reached its nadir. The Japanese had swept most of the Pacific. Midway, an island speck in the Central Pacific, stood between Japan and Hawaii while Australia hung by a slender thread.

As a result the "top brass" diverted the Red Arrow Division to the Pacific primarily to bolster Australian defenses. At the same time, General MacArthur made a bold tactical decision: to carry the fight to the enemy by invading New Guinea, a Japanese stronghold. This plan precipitated a bloody, three-year battle for supremacy.

The New Guinea Campaign evolved into near continuous war on the sea, in the air, and on the land. On land it became a brutal conflict in which the enemies were the Japanese, the jungle, and disease. It continued undiminished until the Japanese surrender in August 1945. Unfortunately, it became a forgotten war as public attention focused mostly on the war in Europe.

The Battle of Driniumo River on July 10 -11, 1944, was an example of this relentless warfare. On the night of July 10, the Japanese unleashed ten thousand troops, who poured across the American defenses. The fighting occurred in a steaming jungle with visibility less than a rifle's length. During the afternoon of July 11, superior Allied aerial and naval bombardment carried the day forcing the Japanese to retreat, thereby saving the American infantry.

SERGEANT ENDL'S LAST WORDS

Sergeant Endl's company was part of a battalion movement that had just completed a thirty-hour forced march through the jungle which brought his unit face to face with the Japanese front line. When his platoon leader was wounded, Endl assumed command. He realized that a dozen men had been wounded and were lying helpless on the trail. Without orders, Endl decided to rescue his fallen buddies knowing that the Japanese took no prisoners. Calmly appraising the situation, Endl said, "I'm gonna get them."

From the Forest to the Battlefield

Lieutenant Colonel Samuel Scott, his Battalion Commander said

> Although he had long missed the point of exhaustion where most men would have been exhausted, Sergeant Endl engaged the enemy in an honorable and heroic fight. The eight to ten-minute lull enabled the second and third platoon to withdraw and reorganize with the rest of the company to successfully prevent the enemy from advancing to the village of Anamo.
>
> Single-handedly he held up the enemy advance so that the other men could come up from the rear and crawl forward to evacuate the wounded. He almost made it. He was shot in the back while carrying his fourth buddy out of harm's way.

Staff Sergeant Edward Lane, a squad leader, had high praise of his fellow NCO:

> They were advancing on him. Some of the Japs had fixed bayonets but that didn't stop him. I saw six or eight Japs all around Endl and when he brought out the first three of the wounded, he laid them down on the trail fifteen feet from me. I saw him go back for the fourth man, still firing and fighting...If it hadn't been for Endl's charging and fighting off the enemy to get the wounded men, we wouldn't have gotten them out...I feel that we'd all have been pocketed by the Japs and pushed back to Anamo... He sure fought a heavy one-man fight to save his buddies.

Private First Class Daniel Inko was awestruck by End's cool approach:

> We were pinned down by the first fire of the Japs; and when he reported this, our commanding officer built up both flanks and ordered the withdrawal. But Sergeant Endl knew that four scouts had been cut off and he said he was going to get them back on line. I last saw him as he went forward into a really fierce fire. But at all times during this fighting he was the most calm and efficient man I ever saw.

Commander of the Sixth Army, Lieutenant Walter Kruger added his tribute:

> In the type of jungle fighting peculiar to this theater, the recovery of the dead and wounded is a major problem. No unit will willingly abandon its dead nor leave the wounded comrades to the known and unmerciful acts of the Japanese...Knowing full-well the obvious dangers, Staff Sergeant Endl voluntarily elected to perform, single-handedly, an exceedingly courageous act...He reflects great honor and credit on the military service and on the infantry.

Even General MacArthur weighed in on Endl's actions: "Staff Sergeant Endl's heroic self-sacrifice saved the lives of many of his comrades, enabled his company to withdraw, allowed the company to set up a perimeter defense, and to stop the enemy attack."

MEDAL OF HONOR CITATION

For conspicuous gallantry and intrepidity at the risk of his life above and beyond the call of duty near Anamo, New Guinea, on 11 July 1944. S/Sgt. Endl was at the head of the leading platoon of his company advancing along a jungle trail when enemy troops were encountered and a fire fight developed. The enemy attacked in force under heavy rifle, machinegun, and grenade fire. His platoon leader wounded, S/Sgt. Endl immediately assumed command and deployed his platoon on a firing line at the fork in the trail toward which the enemy attack was directed. The dense jungle terrain greatly restricted vision and movement, and he endeavored to penetrate down the trail toward an open clearing of Kunai grass. As he advanced, he detected the enemy, supported by at least 6 light and 2 heavy machineguns, attempting an enveloping movement around both flanks. His commanding officer sent a second platoon to move up on the left flank of the position, but the enemy closed in rapidly, placing our force in imminent danger of being isolated and annihilated. Twelve members of his platoon were wounded, 7 being cut off by the enemy. Realizing that if his platoon were forced farther back, these 7 men would be hopelessly trapped and at the mercy of a vicious enemy, he resolved to advance at all cost, knowing it meant almost certain death, in an effort to rescue his comrades. In the face of extremely heavy fire he went forward alone and for a period of approximately 10 minutes engaged the enemy in a heroic close-range fight, holding them off while his men crawled forward under cover to evacuate the wounded and to withdraw. Courageously refusing to abandon 4 more wounded men who were lying along the trail, he brought them back to safety one by one.. As he was carrying the last man, he was struck by a heavy burst of automatic fire and was killed. By his persistent and daring self-sacrifice and on behalf of his comrades, S/Sgt. Endl made possible the successful evacuation of all but one man, and enabled the two platoons to withdraw with their wounded and to reorganize with the rest of the company.

MEDAL OF HONOR PRESENTATION

Colonel George MacMillan, Company Commander of Camp McCoy, presented Endl's Medal of Honor to his widow, Anna Marie Endl, at Janesville, Wisconsin, on March 27, 1945. She later presented her husband's Medal of Honor to the Wisconsin Veterans Museum in Madison, Wisconsin, where it is on permanent display.

HONORS

Endl is honored at the Veterans Museum at Madison, Wisconsin.

In 2015 the Wisconsin Army National Guard installed Endl in its Hall of Fame.

Endl has two streets bearing his name: Sendal, New Guinea, and Fort Benning, Georgia.

Within the city limits of Fort Atkinson, Wisconsin, there is a Gerald Court as well as an Endl Park.

While at the dedication of the Veterans Museum, Joanne Schudda, whose husband is a cousin of Endl, said

My aunt and I spent a lot of hours where she talked about him; and I felt like I really knew him through her, even though I never met him. I felt kind of close to my aunt because she brought him to life for us. I just feel like I am sort of representing her. It's just a good thing to be part of something that the man did for us, not just for his men, but for us. It makes you feel proud.

BURIAL SITE

Endl's remains were reinterred at Saint Joseph Catholic Cemetery at Fort Atkinson, Wisconsin, in 1948.

LEROY JOHNSON

BIRTH DATE: December 6, 1919

BIRTH PLACE: Caney Creek, Louisiana

DEATH: December 15, 1944. KIA.

MEDAL OF HONOR ACTION: Limon, Leyte, Philippines Islands. December 15, 1944.

RANK: Sergeant

UNIT: Company K, 126th Infantry Regiment, 32nd Infantry Division

YEARS OF SERVICE: November 1943 - December 15, 1944

AWARDS: Medal of Honor, Silver Star, Purple Heart (2), Combat Infantryman Badge

CCC: F-4, Leesville, Louisiana. June 1937 - September 1938. DG-82, Wells, Nevada. October 1938 - April 1939.

LEROY JOHNSON

Leroy was born on December 6, 1919, in Oakdale, Louisiana, to Leander and Eileen Johnson. He was one of nine children, five girls and four boys. He dropped out of school after seventh grade. Physically not imposing, he was a skinny kid, weighing 110 pounds on a five-foot seven-inch frame. He worked occasionally at wood cutting and post making. Upon entering the CCC, he listed his previous occupation as working on his father's farm.

CCC EXPERIENCE

Leroy served in the CCC from June 1937 to April 1939. He first served at Camp F-4 in Leesville, Louisiana, and then at Camp DG-82 near Wells, Nevada. His occupation in Louisiana was road construction. While at DG-82, he worked on rodent control. His evaluations were poor at Camp F-4, but at the Nevada camp, his superiors evaluated him as average.

But he had a weakness: a proclivity to go AWOL. His absence on May 2, 1938, involved a car accident. He and his CCC buddies drove to a local dance and while traveling at a great speed, the driver swerved to avoid hitting a herd of cows. In the process the car overturned throwing the boys out of the vehicle.

Dewitt Owens, the owner of the cows, said the young men were under the influence of liquor. In his affidavit Johnson, the driver, admitted that the truck had bald tires and that he was speeding. J. E. Hardy, a witness to the crash, said, "I rushed to the victims. One boy was on the ground. When I lifted his head his breath smelled of liquor. He identified himself as Leroy Johnson." Although Johnson's pals were knocked unconscious, neither needed hospitalization. Johnson, on the other hand, suffered severe abrasions on his back, a puncture on his knee, and a broken right clavicle.

Even though the young men had broken several CCC regulations, officials never brought charges against the boys. Nothing exists in Johnson's record regarding any resolution of the incident. Apparently in the clear, Johnson reenlisted in the CCC shortly afterward and transferred to Nevada.

One must look at Johnson's behavior within the times it had occurred. The Great Depression had profound negative effects upon the family unit. Values were shunted as individual survival became paramount. In that day-to-day struggle, discipline suffered considerably or disappeared completely.

Johnson was attracted to the CCC for two reasons: a job and a monthly allotment for his family. He failed to take into account the nature of *quid pro quo* (something for something). In exchange for a job and relief for his family, he had to accept the conditions of working in a structured organization with specific rules and regulations. Like so many other young men who enlisted in the CCC, this realization had to have come as a huge shock, especially when compared with their previously unfettered life.

From the Forest to the Battlefield

Many CCC inductees immediately ran afoul of the system. Some were shocked; others persevered. Many simply walked away. Johnson did not seem to understand that he could not go to a dance just because he wanted to. His experiences in early life help explain his frequent AWOLs.

Johnson was fortunate because he received a second chance and could transfer to a Nevada CCC camp, far from the temptations of Louisiana. There his record was clean and his ratings average. It appeared as if Johnson had matured and learned how to fit into the system. He received an honorable discharge from the CCC.

MILITARY EXPERIENCE

Of course, the CCC was only a prelude to what was to come a few years later. When Johnson joined the Army, he found himself in a comparable situation. Only this time, he carried a rifle not a shovel. Familiar with the Army's structure, he steered clear of the pitfalls. Ultimately, he survived rigorous training and months of combat, eventually becoming a leader within a system that, at one time, he had almost failed.

Like many young men in the Great Depression, Johnson found that the military offered him a respite from hard times. Two weeks before Pearl Harbor, he joined the US Army. He was placed in the 32nd Infantry Division.

The 32nd Infantry Division, the Red Arrow Division, was the first division moved entirely by ship convoy into a combat zone. The unit briefly trained in Australia and went into combat on the island of New Guinea, a campaign that pitted a jungle-trained enemy against a green American outfit. This campaign was bloody, slow, and costly as the 32nd Division suffered major losses. But the Japanese threat of invasion of Australia had been eliminated and marked the beginning of General Douglas MacArthur's planned return to the Philippines.

Sergeant Leroy Johnson belonged to Company K of the 126th Infantry Regiment, the 32nd Division. On April 6, 1944, he was awarded a Silver Star and a Purple Heart for moving his squad successfully against a heavily entrenched enemy position at Sanananea (Papuan Campaign-New Guinea).

After a brief respite, the 32nd Division landed on Leyte, Philippines, on November 15, 1944. At this point, the 32nd had become a battle tested outfit, skilled in jungle warfare.

Once again, the Japanese had planned well, devising a brilliant defensive strategy. Advancing on jungle trails not wide enough for a jeep, the American infantryman had to attack well prepared Japanese positions, frequently taking heavy losses. Bitter hand-to-hand fighting occurred near Limon where Sergeant Johnson lost his life.

MEDAL OF HONOR CITATION

Sergeant Leroy Johnson was squad leader of a 9-man patrol sent to reconnoiter a ridge held by a well-entrenched enemy force. Seeing an enemy machinegun position, he ordered his men to remain behind while he crawled to within 6 yards of the gun. One of the enemy crew jumped up and prepared to man the weapon. Quickly withdrawing, Sgt. Johnson rejoined his patrol and reported the situation to his commanding officer. Ordered to destroy the gun, which covered the approaches to several other enemy positions, he chose 3 other men, armed them with hand grenades, and led them to a point near the objective. After taking partial cover behind a log, the men had knocked out the gun and begun an assault when hostile troops on the flank hurled several grenades. As he started for cover, Sgt. Johnson saw 2 unexploded grenades which had fallen near his men. Knowing that his comrades would be wounded or killed by the explosion, he deliberately threw himself on the grenades and received their full charge in his body. Fatally wounded by the blast, he died soon afterward. Through his outstanding gallantry in sacrificing his life for his comrades, Sgt. Johnson provided a shining example of the highest traditions of the U.S. Army.

MEDAL OF HONOR PRESENTATION

Sergeant Johnson's Medal of Honor was presented posthumously to his mother, Mrs. True Johnson.

A LETTER FROM JOHNSON'S COMPANY COMMANDER, JOHNNY B. WAX

Dear Mr. and Mrs. Johnson,

Several times during the last few months I have received good news, but none made me happier than when I picked up the last Monday's *Times Picayune* and learned that your son had been awarded the Congressional Medal of Honor. He was a fine boy and every inch a soldier...I witnessed the incident for which he was awarded the nation's highest award. After receiving his fatal wound, he managed to get up, take three staggering steps, and reach the three of us who were rushing up the hilltop to help him. We lowered him rapidly down the hill and he died within a few minutes. Nothing can bring him back to life but I am sincerely glad that a grateful nation could in some way, even so small, show their appreciation for what he did. His name and the sacrifice he made will always stand out in a division that has been outstanding throughout the war.

HONORS

Sergeant Johnson's monument, erected in 1995, stands on 8th Street in Oakdale, Louisiana.

A bronze plaque commemorating Sergeant Johnson hangs on the wall of the Oberlin, Louisiana, Court House. This plaque was formerly at Camp Leroy Johnson, New Orleans, Louisiana.

From the Forest to the Battlefield

Leroy Johnson Drive is located on the campus of the University of New Orleans.

A MEMORIAL DAY TRIBUTE

Excerpts from A MEMORIAL DAY STORY FOR THE AGES, 24,550 EXTRA DAYS OF LIFE (Reprinted from the *Creekbank blog*)

A phone call from Master Sergeant James Clemenson to Curt Iles of the Creekbank *blog*:

> Sir I am contacting you because of your research on the Medal of Honor winner, Sgt Leroy Johnson. My father (Herman Clemenson) was with Johnson the night he saved my father's life with this brave act....Later on that day, he held his best friend as he died. The next day my father received severe grenade wounds that ended his active service. He has nearly seventy years' extra life due to the heroic act of a fellow soldier named Sergeant Leroy Johnson.

Illes wrote, "Clemenson died in 2011. He lived 24,550 days after Sgt. Leroy Johnson saved his life on December 15, 1944. That's sixty-seven years, two months, and seventeen days." Iles completed his blog in a fitting tribute:

> Memorial Day 2012 is a day to remember the sacrifice of men and women who are willing to die to buy the daily freedom we enjoy. For every American it should be a time of gratitude, thoughtfulness, and remembrance. Remembrance of a soldier's story of the ultimate sacrifice.

BURIAL SITE

Originally interred at Limon, Leyte, Philippines, Johnson's remains were later moved to the American Military Cemetery near Manila, Philippines. He is buried there along with 17,000 other American soldiers.

WILLIAM R. SHOCKLEY

BIRTH DATE: December 4, 1918

BIRTH PLACE: Bokoshe, Oklahoma

DEATH: March 31, 1945. KIA.

MEDAL OF HONOR ACTION: Villa Verde Trail, Luzon, Philippines. March 31, 1945.

RANK: Private First Class

UNIT: Company L, 128th Infantry Regiment, 32nd Infantry Division

YEARS OF SERVICE: January 1940 - March 31, 1945

AWARDS: Medal of Honor, Purple Heart (2), Bronze Star, Combat Infantryman Badge

CCC: F-224, Saugus, California. April 1939. Camp F-94, Fresno County, California. May-July 1939.

WILLIAM R. SHOCKLEY

William Ralph Shockley and his wife, True, were rootless American farmers who searched for employment in Oklahoma, Arkansas, and finally California. Their first child, William, was born in Bokoshe, Oklahoma. Their next three children were born in Arkansas. Their last child was born in Fresno County in 1935. They were Okies by definition. Their lot in life in the "promised land" differed little from life in Oklahoma and Arkansas. William eked out a living on a rented farm. Later he worked occasionally as a ranch hand. His income in 1940 was $240.00.

Young William completed eighth grade at Caruthers Elementary School in Caruthers, California, before dropping out of school. He, too, worked as a ranch hand, but his employment was sporadic. He never found steady employment until joining the Civilian Conservation Corps in April 1939. Sadly, his hitch in the CCC ended abruptly four months later.

Initially, he served at F-224 at Camp Trimmer near Saugus, California. He transferred in late May 1939 to Camp F-94, Fresno County. At Camp F-94, he ran into disciplinary problems. He went AWOL over the Fourth of July. He had been ordered to remain at camp on fire watch duty, but he wanted to go home. On July 1, he left his post for four days. Upon his return the Commanding Officer held a trial and found him guilty. He paid dearly for his weekend off: sixteen extra days of work, forfeiture of four days' pay, and confinement to camp for one week.

This experience did not sit well with William. A few days later he left camp again, only this time permanently. At the end of the month, July 31, 1939, his company commander charged him with desertion. Since the Uniform Code of Military Justice did not apply to CCC enrollees, he was removed from the rolls, and his mother lost her monthly stipend. This was yet another case of a young man not ready to submit to the necessary discipline of the CCC.

After returning home he endured five more months of chronic unemployment. Upon entering the service in January 1940, he listed his occupation as a truck driver. The federal census in 1940 indicated that he had worked for ten weeks the previous year, and that his earned income had been $110.00.

William Shockley was initially stationed at The Presidio, an historic army fort overlooking San Francisco Bay. Later he transferred to the 126th Regiment of the 32nd Infantry Division, the Red Arrow Division, which had been recently activated. His journey to the jungles of New Guinea and the Philippines had begun.

Originally, the 32nd had trained for combat in Europe; however, at Fort Devens, Massachusetts, their orders for Northern Ireland were abruptly changed. Fearing the fall of Port Moresby, a potential staging ground for the Japanese invasion of Australia, General MacArthur petitioned for immediate help to carry the battle to New Guinea, an island north of Australia, controlled by the Japanese.

Logistically, it was an enormous operation. The 32nd Division crossed the United States and arrived in San Francisco, where a massive convoy transported them to the "land down under" in late May 1942. With little jungle training, the first elements of the division saw action against the Japanese during that September. Soon, the entire division was engaged in combat.

The Papuan Campaign ultimately was a victory bought at a huge price, not only in terms of battlefield casualties but also with regard to jungle diseases. Heavy losses prompted officials to recall the division back to Australia for retraining and refitting.

The 32nd went back into action in January 1943 participating in amphibious landings at Saidor and Aitope, on the northern coast of New Guinea. The brutal battles continued there as the Japanese and the jungle proved to be formidable. It was not until August that the Japanese presence was eliminated, thereby allowing the division to rest.

Shockley first won distinction at Saidor by leading a squad against a heavily defended position and forcing the enemy soldiers to withdraw. For this action he was awarded a Bronze Star as well as the Purple Heart. He also became eligible to wear the Combat Infantryman Badge, a highly-coveted award.

By November 1944, they landed at Leyte, Philippines Islands, where the division fought until Christmas before moving on to Luzon. The 128th Infantry Regiment, part of the 32nd Infantry Division, bore the brunt of the 115 days' struggle to secure the Villa Verde Trail, a winding, twenty-seven miles, goat path. The trail consisted of sharp ridges and deep valleys that required small unit tactics, that is, four-man attack squads with support by a twelve- man squad. The Japanese defended the trail from dug-in, heavily fortified positions, where frequently the opposing forces were but a few yards apart. Much of the combat was hand-to-hand. It was in these conditions that Shockley, a member of Company L, 128th Infantry Regiment, 32nd Division, lost his life.

THE LAST WORDS OF PFC. SHOCKLEY: *I will remain until the end.*

On March 31,1945, Shockley's company had gained control of Hill 504 near the Villa Verde Trail. That evening, the Japanese counter attacked. Begun as a heavy artillery charge, the enemy followed up with a banzai charge against Shockley's badly undermanned company. It was a ferocious battle. The Japanese attacked, fell back, regrouped, and then charged fearlessly again and again. Shockley saw that the position was untenable and recognized the need for his company to escape before being overrun.

From the Forest to the Battlefield

Private John I. Allen, a member of Shockley's machine squad, provided this eyewitness account:

> We were in an advanced position when the Japanese counter attacked. They were in great numbers and had worked their way within yards where he had set up our machine guns. Private Shockley saw the situation and he told us to withdraw. He was at his gun and he said he was going to stay until the end-- that he would cover us until we got back to our line. The Japs had worked in on either side and threatened to cut us off. As we withdrew, he beat off one enemy attack. But in that assault, the Japs got into our foxholes on either flank and they took up the attack from there. He got up and shifted the machine gun to cover the new threat and when they came in, he was firing at them. He was shot through the chest as they closed in.

Sergeant Clifford Calhoun, who was leader of a machine squad that had taken up position on a hill near the trail, also attested to Shockley's valor:

> When Private Shockley insisted that only one man remain behind at the machine gun, I saw the squad safely on its way. The Japs were throwing hand grenades and dynamite charges. Twice during the rush the machine gun developed stoppages. Under the fire that came from different sides, Private Shockley cleared the weapon, resumed firing, and drove them off. They had gotten to the foxholes vacated by our men and they took the fight to him. He got up, shifted his machine gun and laid his fire along those lines. They charged again and finally overran his position. He died the way he said he would, firing to the last.

MEDAL OF HONOR CITATION

He was in position with his unit on a hill when the enemy, after a concentration of artillery fire, launched a counterattack. He maintained his position under intense enemy fire and urged his comrades to withdraw, saying that he would "remain to the end" to provide cover. Although he had to clear two stoppages which impeded the reloading of his weapon, he halted one enemy charge. Hostile troops then began moving in on his left flank, and he quickly shifted his gun to fire on them. Knowing that the only route of escape was being cut off by the enemy, he ordered the remainder of his squad to withdraw to safety and deliberately remained at his post. He continued to fire until he was killed during the ensuing enemy charge. Later, four Japanese were found dead in front of his position. Pfc. Shockley, facing certain death, sacrificed himself to save his fellow soldiers, but the heroism and gallantry displayed by him enabled his squad to reorganize and continue its attack.

MEDAL OF HONOR PRESENTATION

E.E. Basye, mayor of Selma, California, presided over the ceremony. Mrs. True Shockley accepted her son's Medal of Honor from Colonel J.J. France, Commanding Officer of the 9th Service Command Rehabilitation at Turlock California Center. The presentation was held in the Selma High School auditorium where the high school band played appropriate music selections.

BURIAL SITE

William R. Shockley is buried at Floral Memorial Park in Selma, California.

WILLIAM J. CRAWFORD

BIRTH DATE: May 19, 1918

BIRTH PLACE: Pueblo, Colorado

DEATH: May 15, 2000

MEDAL OF HONOR ACTION: Altaville, Italy. September 13, 1943.

RANK: Private

UNIT: Company I, 3rd Battalion, 142nd Infantry Regiment, 36th Infantry Division

YEARS OF SERVICE: July 1942 - 1945. Reenlisted 1947 - 1967.

AWARDS: Medal of Honor, Prisoner of War Medal, Others

CCC: F-33, Manitou Springs, Colorado. April - September 1937.

WILLIAM J. CRAWFORD

George Crawford (1884-1953) was born in Kansas but moved to Colorado as a youngster. He became a blacksmith and later married Milly Henson (1885-1919) in 1908. They had three children: Ida (1910), George (1912), and William (1919). When William was an infant, his mother died leaving a devastated husband who never fully recovered from her loss. He grieved so deeply that he was incapable of caring for his children.

Consequently, Milly's father and mother, Charles and Ida Henson, took the children and raised them as their own. Charles Henson managed a grocery store for much of his life, and William gradually became a great deal of help.

Young Bill graduated from Central High School at Pueblo in 1936. He was a good student and particularly liked history. A member of the Boy Scouts, he delivered the local paper and delivered groceries from his grandfather's store. He had a bit of a mischievous streak. His favorite story was how he liked to disconnect the local trolley while the conductor was busy with his passengers!

Later, he took up boxing as a means of recreation. A lightweight, he was nearly six feet tall and weighed only 130 pounds, but his height and long arms gave him a significant advantage. In fact, he became a local Golden Gloves champion. When asked why he didn't turn professional, he said, "I probably could have but the war came along and interrupted my plans."

CCC EXPERIENCE

William Crawford enrolled in the CCC for the standard enlistment of six months. He served in Company 1819 at Camp F-33, Manitou Springs, Colorado, from April to September 1937. His duty was road construction. His performance was judged satisfactory throughout the enrollment period. He assigned his allotment to Charles Henson, his grandfather.

Crawford took two evening courses in safety and fire prevention, scoring well in each course. His personal evaluations made by his company commander, his camp superintendent, and his educational adviser were the same: very good. Prior to his discharge, the doctor listed him as in good health even though this six foot young man weighed only 130 pounds, the same as when he enlisted. Arguably, his weight reflected increased muscle mass due to his strenuous work on the road crew. He was honorably discharged on September 31, 1937.

After returning home, Crawford worked at several odd jobs such as painting houses and barns. He continued working at his grandfather's store and in 1939 worked seven days a week for fifty-two weeks earning $350.00.

MILITARY EXPERIENCE

Crawford joined the Army on July 29, 1942. After basic training, he was assigned as an infantryman to Company I, 3rd Battalion, 142nd Infantry Regiment of the 36th Infantry Division. On September 9, 1943, the division invaded Italy at Salerno. Four days later, Private Crawford had his date with history near the town of Altavilla.

Crawford's company had been assigned the mission of taking Hill 424 that had been fortified with dug-in machine gun emplacements. As his platoon advanced on their objective, it came under intense machine gun fire, stalling forward movement. Sergeant Robert C. McMillan said, "Crawford had no orders to move. But he realized the importance of the enemy position and moved forward on his own initiative."

Under heavy fire, Crawford inched ahead and took out the first machine gun nest. As his comrades moved up, they were stopped again by the murderous cross fire from two additional machine gun nests. Once again, Crawford voluntarily advanced ahead of his unit while bullets sprayed around him. First, he swerved to his left and took out the machine gun emplacement with a single hand grenade, killing the crew. Then he advanced toward the second one and took that one out, too. After that he jumped into the machine gun nest and turned the weapon against the fleeing enemy.

"I was eyewitness to this," said Sergeant D.C. Robinson. "His courageous efforts were largely responsible for the continued advance of his unit toward their objective."

The furious fighting continued throughout the afternoon. By evening the company had set up defensive positions. As darkness fell, the men of Crawford's platoon marveled at how they were still alive. All knew that they were living because of the heroism of Crawford. However, when they looked for him, he was nowhere to be found.

Unbeknownst to his comrades, Private Crawford remained behind German lines to help a wounded comrade. During the fight, others around him died. "I was untouched for some reason," he said. "The Lord was looking over me." But the Germans soon captured him.

Thus, he began a four-week trek to Hammerstein, West Prussia, Germany, six hundred miles northeast from Altavilla, Italy. There, he spent the duration of the war. Since his POW status had not been verified by the Germans, the Army reported him as killed in action. It was not until the end of the war that his family learned of his capture. By fall 1945, he returned to the United States after being held captive 686 days.

His recollection of his captivity and subsequent march to freedom is revealing

I accepted the Lord on September 1943 at Stalag II B at Hammerstein, Germany. At that time, the camp had received Bibles, hymnals, and an accordion. We organized a "Born-Again" evangelistic worship service. A German officer escorted some of us out of the prison compound to a large meeting hall in Hammerstein. We had to give this up when the Russian Army came through Poland...

PRISONER OF WAR CAMPS IN GERMANY

Over one hundred POW camps were scattered throughout Germany and housed nearly 95,000 Americans. There were separate camps for enlisted men, officers, and Allied airmen. The captives lived a life of boredom and uncertainty. Hardship was ever-present. Mistreatment was common and brutality was always a real possibility. At best, the food was poor. The average daily ration for each man was three potatoes, a cup of soup, a tiny piece of bread, ersatz coffee, and perhaps a tiny amount of margarine. There were never enough blankets, and the few the Germans issued were called "tablecloths" because they were so thin. Mail was erratic, and Red Cross packages were irregularly distributed, but religious services were permitted.

The fictional life of *Hogan's Heroes* did not exist in these stalags. Instead tedium and lethargy were commonplace. What few books existed were "dog-eared" from use. Recreation was obviously limited. The war was far away with no end in sight.

But from this milieu, a rare exception occurred. A German guard had been boasting about Max Schmeling's ability as a boxer. The Americans responded in kind. Other guards entered the verbal fray. Someone mentioned that Crawford was a boxer. The guards offered one of their own as a challenge. It was to be a bare-knuckle fight. Everybody anticipated the event.

Crawford knocked out his opponent. The outcome greatly increased the morale of the American POWs.

By March 1945 many camps had been liberated by advancing Allied troops on the Western Front. It was a different situation for the camps east of Berlin where the Russians were closing in. Weeks before the fall of Berlin, the Germans opened the stalags to flee from the onrushing Russian Army. But they maintained control of the POWs.

We had to march westward to escape the Russian Army. We were liberated by the American Army after marching for fifty-two days and almost five hundred miles. I carried my Bible on my back and my new testament in my left-hand shirt pocket. How I survived, the Lord only knows.

These marches to freedom were brutal. The POWs who were too ill to move stayed on to be liberated by the Russians. The remainder of the captives walked about twenty miles a day, slept in open fields or barns, and survived on a minimum of rations. These marches averaged about two hundred miles. Crawford's walk to freedom was twice as long.

MEDAL OF HONOR CITATION

For conspicuous gallantry and intrepidity at risk of life above and beyond the call of duty in action with the enemy near Altavilla, Italy, 13 September 1943. When Company I attacked an enemy-held position on Hill 424, the 3d Platoon, in which Pvt. Crawford was a squad scout, attacked as base platoon for the company. After reaching the crest of the hill, the platoon was pinned down by intense enemy machinegun and small-arms fire. Locating 1 of these guns, which was dug in on a terrace on his immediate front, Pvt. Crawford, without orders and on his own initiative, moved over the hill under enemy fire to a point within a few yards of the gun emplacement and single-handedly destroyed the machinegun and killed 3 of the crew with a hand grenade, thus enabling his platoon to continue its advance. When the platoon, after reaching the crest, was once more delayed by enemy fire, Pvt. Crawford again, in the face of intense fire, advanced directly to the front midway between 2 hostile machinegun nests located on a higher terrace and emplaced in a small ravine. Moving first to the left, with a hand grenade he destroyed 1 gun emplacement and killed the crew; he then worked his way, under continuous fire, to the other and with 1 grenade and the use of his rifle, killed 1 enemy and forced the remainder to flee. Seizing the enemy machinegun, he fired on the withdrawing Germans and facilitated his company's advance.

MEDAL OF HONOR PRESENTATION

At Camp Carson, Colorado, on May 11, 1944, Major General Terry Allen presented William Crawford's Medal of Honor posthumously to Crawford's father, George Crawford.

A reporter who obviously knew about the family's history astutely recorded his observations:

> The grizzled old blacksmith from Pueblo, Colorado, shifted his feet uncomfortably, he felt out of place before a crowd of soldiers no less to face a two-star general....It was not a happy occasion, but it was a ceremony the man who had tasted grief far too often could not avoid. "Your son was a hero," General Allen said to the father who struggled to keep tears from falling down his cheeks...Slowly the elder Crawford stretched his work-hardened hands forward to accept the award, though prestigious, would never replace the son that he had lost. As he turned away, no longer could his tears be restrained. So he slowly walked away alone, hiding them in his solitude.

LIFE AFTER WORLD WAR II

When he returned from overseas, Bill married Eileen Bruce on January 13, 1946. They had two children. He reenlisted in 1947 and served most of his duty as an Army recruiter at Pueblo, Colorado. He and his wife built a house near Palmer Lake, not too far from Pueblo, where he became quite active in civic affairs. After retirement in 1967, he missed the military. He applied for a janitor's position at the Air Force

Academy. When asked why he took that job, he said, "There are young people there." For several years he took care of a dormitory of one hundred cadets where he mopped and buffed the floors, emptied the trash bins, and cleaned the toilets.

Later, James Moschgat, a retired USAF Colonel, who lived in that dorm recalled

> Maybe it was his physical appearance that made him disappear into the background. Bill didn't move quickly, and in fact, you could say he shuffled a bit, as if suffering from some sort of injury. His gray hair and winkled face made him appear ancient to a group of cadets. Face it, Bill was an old man working in a young man's environment. What could he have to offer us on a personal level?

One day in 1976, Moschgat was reading a book about recipients of the Medal of Honor, and he stumbled across Crawford's entry. "Holy cow," he said to his buddy, "You're not going to believe this but our janitor is a Medal of Honor recipient!" When he showed Crawford the page, Crawford said, "Yep, that's me." Moschgat was stunned. Then he asked, "Why didn't you tell us about it?" Crawford answered, "That was one day in my life and it happened a long time ago."

After that the relationship between Crawford and the cadets blossomed. He got to know everyone of the cadets in his building. In fact, he became their mentor. As his reputation grew, cadets sought him out just to talk with him or to say hello. To the cadets, he became a treasure and a much-loved individual.

THE SECOND MEDAL OF HONOR PRESENTATION

On May 30, 1984, President Ronald Reagan made the annual commencement address at the US Air Force Academy. After concluding his address, he indicated he had some unfinished business to conclude. He said

> Now there's something I want to do that means a lot to me, and, I'm sure, will mean a lot to you. We're graced with the company of a man who believed so much in the values of our nation that he went above and beyond the call of duty. In July of 1944 a grateful nation bestowed the Medal of Honor on a soldier, a private, for extraordinary heroism on Hill 424 near Altavilla, Italy. The soldier could not accept the award that day. He was a prisoner of war, and his father accepted it on his behalf. Since early in this century, it has been customary for the President to present the Medal of Honor. Well, nearly forty years have gone by, and it's time we do it right. A native son of Colorado and certainly a good friend of the Air Force Academy will forever be in the select company where the heroes of our country stand. It gives me great pleasure to ask Mr. William J. "Bill" Crawford, formerly of the 36th Infantry Division, to come forward.

The entire assembly rose to their feet. Crawford's citation was read before the President placed the Medal of Honor around his neck.

From the Forest to the Battlefield

HONORS

At Sergeant Crawford's death, Governor Bill Owens, Governor of Colorado, ordered all the flags to be flown at half-staff in Crawford's honor.

In 2010 the Colorado State Fair honored all veterans on Military Appreciation Day. Specifically, at the forefront of the celebration were the four recipients of the Medal of Honor from Pueblo.

There is a Medal of Honor Memorial near the Pueblo Convention Center featuring four life-sized statues of Pueblo's Medal of Honor recipients.

In 2010 the Crawford House opened in Pueblo, Colorado. It is a shelter, a mental health facility, and a residential facility for veterans.

There is a Crawford Memorial located at Palmer Lake, Colorado, where a life-sized statue of Crawford stands overlooking the garden.

The city of Pueblo has a Heroes Plaza.

Pueblo sponsors an annual essay contest based on the values of Pueblo's four Medal of Honor recipients.

In 1958 Crawford was one of the Medal of Honor recipients to serve as an Honor Guard for the burial of the Unknown Soldiers from World War II and the Korean War.

CRAWFORD'S DEATH

William R. Crawford died on March 15, 2000, at his home in Palmer Lake. He was survived by his wife, Eileen, a son, Daniel, a daughter, Beverly Jean Kite, and a sister, Frieda Kahle, five grandchildren, and four great-grandchildren.

His son-in-law, Pastor Ed Kite, delivered the main eulogy, calling the deceased "our silent hero." A friend, Pete Lemon, recalled that Bill, "Always had a smile on his face. He always had a handshake. He always had a story."

Over three hundred people braved a pending snow storm to attend the funeral. Also in attendance were Pueblo's three other Medal of Honor recipients: Carl Sitter and Jerry Murphy, representing the Korean War, and Drew Nix, a representative from the Viet Nam War. The Cadet Chorale provided the music, and another group of cadets acted as pall bearers.

BURIAL SITE

William R. Crawford's remains are interred at the United States Air Force Academy Cemetery.

JAMES M. LOGAN

BIRTH DATE: December 19, 1920

BIRTH PLACE: McNeil, Texas

DEATH: October 9, 1999

MEDAL OF HONOR ACTION: Salerno, Italy. September 9, 1943.

RANK: Sergeant

UNIT: 3rd Battalion, 142nd Infantry Regiment, 36th Infantry Division

YEARS OF SERVICE: 1936 - March 1945. Joined Texas National Guard in 1936. Federal service in 1940. Left Texas National Guard on May 24, 1945.

AWARDS: Medal of Honor, Distinguished Service Cross, Purple Heart, Bronze Star (2), Italian Cross of Valor

CCC: SP-29, Ottine, Texas. January - March 1937.

JAMES M. LOGAN

His parents, Charles M. Logan (1886-1956) and Maggie Mae Williams Logan (1884-1964) were Texans who struggled to survive. During World War I, Charles was not eligible for military service because he was blind in one eye. In 1918 the couple married. They had two children: a boy, James, born in 1920, and a girl, Wanda, born in 1924. During the 1920s, Charles Logan worked sporadically in construction. Later he sold sewing machines.

Little else is known about James's father. For example, the Army press release announcing Logan's becoming a Medal of Honor recipient specifically states, "...Sergeant Logan is from Luling, Texas, where his mother, Mrs. Maggie M. Logan, and his sister, Mrs. G. A. Welch, live at 416 Austin Street." There is no mention of his father.

"Things were pretty tough as a child," James said. "I was used to hunting and fishing so my family could eat." He quit school in seventh grade and sold books door-to-door for a brief time. Then he caddied at a golf course near the San Marcos River. When not caddying, James fished golf balls out of the river and sold them to the golfers at a dime apiece.

A sturdy young man, James was five foot seven inches tall and weighed 130 pounds. He looked older than his chronological age, a fact that enabled him to join the Texas National Guard at age fifteen. As a guardsman, he earned a dollar a day.

CCC EXPERIENCE

When he was seventeen, James joined the CCC and was stationed at Camp SP-29 at Ottine, Texas, not too far from his home. His CCC career lasted less than three months because he suffered from nocturnal enuresis. Most of the time, he was a patient in the camp hospital. While in the hospital, he took a couple of basic courses offered by the camp: arithmetic and writing. He was honorably discharged from the CCC on March 9, 1937.

MILITARY EXPERIENCE

Upon his return home, Logan continued his membership in the Texas National Guard. In November 1940 his outfit was nationalized into the US Army at Camp Bowie, Texas. Eventually Logan became a rifleman in Company I, 3rd Battalion, 141st Infantry Regiment, 36th Infantry. The 36th Division, also known as the Arrowhead Division, became a storied Army division that fought in Italy, France, and Germany. By the end of the war the men of the 36th Division had reached Austria.

After its mobilization the 36th Division participated in the Louisiana War Games and the Carolina maneuvers during 1941 and 1942. Just prior to shipping overseas, the Arrowhead Division participated in amphibious mock assaults at Martha's Vineyard. The next stop was North Africa where it trained for an additional five months before becoming the vanguard of the American assault at Salerno, Italy. There Logan participated in action that led to his recommendation for the Medal of Honor.

From there the division moved to Monte Cassino, where it participated in attacks on the Gustav Line in the winter of 1943-44. The division suffered heavy losses trying to cross the Rapido River that winter. Prior to the attack, Logan slipped in the mud and fell, breaking his elbow. He was in the hospital when his unit stormed across the river. The 36th suffered nearly two thousand causalities in that battle. The losses decimated the unit so much so that Command pulled the division out of the line for nearly two months. When It next resumed action near Anzio, Logan was back with his unit.

As the Germans pulled back, the division took Velletri, the last military obstacle prior to Rome. A few days later, he received the Medal of Honor for his action at Salerno on September 9, 1943.

MEDAL OF HONOR CITATION

For conspicuous gallantry and intrepidity at risk of life above and beyond the call of duty in action involving actual conflict on 9 September 1943 in the vicinity of Salerno, Italy. As a rifleman of an infantry company, Sgt. Logan landed with the first wave of the assault echelon on the beaches of the Gulf of Salerno, after his company had advanced 800 yards inland and taken positions along the forward bank of an irrigation canal, the enemy began a serious counterattack from positions along a rock wall which ran parallel with the canal about 200 yards further inland. Voluntarily exposing himself to the fire of a machinegun located along the rock wall, which sprayed the ground so close to him that he was splattered with dirt and rock splinters from the impact of the bullets, Sgt. Logan killed the first 3 Germans as they came through a gap in the wall. He then attacked the machinegun. As he dashed across the 200 yards of exposed terrain a withering stream of fire followed his advance. Reaching the wall, he crawled along the base, within easy reach of the enemy crouched along the opposite side, until he reached the gun. Jumping up, he shot the 2 gunners down, hurdled the wall, and seized the gun. Swinging it around, he immediately opened fire on the enemy with the remaining ammunition, raking their flight and inflicting further casualties on them as they fled. After smashing the machinegun over the rocks, Sgt. Logan captured an enemy officer and private who were attempting to sneak away. Later in the morning, Sgt. Logan went after a sniper hidden in a house about 150 yards from the company. Again the intrepid Sgt. ran a gauntlet of fire to reach his objective. Shooting the lock off the door, Sgt. Logan kicked it in and shot the sniper who had just reached the bottom of the stairs. The conspicuous gallantry and intrepidity which characterized Sgt. Logan's exploits proved a constant inspiration to all the men of his company, and aided materially in insuring the success of the beachhead at Salerno.

LOGAN RECOMMENDED FOR THE MEDAL OF HONOR AGAIN

On June 1, 1944, near Velletri, Italy, Logan risked his life repeatedly to break up a German counterattack. He killed fifteen and captured another twenty-five Germans. He was recommended for the Medal of Honor again. But protocol indicated that no person could acquire two Medals of Honor. As a result, the recommendation was downgraded to the Distinguished Service Cross, the nation's second highest award for valor. At that time he was only the second member of the Armed Forces during World II War to have received both medals.

The US Army Press Release gave this account of his actions at Velletri:

> The enemy counterattack, delivered by at least one company armed with machine guns, machine pistols, rocket launchers and rifles and supported by mortars was launched before Sergeant Logan's squad had time to seek covered positions. Not willing to risk the lives of his men by ordering them to attack under intense enemy fire, Sergeant Logan ran toward the enemy armed with hand grenades, a rifle, and a grenade launcher. He darted from one enemy position to another firing rifle grenades and throwing hand grenades until he had exhausted his supply. Then he circled back to his original position where he took a BAR from one of his men. He fired it until it jammed from heat. He picked up another BAR and with his squad loading magazines he sprayed the enemy positions until the enemy broke in disorder with Sergeant Logan running after them. With his squad following him, he pursued the retreating enemy through the vineyard until all the ammunition they possessed had been fired.

According to the Distinguished Service Cross Citation:

> Through Sergeant Logan's superb initiative, his reckless daring, his undeniable leadership. and his total disregard for his personal safety, the enemy's plan was broken... Moreover, his action was contributory to the fall of Velletri, Italy.

He was wounded by shrapnel that day, thereby becoming a recipient of the Purple Heart. He also received the Bronze Star with two clusters, the Italian Cross of Valor, and several service medals.

MEDAL OF HONOR PRESENTATION

Sergeant Logan received the Medal of Honor from Lieutenant General Alexander M. Patch at a military ceremony outside of Naples, Italy, on June 6, 1944. The Army did not want its Medal of Honor recipients to continue in combat. Subsequently, Logan was transferred to Fort Sam Houston, Texas, where he was assigned to the 4830th Service Unit. He said, "I went on a bond drive after that." Apparently not a happy experience, Logan said, "They liked to kill me with that."

LIFE AFTER WORLD WAR II

Logan was discharged from the US Army on March 6, 1945. A few months later he left the Texas National Guard and took a job with Humble Oil Company (Exxon Company) as an oilfield roustabout. His reason was basic, "I needed something to eat." He worked in that capacity at Luling and then Kilgore, Texas, where he moved in 1953. Logan retired in 1978. He lived on his pension from Exxon, his Social Security annuity, and a monthly stipend for being a Medal Of Honor recipient.

Haunted by his poverty-stricken childhood and lack of education, Logan never roamed much from Kilgore, Texas. He never returned to Italy. He said, "I can't afford it." Asked why he rarely attended the 36th Division reunions, his answer was similar. "Those hotels cost $90.00 a day and those things last for two or three days. I can't afford it."

Tragedy dogged him in later life. His first wife, Agnes, died of lung cancer in 1968. A year later his eldest son, James, died in a car accident.

He married again, but this marriage failed. Once during a nasty argument, his second wife, in a fit of rage, tossed Logan's Medal of Honor into the trash. It was gone. Obviously very unhappy, he said, "It ain't easy getting a replacement. They don't like to mail those things out. It took me more than a year." He had a bout with colon cancer but survived. His major solace was working on his ranch that he bought in 1953. After retirement, he lived alone there with his two poodles while working his small ranch of twenty-eight cattle. His main loves were his dogs and an occasional cigar.

Frequently, reporters came to interview him. He received them kindly and answered the questions in a forthright manner. Robert Buckman from the *Houston Press* asked him, "How did you dodge all those bullets?" He replied, "There weren't many bird, squirrel, or rabbit hunters among that bunch we were fighting."

Logan admitted that he had lost a lot of good friends in Italy. "I used to do a lot of dreaming of it. But it don't bother me so much anymore."

He seemed bitter about how some Medal of Honor recipients "cashed-in" on their experiences. "Some people made a lot of money from the Medal of Honor, others didn't get anything. I never got a cent," he told Robert Buckman.

Upon the fiftieth anniversary of his becoming a recipient of the Medal of Honor, he said, "It was something I did for the good of I Company. I don't even think much about it today. It's a different time---a different place."

HONORS

On May 30, 1997, the Texas Legislature honored Sergeant Logan by presenting him with the Texas Legislative Medal of Honor. He was the first recipient of this award, an award that goes to a former Texas National Guard member who also had received the Medal of Honor. After the ceremony, he was the guest of honor at the House Chamber in Austin, Texas. George W. Bush, Governor of Texas, said, "You have earned the gratitude of the nation and of the State of Texas. I honor your courage, and I thank you for your service."

In that same year, the Kilgore National Guard dedicated its new wing of the armory to Sergeant Logan.

LOGAN'S DEATH

James M. Logan, an American hero at the invasion of Salerno, Italy, died October 9, 1999, at a hospital in Longview, Texas. Cancer had accomplished what the Germans could not do. On that date, Logan entered the Pantheon of Great Texans. He was one of only thirty-one servicemen from the Lone Star State who had received the Medal of Honor during World War II. His exploits on the battlefield became legendary for they represented how an ordinary man could rise to great heights when his country called.

BURIAL SITE

Sergeant James Logan is buried at the Texas State Cemetery at Austin, Texas. He was predeceased by his wife, Agnes Pauline Logan, and a son, James. He was survived by his son, Paul, four grandchildren, and a great-granddaughter.

THOMAS E. McCALL

BIRTH DATE: May 9, 1916

BIRTH PLACE: Burrton, Kansas

DEATH: September 19, 1965

MEDAL OF HONOR ACTION: San Angelo, Italy. January 22, 1944.

RANK: Staff Sergeant

UNIT: Company F, 143rd Infantry Regiment, 36th Infantry Division

YEARS OF SERVICE: June 1938- September 19, 1965

AWARDS: Medal of Honor, Silver Star, Bronze Star, Purple Heart, Combat Infantryman Badge

CCC: SCS-2, Lafayette, Indiana. October 1936 - April 1937.

THOMAS E. McCALL

Thomas Edward McCall was born in Burrton, Kansas, on May 9, 1916. Burrton is a small town in south central Kansas, north of Wichita. Richard and Josephine McCall, both Kentuckians, were married in 1898. They had four sons and three daughters. Thomas was their sixth child. Both parents had little formal education, and Richard McCall was a general laborer with limited income.

When Thomas was a child, the family moved to Attica, Indiana. This small town in Fountain County was where Paul Dresser wrote the state song, "On the Banks of The Wabash, Far Away" in 1897. Tommy attended elementary school and completed eighth grade.

CCC EXPERIENCE

Thomas enrolled in the CCC on October 15, 1936. He was assigned to Camp Tecumseh, SCS-2, Company 1587, in Lafayette, Indiana. Camp Tecumseh was located on the west bank of the Wabash River, four miles north of Lafayette. Projects of this soil conservation camp included planting jack pine and black locust, constructing check dams, and making sod waterways.

Thomas designated his brother, Russell, as the recipient of the twenty-five dollar family allotment. Thomas was a tall, lanky, twenty-year-old at six foot one inches tall and weighed 162 pounds at the time of his enrollment. He had experience as a wood cutter and a farm hand. Furthermore, he had worked as an extra at Lafayette Motor Parts. Thomas did not adapt to the CCC camp lifestyle. His performance as a laborer was rated as unsatisfactory. He was discharged on April 15, 1937, for "refusal to work." He left Camp Tecumseh owing the camp exchange one dollar.

MILITARY EXPERIENCE

Thomas E. McCall was destined to be a military man. By 1965 he had served in the National Guard, Army, and the Air Force. It all started when Thomas joined the Indiana National Guard in the mid-1930s. In June 1938, he enlisted in the Army at Veedersburg, Indiana. He served in North Africa and Italy. He was awarded the Combat Infantryman Badge for exemplary conduct against the enemy in September 1943. Shortly afterward, he was awarded the Purple Heart. He was awarded a Silver Star for heroic action on December 15, 1943. McCall moved alone against the enemy to set up machine gun positions to support the assault on the Germans. Finding the desired position infested with the enemy, he obtained a Browning automatic rifle, charged the position, and cleared the area. He was wounded in this attack but remained with his machine gun section.

By early 1944 Thomas was a Staff Sergeant with Company F of the 143rd Infantry Regiment, 36th Infantry Division (T-Patchers), and was stationed near San Angelo, Italy. The Allies were preparing for the Battle of Monte Cassino. The battle plan involved four assaults. The southern end of the Lin Valley was protected by large hills overlooking the town of Cassino and atop the hill sat the historic Abbey of Monte Cassino. The area was further protected by the fast flowing Rapido and Gangliano Rivers. The Germans recognized the defensive value of the terrain and built the western anchor of the Gustav Line through this area. The Allies knew they had to drive back the enemy if they were to break through to Rome. On January 22, 1944, the fifth day of the first assault, Thomas McCall was in command of a machine gun section assigned to provide fire support for the advancing troops. Company F advanced to the Rapido River in darkness. Under heavy fire from enemy mortars, machine guns, and artillery, the Americans crossed an ice- covered bridge. Many casualties occurred upon reaching the west bank and reorganization was necessary. Staff Sergeant McCall organized his men into an effective unit and led them forward through the muddy terrain. After moving through barbed wire, McCall set up his two squads at a vantage position to cover the battalion's front. A shell landed near one of the positions and wounded the gunner, killed the assistant gunner, and destroyed the weapon. With enemy fire surrounding him, Thomas crawled to the wounded gunner and dragged him back to a position of cover. When the members of the second machine gun section were wounded, McCall was the only remaining member of his section. He ran firing his machine gun from his hip within thirty yards of an enemy machine gun nest. He fired two bursts into the nest killing or wounding the Germans and put their weapon out of action. McCall advanced on a second machine gun position again firing from the hip and killed all four of the crew. In the face of overwhelming enemy fire, McCall was last seen courageously moving toward a third machine gun nest placed fifty yards behind the other two nests.

Thomas McCall was listed as MIA (Missing in Action) and later his parents were notified that he was presumed dead. The Medal of Honor was presented posthumously to his father, Richard McCall. But when the war in Europe ended, it was discovered that McCall had been wounded, captured, and held as a prisoner of war for sixteen months. After he was repatriated in July 1945, Thomas spent twenty months in hospitals. While McCall survived the Battle of Monte Cassino, many did not. Of the 140 men in Company F, all three officers were wounded and only fifteen enlisted men, many wounded, made it back across the Rapido River. This battle for Rome raged from January 17 - May 18, 1944, and cost the Allies 50,000 casualties before the Germans were driven from their position.

MEDAL OF HONOR CITATION

For conspicuous gallantry and intrepidity at risk of life above and beyond the call of duty. On 22 January 1944, Company F had the mission of crossing the Rapido River near San Angelo, Italy. For the defense of these positions the enemy had prepared a network of machinegun positions covering the terrain to the front with a pattern of withering machinegun fire, and mortar and artillery positions zeroed in on the defilade areas. S/Sgt. McCall commanded a machinegun section that was to provide added fire support for the riflemen. Under cover of darkness, Company F advanced to the river crossing site and under intense enemy mortar, artillery, and machinegun fire crossed an ice-covered bridge which was continually the target for enemy fire. Many casualties occurred on reaching the west side of the river and reorganization was imperative. Exposing himself to the deadly enemy machinegun and small arms fire that swept over the flat terrain, S/Sgt. McCall, with unusual calmness, encouraged and welded his men into an effective fighting unit. He then led them forward across the muddy, exposed terrain. Skillfully he guided his men through a barbed-wire entanglement to reach a road where he personally placed the weapons of his two squads into positions of vantage, covering the battalion's front. A shell landed near one of the positions, wounding the gunner, killing the assistant gunner, and destroying the weapon. Even though enemy shells were falling dangerously near, S/Sgt. McCall crawled across the treacherous terrain and rendered first aid to the wounded man, dragging him into a position of cover with the help of another man. The gunners of the second machinegun had been wounded from the fragments of an enemy shell, leaving S/Sgt. McCall the only remaining member of his machinegun section. Displaying outstanding aggressiveness, he ran forward with the weapon on his hip, reaching a point 30 yards from the enemy, where he fired 2 bursts of fire into the nest, killing or wounding all the crew and putting the gun out of action. A second machinegun now opened fire upon him and he rushed its position, firing his weapon from the hip, killing 4 of the gun crew. A third machinegun, 50 yards in rear of the first two, was delivering a tremendous volume of fire upon our troops. S/Sgt. McCall spotted its position and valiantly went toward it in the face of overwhelming enemy fire. He was last seen courageously moving forward on the enemy position, firing his machinegun from his hip. S/Sgt. McCall's intrepidity and unhesitating willingness to sacrifice his life exemplify the highest traditions of the Armed Forces.

LIFE AFTER WORLD WAR II

Thomas McCall married Maxine Jefferies in 1946 in Lafayette, Indiana. They lived in Lafayette between his interrupted military stints in the National Guard, Army, and Air Force, covering nearly three decades. In addition to serving in both World War II and the Korean War, McCall served as a Senior Army Advisor to the District of Columbia National Guard. Furthermore, he performed National Guard military police duty at the Pentagon.

NEWSPAPER ACCOUNTS OF HIS MILITARY CAREER POST MEDAL OF HONOR:

Wisconsin Rapids Daily Tribune. August 3, 1945:

> Former POW Thomas McCall will not be discharged until the war is over. "I want to take a crack at those Japs," he said. He was thought dead so his Medal of Honor was issued posthumously to his par*ents.*

From the Forest to the Battlefield

Dixon Evening Telegram. Dixon. Illinois. August 7, 1951:

Thomas McCall attempted to reenlist in the US Army today. It will be up to the Pentagon to decide. McCall said, "I felt lost since I got out of the service last February." When asked where he wants to go he said, "I signed up for the Far East since I want to see what's *going on there.*" On August 9, the Army welcomed its hero back to the fold as a Master Sergeant. They waived his physical problem.

Charleroi Mail. Charleroi, Pennsylvania. November 8, 1951:

Master Sergeant Thomas McCall was wounded in his 3rd day of Korean War combat. He had risked his life to crawl back and rescue a wounded comrade. He was struck in the chest. He said he volunteered for Korea because "I don't feel at home unless artillery and machine gun fire is zapping around my head."

FATEFUL DAY

The Conowingo Dam in northeastern Maryland is a large hydroelectric dam in the lower Susquehanna River. Completed in 1928, the dam with its fifty-three flood gates supports a nine-thousand-acre reservoir. This reservoir with its many recreational opportunities was the site of Thomas McCall's death on Sunday, September 19, 1965. Thomas McCall and his son were enjoying a father-son fishing trip. A siren sounded warning fishermen to head for shore as a flood gate was opening. The anchor was stuck so they started swimming to shore in the unexpected rush of water. Thomas kept his son's head above the waves and the boy was rescued by onlookers in a boat. Meanwhile, Thomas went under. Rescue attempts failed. Army Master Sergeant Thomas E. McCall courageously sacrificed his own life to save his eight-year-old son. This happened just two months before McCall planned to retire after almost thirty years in the military.

HONORS

The Military Order of the Purple Heart, Thomas McCall Chapter 1922, located in West Lafayette, Indiana, is named after Thomas McCall.

BURIAL SITE

Thomas Edward McCall is buried in Springville Cemetery, Lafayette, Indiana. He was survived by his wife, Maxine, and his sons of Oxon Hill, Maryland, a suburb of Washington, DC. Thomas was also survived by three brothers and three sisters.

HOMER L. WISE

BIRTH DATE: February 27, 1917

BIRTH PLACE: Baton Rouge, Louisiana

DEATH: April 22, 1974

MEDAL OF HONOR ACTION: Magliano, Italy. June 14, 1944.

RANK: Staff Sergeant

UNIT: Company L, 142nd Infantry, 36th Infantry Division

YEARS OF SERVICE: 1941- July 21, 1945. 1947 - December 21, 1966.

AWARDS: Medal of Honor, Silver Star, Bronze Star, Purple Heart (3), Combat Infantryman Badge, Croix de Guerre, (France), Croce di Guerra, (Italy), Others

CCC: P-58, Olla, Louisiana. April 1935 - June 1936. SCS-5, Ruston, Louisiana. October 1937 - August 1938.

HOMER L. WISE

The story of Homer Lee Wise begins in the Deep South. Homer was born on February 27, 1917, in East Baton Rouge Parish, Louisiana. He was raised by his grandparents, William T. Wise and Harriet F. Wise, on a farm on Denton Road. Willie and Hattie had three children: John, Edna, and Woodrow. According to the 1930 US Census, there were four grandsons in the household: Homer and his brother, Edward, and Ramsey and Leone Shaffer. Homer loved to hunt and fish. He attended elementary school and worked on the farm. Homer left home as a young teenager and traveled to Texas where he worked at odd jobs.

CCC EXPERIENCE

At age eighteen, Homer Wise enrolled in the CCC on April 17, 1935, in Lafayette, Louisiana. He was assigned to Camp P-58, Company 1492, in Olla, Louisiana. Homer reported that he had never worked except on a farm. The twenty-five-dollar allotment was sent to his grandfather, Willie Wise. At the time of his enrollment, Homer was close to six-foot-tall and weighed 147 pounds. It was noted on his medical exam record that he had moderate flat feet. Camp P-58 was known as Camp Urania Forest. The camp was in the area owned by the Urania Lumber Company. The company began fostering forestry research in 1910 by cementing ties with the Yale University Forestry School and the United States Forest Service. Henry Hardtner, the owner of the company, is recognized as the "Father of Reforestation" in the South. Homer spent fourteen months at Camp P-58 working in the forests. His work was rated satisfactory. He was honorably discharged on June 16, 1936, "to respond to urgent proper calls for his continued presence elsewhere."

Homer reenrolled in the CCC on October 5, 1937, in Baton Rouge. He was now twenty years old and eleven pounds lighter than when he first joined the CCC. This time he was assigned to Camp SCS-5, Company 4410, in Ruston, Louisiana. Homer reported that he had previously worked in a sawmill for six months. Also, he indicated he would like to be an oil field worker in the future. For unknown reasons Homer was AWP (Away With Permission) on April 4, 1938, and again for five days from August 8 - August 12, 1938. He was AWOL for three days from May 31 - June 2, 1938. It was reported that there were "no incapacitations due to his own misconduct." Camp SCS-5 performed soil erosion work, and the Project Superintendent wrote that Homer was "very satisfactory as a workman in the field." He was honorably discharged on August 26, 1938. When Homer left SCS-5, he owed the US Government $2.24 for lost property, and an additional $7.90 was owed to Company 4410. Although not in currency, Homer Lee Wise would ultimately repay his country by risking his life under heavy fire during World War II.

From the Forest to the Battlefield

MILITARY EXPERIENCE

After his CCC days, Homer went to Texas to work. He was a parking lot attendant as well as a filling station attendant. He earned $960 in 1939. In September 1941 Homer enlisted in the Army. His first assignment was Camp Wilson near San Antonio, Texas. After basic training Homer traveled through the Deep South with the 36th Infantry Division. The division ended up at Camp Edwards on Cape Cod in August 1942. There Sergeant Wise met Madolyn DiSesa while she was on vacation. They became engaged in January 1943. From April 1943 Homer trained with the 36th Infantry Division in North Africa. He entered combat for the first time on September 9, 1943, when he was one of the first men to land at Salerno. He continued to serve in the Italian Campaign for the next year. Sergeant Wise saw heavy fighting in Italy and was soon a battle- tested soldier. To his men he was known as "Blackie." He fought in Naples and Rome and on January 7, 1944, Homer was awarded a Silver Star.

Captain Eric Anderson recalling the battles in Italy said

> I joined the 142nd Infantry when it came back from the Rapido River. We camped at the base of Mount Vesuvius which blew its top that night. We had about a foot of ashes on us the next morning. We had to move to a new area. Two days later, we had a parade, and General Clark gave Charles Kelly the Medal of Honor. The sergeant standing next to me said, "I'm going to get one of those on the next trip up." He was awarded it just north of Rome. His name was Sergeant Homer Wise.

On June 14, 1944, near Magliano, Italy, the American forces were pushing inland from a bloody beachhead. Early in the day, the platoon was pinned down by savage enemy fire, and the men were forced to dig in. It was a very hot day, and artillery fire had set the dry grasses on fire. A fellow soldier lay seriously wounded and exposed on the battlefield. Under extreme enemy fire, Homer left his position of cover and went to the front to rescue his bleeding comrade. A medic crawled to his side, and they carried the soldier one hundred yards to safety where he could receive aid.

The platoon attempted to advance again when Homer spotted a German officer and two enlisted men with automatic rifles. "I'll get them," he yelled, and ran toward the enemy, holding his fire. The three soldiers were desperately firing at him. Wise at last opened fire with his Thompson submachine gun and killed all three Germans.

Sergeant Wise returned to his men and led them forward for a short distance when they were stopped by heavy rifle and machine gun fire. Homer fell into a crowded foxhole. He knew what had to be done. Homer yelled, "Don't give me any crap about signed orders! Just gimme an M-1 and a batch of anti-tank grenades so I can get us the hell outa this mess." The captain sharing the shallow pit with Homer handed over the rifle and grenades. Once again exposed and alone, Sergeant Wise began to fire on the Germans.

107

From the Forest to the Battlefield

Those that weren't dead fled. Homer followed them firing his submachine gun from his hip and his men were able to move forward.

Heavy machine gun fire from the front and both flanks pinned them down once again. Homer picked up an automatic rifle and walked through a hail of flying bullets to knock out the Germans to the front. The platoon advanced one more time.

The American soldiers were now approaching their objective, Hill 163, but German emplacements on the slopes rained bullets down on them. An American tank fired its 75mm gun at the enemy, but deadly fire forced it to "button up" when one tread was shattered. Sergeant Wise saw a machine gun mount on the abandoned tank turret. One of his men warned him the gun was jammed. Wise boldly leaped up on the tank, unjammed the gun, and fired 750 rounds from the tank, taking out the flanking German positions. Due to Homer's amazing agility and initiative, Company L had achieved their objective and took Hill 163.

Homer Wise, squad leader of Company L, had achieved his objective, too. The tall, blue eyed, young man from Baton Rouge, Louisiana, had courageously earned his Medal of Honor.

Commanding Officer, John T. Johnson, described what he saw that day:

> The unhesitancy with which Sergeant Wise repeatedly put himself into positions where any escape seemed miraculous demonstrated a courage unfathomable. His exceeding gallantry and insuperable devotion to duty was a source of admiration to all who witnessed his intrepid acts, and the memory of it will perpetually inspire fighting men.

On June 18, only four days after his Medal of Honor action, Homer suffered a shrapnel wound to the head and was awarded a Purple Heart. Beginning in August 1944, Sergeant Wise participated in the Allied invasion of southern France. On August 16 he earned a Bronze Star and on August 22 a second Purple Heart for a bullet wound inflicted by a sniper. Wise was again shot by a sniper on September 22 and earned a third Purple Heart for his wound.

He was removed from combat in November and formally presented with the Medal of Honor by Lt. General Alexander M. Patch, commander of the Seventh Army, in Epinal, France, on November 28, 1944. General Patch turned to the five general officers in attendance and said, "Gentlemen, let's give this man a salute." He then said to Sergeant Wise, "I wish we had an Army of soldiers like you." It was also reported in the *Stars and Stripes* that Patch said, "Sergeant, I hope you will stay with us, and I'm prepared to promote you to captain." Homer responded, "General, thank you, but I'd rather be a live sergeant than a dead captain." (At that point in the war, the fatality rate for officers was very high.)

MEDAL OF HONOR CITATION

While his platoon was pinned down by enemy small-arms fire from both flanks, he left his position of comparative safety and assisted in carrying 1 of his men, who had been seriously wounded and who lay in an exposed position, to a point where he could receive medical attention. The advance of the platoon was resumed but was again stopped by enemy frontal fire. A German officer and 2 enlisted men, armed with automatic weapons, threatened the right flank. Fearlessly exposing himself, he moved to a position from which he killed all 3 with his submachine gun. Returning to his squad, he obtained an M1 rifle and several antitank grenades, then took up a position from which he delivered accurate fire on the enemy holding up the advance. As the battalion moved forward it was again stopped by enemy frontal and flanking fire. He procured an automatic rifle and, advancing ahead of his men, neutralized an enemy machine gun with his fire. When the flanking fire became more intense he ran to a nearby tank and exposing himself on the turret, restored a jammed machine gun to operating efficiency and used it so effectively that the enemy fire from an adjacent objective.

LIFE AFTER WORLD WAR II

Sergeant Wise had been wounded three times between June 1944 and September 1944; therefore, he was entitled to a trip home. Back in Stamford, his fiancée, Madolyn DiSesa, hadn't had a letter from him in three weeks. Her worry turned to excitement when she heard that Homer had been awarded the Medal of Honor. She told a *Stamford Advocate* reporter on November 29, 1944, "Now H.L. will be coming home!" (Homer preferred to be called H.L. rather than his given name of Homer). The tall, blonde Madolyn also said, "He'll probably be more nervous when we finally meet than he was during all those campaigns. He's very modest and he'd give up his uniform for civvies in a minute, but he never gripes about the Army in his letters. He just figures it's something that has to be done and he's doing his best in a big job."

On February 12, 1945, Homer Lee Wise married Madolyn DiSesa. On July 21, 1945, the twenty-eight-year-old soldier was honorably discharged from the Army. Homer worked at a local college and settled into life in his adopted hometown of Stamford.

Homer fit right into the community. He had morning coffee at Chat N' Chew across the street from the Town Hall. A frequent visitor at the local radio station, WSTC, he dropped off public service announcements encouraging young men to enlist in the Army. He joined a local service club. In a nutshell, Homer Wise was an involved, caring citizen.

From the Forest to the Battlefield

The couple made their home on Tree Lane in Springdale near downtown Stamford, where Homer kept a beautiful yard and built a bridge over a small brook in the back. He liked to play penny poker with his in-laws and fix steaks on the grill. Homer and Madolyn's son, Jeffery, was born in 1949.

He returned to military service in 1947. He was the Director of Army Recruiting in Stamford through 1959, interrupted by a two-year tour of duty in Germany from 1952-1954. From 1961 to 1963 he served at the Army Garrison at Croix Chapeau, France. He was on US Army assignment at Fort Devens, Massachusetts, from 1963 to 1965, and served in Italy from 1965 to 1966. After serving twenty-three years, he retired from the Army as First Sergeant on December 26, 1966.

Despite his attempts to remain unnoticed, H. L. was recognized as a highly-decorated Medal of Honor recipient. On May 27, 1958, he was one of six honorary pall bearers at the dedication of the Tomb of the Unknowns presided over by President Dwight D. Eisenhower. Homer was also a guest of the President at the inaugurations of Presidents Dwight Eisenhower, Richard Nixon, and Lyndon Johnson.

At a dinner of the Western Connecticut Council of the U.S. Navy League in 1957, Homer was working as a waiter. Word spread that a Medal of Honor recipient was waiting on them. The Navy officers brought Wise to the head table, bumping two Vice Admirals and a Rear Admiral from their seats!

Later, Homer was a hero once again when he noticed an intruder attempting to break into his neighbor's house. He grabbed the burglar and held him until the police arrived.

After retirement from the military, Homer continued to be a devoted husband and father. Also, Homer was a loving uncle to his niece, Jean, having carried her baby photo throughout the war. Homer worked as a mail supervisor at a bank and waited tables to earn extra money to send his son to college. On a sad note, Jeffery died at age forty in 1990.

On April 21, 1974, at age fifty-seven, Homer collapsed at his job as a mail supervisor at a Darien bank. He died in the hospital the next day. An artificial artery that had allowed him to survive a war wound had collapsed causing his death. His wife, Madolyn, remained a widow for twenty-eight years. She died in 2002.

MEMORIES OF A HUMBLE MAN

All his life Homer Wise never talked about what he saw or did during World War II. If people asked him about it, he would make a joke or find a way to side-step a reply. He would tell his family and friends, "I really would like to slip into society without too much attention." His only son, Jeffery, never knew about his Medal of Honor until a classmate told him when he was twelve years old.

From the Forest to the Battlefield

Tony Pavia interviewed Madolyn Wise for his book about Stamford's World War II veterans. She told him Homer worked as a waiter at Lou Singer's steakhouse, and customers sometimes went up to him and said, "You're the Medal of Honor winner...you're not going to wait on me." The customers would then ask the boss if Homer could join them for dinner. He was mortified by that. People would also ask him how many men he had killed and he had a hard time with that," said Pavia.

Homer's niece, Jean Rinaldi, never realized the magnitude of her uncle's military honors until after his death. "He was an ordinary person and he was my uncle. I didn't think of him like a hero," remarked Rinaldi in 2009.

MISSING MEDAL OF HONOR

The whereabouts of Homer's Medal of Honor is unknown. After her son, Jeffery, died in 1990, Madolyn Wise moved to a condominium in Stamford. Jean Rinaldi, Homer's niece, remembers the medal hanging on the wall. Rinaldi believes her aunt gave the medal to Evans Kerrigan. Evans, a former Marine, served in Korea and wrote books about military medals. He was very involved in Chapter 1932 of the Military Order of the Purple Heart. "She gave the medals to me and I gave them to Eddie Page. Eddie was going to hold them until we got a permanent meeting place for our chapter," said Kerrigan. Unfortunately, Eddie Page died and his widow, Betty, only knows the medals were not kept in their home. "I wish I did have it. That is so sad they can't find it," remarked Betty Page in 2008. Evans Kerrigan died on November 24, 2014. The location of Homer's Medal of Honor remains a mystery.

A STATUE FOR HOMER WISE

James Vlasto first met Homer Wise in 1956. They were friends until Homer's death in 1974. For over thirty years, Vlasto thought about a way to honor his friend. After he retired in 2008, Vlasto formed The Homer L. Wise Memorial Committee. The fourteen-member committee spent half a decade raising money for a statue and dedication ceremony. By 2013 the nonprofit organization had raised $82,000 and the statue, sculpted by Janice Mauro, was dedicated at Veterans Park in Stamford on May 26, 2013. "If you look at the statue, you will see it's not menacing," said Vlasto. "There's no guns. No hand grenades. No helmets. Just him as a person and a hero."

The six foot three-inch bronze statue is a tribute to the city's only Medal of Honor recipient from World War II. Inscribed at the base of the statue: "Master Sergeant Homer L. Wise, Medal of Honor, June 14, 1944, United States Army." A large crowd assembled for the dedication after the annual Memorial Day parade. Most agreed that Homer, a quiet, unassuming man, would have shunned the limelight. His entire life, Homer Wise never talked about what happened near Magliano, Italy, in 1944.

At the statue dedication in 2013, Joe Rumore, Homer's nephew, commented, "He'd be very proud of the presentation, but I'm sure he wouldn't have much to say about it because he was a private man. He didn't talk at all about his heroics."

Jim Vlasto, director of the statue project, stated, "Homer avoided the spotlight. He did not make speeches. He did not talk about his heroism. He didn't give any interviews, much to his material detriment."

HONORS

A park at the corner of Chester and Bedford Streets in Stamford, Connecticut, is named Homer Lee Wise Memorial Park.

The Homer L. Wise Memorial Highway runs along a portion of Route 137 from West Broad Street to High Bridge Road in Stamford, Connecticut.

On November 15, 2009, at the opening of the Louisiana Military Hall of Fame and Museum in Abbeville, Louisiana, Homer Wise was one of the first of four soldiers inducted into the Hall of Fame.

A memorial marker in honor of Homer L. Wise is located at the Louisiana Military Hall of Fame and Museum in Abbeville, Louisiana.

On November 17, 2009, Homer L. Wise was honored by Governor M. Jodi Rell at an induction ceremony of the Connecticut Veterans Hall of Fame in Hartford, Connecticut.

BURIAL SITE

Homer L. Wise is buried in St. John Roman Catholic Cemetery in Darien, Connecticut.

ORVILLE E. BLOCH

BIRTH DATE: February 10, 1915

BIRTH PLACE: Big Falls, Wisconsin

DEATH: May 28, 1983

MEDAL OF HONOR ACTION: Firezuola, Italy. September 22, 1944.

RANK: First Lieutenant

UNIT: Company E, 338th Infantry Regiment, 85th Infantry Division

YEARS OF SERVICE: February 1942 - 1970

AWARDS: Medal of Honor, Military Cross of Valor (Italy), Free Polish Silver Cross, Others

CCC: F-19, Harding County, South Dakota. April - September 1935. Camp D-1 Army, Fechner, South Dakota. October 1935 -September 1937.

ORVILLE E. BLOCH

Emile and Otillia Bloch came to Wisconsin from Germany in 1899. Later, they moved to Streeter, North Dakota, where Emile worked as a garage mechanic. Naturalized in 1920, they were the parents of nine children. As their family grew, Emile bought farm animals, butchered them, and sold the meat from a small meat shop that he had opened. The store provided the family's livelihood. By 1930 they bought a modest home in Streeter.

Orville, their third child, and the first boy, was born on February 10, 1915, in Big Falls, Wisconsin, prior to the family's move to North Dakota. Small in stature, a little over five feet tall, he was given the nickname "Weenie." A diligent student who always applied himself, he went through school easily, graduating in 1934.

As a sophomore, Orville and seven other local boys organized the first basketball team at Streeter High School. From the money they received from local businessmen, the boys rented a local building for the games. In addition to basketball, Orville played football and track.

In the summertime Orville traveled with his father to buy livestock, learning his father's trade in the process. Later, he applied those skills when he worked for the Swift Company in Rochester, Minnesota. The meat business was not, however, his focus. It was only a means to an end, that is, to secure a college education.

For a couple of summers, he worked for various farmers during threshing season because regular paying jobs were scarce. Orville signed on with the CCC when that agency was in the midst of an enrollment drive in early spring 1935.

CCC EXPERIENCE

Initially Orville volunteered for six months, but because of his positive work habits, the CCC accepted him for additional enrollment periods. He ultimately served for thirty months, first at Camp F-19, Camp Crook, South Dakota, and then at Camp D-1 Army, Fechner, South Dakota. At both camps he worked in the supply department as a property/tool checker. He found this job very challenging considering the enormous number of tools each camp had in its inventory. In addition to the dispensing of tools, Orville had to check them back in again in the evening. He then had to collect and have the necessary tools needed for the following day's work projects. Due to Bloch's close attention to detail, his company commander promoted him to assistant leader, a position that provided another five dollars to his monthly pay.

From the Forest to the Battlefield

Bloch's CCC record was spotless. He took courses in truck driving, handling of explosives, and first aid. His instructors graded him above average in each course. Bloch also received excellent recommendations from his superiors who recommended that Orville attend college. Bloch received an honorable discharge in July 1937.

Aided by a small loan from North Dakota Agriculture College, Bloch began his first year at college. After that time he provided his own way through school, working at various jobs from operating a machine in a meat factory to managing a Piggly Wiggly meat market.

Bloch was an academically sound student whose extracurricular interests were quite wide. He became an excellent marksman on the school's rifle team as well as joining the Reserve Officers Training Corps. As a member of the school's livestock judging team, he competed as far away as Illinois and Texas. At the same time, he wrote for the college agriculture magazine. Between academics and working at whatever job he could find to finance school expenses, Orville Bloch had little free time.

The events at Pearl Harbor on December 7, 1941, changed everything. He dropped out of college, just a few credits shy for graduation. Wanting to be an officer, Orville went directly to the Army, Navy, and the Marine Corps' recruiting offices. Their answers were the same: too short for the military. Undeterred, he traveled to Fort Snelling, Minnesota, and enlisted as a private. He must have seen some ironic humor in the whole matter as he listed his previous civilian job as that of an actor.

Bloch took his basic training at Fort Robinson, Arkansas. There according to an Army Press Release, his superiors recognized "...his physical and mental attributes and his ability to lead." As a result, they recommended him for Officer Candidate School at Fort Benning, Georgia. By October 1942 he had graduated as a Second Lieutenant, thus beginning a brilliant twenty-eight-year military career. His first assignment was Easy Company, 338th Infantry Regiment, 85th Division (Custer Division). From there he trained with his division at Camp Shelby, Mississippi.

For the next year, his division was on the move. First, it participated in maneuvers in Louisiana. Then his unit moved across the country to Camp Coxcomb, California, where the men acquired experience in desert warfare. Declared ready for combat, his unit moved to Fort Dix, New Jersey, for final preparations prior to embarkation. In early January his division arrived in North Africa, where it underwent additional training for amphibious landings. Finally, the division reached Naples, Italy, the jumping- off point for the ultimate assault on the Gustav Line, anchored by Monte Cassino. After the Allies breached the Gustav Line, Bloch's division aided in the Anzio breakout. By June 5, 1944, the Custer Division had helped liberate Rome. After a short rest, the unit advanced northward toward the Po River Valley. It was here that Lieutenant Block achieved his nickname, "The One-Man Army."

MEDAL OF HONOR CITATION

For conspicuous gallantry and intrepidity at risk of life above and beyond the call of duty. 1st Lt. Bloch undertook the task of wiping out 5 enemy machine gun nests that had held up the advance in that particular sector for 1 day. Gathering 3 volunteers from his platoon, the patrol snaked their way to a big rock, behind which a group of 3 buildings and 5 machinegun nests were located. Leaving the 3 men behind the rock, he attacked the first machinegun nest alone charging into furious automatic fire, kicking over the machine gun, and capturing the machinegun crew of 5. Pulling the pin from a grenade, he held it ready in his hand and dashed into the face of withering automatic fire toward this second enemy machinegun nest located at the corner of an adjacent building 15 yards distant. When within 20 feet of the machinegun he hurled the grenade, wounding the machine gunner, the other 2 members of the crew fleeing into a door of the house. Calling one of his volunteer group to accompany him, they advanced to the opposite end of the house, there contacting a machinegun crew of 5 running toward this house. 1st Lt Bloch and his men opened fire on the enemy crew, forcing them to abandon this machinegun and ammunition and flee into the same house. Without a moment's hesitation, 1st Lt. Bloch, unassisted, rushed through the door into a hail of small-arms fire, firing his carbine from the hip, and captured the 7 occupants, wounding 3 of them. 1st Lt. Bloch with his men then proceeded to a third house where they discovered an abandoned enemy machinegun and detected another enemy machinegun nest at the next corner of the building. The crew of 6 spotted 1st Lt. Bloch the instant he saw them. Without a moment's hesitation he dashed toward them. The enemy fired pistols wildly in his direction and vanished through a door of the house, 1st Lt. Bloch following them through the door, firing his carbine from the hip, wounding 2 of the enemy and capturing 6. Altogether 1st Lt. Bloch had single-handedly captured 19 prisoners, wounding 6 of them and eliminating a total of 5 enemy machinegun nests. His gallant and heroic actions saved his company many casualties and permitted them to continue the attack with new inspiration and vigor.

MEDAL OF HONOR PRESENTATION

General Lucian Truscott, Commander of the US Fifth Army, presented Orville Bloch with the Medal of Honor on February 6, 1945, in Italy.

MILITARY CAREER AFTER WORLD WAR II

In 1946 Orville Bloch received his discharge from the US Army. He then went to work as a contact person for the VA Hospital in Fargo, North Dakota. He found the military a greater challenge, so he reentered the service. Bloch went to the Advanced Training School at Fort Benning, Georgia, graduating that same year. For the next twenty-three years, he served his country in Japan, the Canal Zone, and Thailand. In the United States, he served at numerous posts. In 1952 Orville Bloch was appointed to the Third Army Headquarters at Fort McPherson, Georgia, as an intelligence officer. As an assistant in the intelligence phase of the operation, he helped design training for the men of the Third Army. As a major, he had completed work at the prestigious Command and General Staff School at Fort Leavenworth, Kansas. During the Kennedy administration, Bloch served as a senior advisor in combat operations.

As Bloch's responsibilities grew, so did his rank. He was on a fast track to that first star, but ill health cut him down. A severe heart attack in 1970 ended his military career. Bloch was a colonel when he retired.

Orville Bloch met his future wife, Beverly Asplund, at a reception in his honor in his hometown in 1945. Beverly was a graduate of Minot State Teachers College and taught English at Streeter High School. They married in 1945 and eventually had four children: one girl and three boys. As a career Army wife, Beverly experienced extended periods of time when her husband was overseas, but she persevered. She outlived her husband by thirty-one years, passing on at the age of ninety-two in 2014.

Upon retirement, Bloch bought an apple orchard near Chelan, Washington. As the orchard prospered, Bloch became known as a man who was kind to all. A modest man, he was well known as someone who enjoyed giving apples to economically distressed schools. Toward the end of his life, Orville drove back to his hometown in North Dakota with apples for the Streeter school. Shortly after that trip, he passed away on May 28, 1983. Colonel Bloch was survived by his wife, Beverly, their four children, and several grandchildren.

HONORS

In 1962 Bloch became the Vice President of the Congressional Medal of Honor Society.

In 1965 North Dakota State University bestowed on Orville Bloch the Outstanding Alumni Achievement Award.

Bloch also became a member of the Bison Hall of Fame from North Dakota State University.

In 1978 Orville Bloch received the North Dakota Legion of Merit.

The US Army named the Battle Projection Building in Chicago in Bloch's name.

In 1991 Bloch was installed in the Infantry Officers Hall of Fame at Fort Benning, Georgia.

The Joint Base of Lewis and McCord in the state of Washington named a street in Bloch's honor.

In 2007 the North Dakota Medal of Honor Association installed a plaque in Bloch's name at Roosevelt Park in Minot, North Dakota.

BURIAL SITE

Orville Bloch was laid to rest at the Evergreen-Washelli Memorial Park in Seattle, Washington. Six recipients of the Medal of Honor attended his funeral.

GEORGE D. KEATHLEY

BIRTH DATE: November 10, 1907

BIRTH PLACE: Olney, Texas

DEATH: September 14, 1944. KIA.

MEDAL OF HONOR ACTION: Mount Altuzzo, Italy. September 14, 1944.

RANK: Staff Sergeant

UNIT: Company B, 338th Infantry Regiment, 85th Infantry Division

YEARS OF SERVICE: May 15, 1942 - September 14, 1944

AWARDS: Medal of Honor, Bronze Star, Purple Heart, Combat Infantryman Badge

CCC: Superintendent, SCS-16, Lamesa, Texas. September 1939 - May 1942.

GEORGE D. KEATHLEY

William Keathley, a newcomer to the Lone Star State, had moved to Texas from Tennessee. He became a teacher in a one-room school. There he met his future wife, Bertha Mary Leberman, who was his student. Later, his wife inherited a 640-acre farm where they raised their family. As with most Texas farmers, William Keathley raised wheat, corn, cotton, and cattle.

George D. Keathley was born in Olney, Texas, on November 10, 1907. He went to high school in Olney, Texas, but did not complete his education there. He moved to Lawton, Oklahoma, where his older brother had a small business. Young George worked there while completing high school. An above average student, he found that math and science were to his liking. After high school he enrolled at Cameron State School of Agriculture and Junior College. Here he ultimately received an Associate degree in Agriculture. Working as a tool dresser and later as a plumber, George saved enough money to enroll at Texas A&M. After two years, he left school as his finances were depleted. Not giving up his goal, he doggedly pursued his degree, attending summer sessions in 1936, 1939, and 1940. Keathley, however, never acquired his degree.

Whether Keathley ever received his Texas A & M diploma was a moot point. His major goal in life was to improve conditions in agriculture. According to family members, "He had a long-held desire to do something about soil erosion and to improve farming methods." For almost four years, he worked with the Soil Conservation Service and then with the CCC. At both jobs, he taught and implemented "scientific farming" to Texas farmers.

THE PLIGHT OF AGRICULTURE IN TEXAS-POST 1918

Two generations of intense farming had greatly weakened the prairie grass that covered and protected the soil. When the Great War occurred, demand for the staple crops increased dramatically as well as the price for those crops. Therefore, farmers broke more ground for farming, which placed even greater stress on the land. The four-year span from 1914 to 1918 was a halcyon time for farmers. When the war ended, however, commodity prices went from boom to bust overnight. To stay even, the farmers simply broke more ground to raise more products. But prices continued to plummet.

Exacerbated by a decade of drought, the once rich Texas soil had disappeared into the multitude of dust storms that ravished the state. In 1934 a mammoth dust storm carried soil from Texas over a thousand miles into New England. In fact, that storm spread a coat of dust covering the Hyde Park estate of President Franklin D. Roosevelt. Corn, wheat, and cotton crops withered in the fields. The scenario was likened to that of Biblical pestilential proportions.

By this time most farmers were in a complete state of panic, feeling that their soil was depleted and would never produce again. All that time, they failed to realize that thousands of tons of soil were disappearing by erosion caused chiefly through two generations of poor farming practices.

THE NEW DEAL'S RESPONSE

By the middle 1930s, President Franklin D. Roosevelt's New Deal had established the Soil Conservation Service to aid agricultural recovery. At the same time, the CCC moved thousands of men into the heartland of America to deal with what many thought of as a hopeless situation.

The Soil Conservation Service preached scientific farming. It was neither mystical nor academic. It was more like an application of common sense farming born out of research done at agricultural schools such as Cameron College and Texas A&M. The SCS thrust Keathley into this environmental crisis. Possessing four years of college in agriculture, he and his colleagues had to convince reluctant farmers to change their basic attitude toward farming, a truly daunting task.

These men became the shock troops for the application of the basic concepts of scientific farming. They had to persuade skeptical farmers to rotate crops, to practice contour farming, to use plant nutrients, and when necessary, to allow land to lay fallow. When those farms showed improvement, he and his colleagues used them as teaching tools to influence others. Slowly, the agency gained the trust of the local people. When the drought finally showed signs of weakening by the early 1940s, six thousand Texas farms had been converted to contour farming.

SUPERVISOR OF A CCC CAMP

From 1935-1939, Keathley had advanced in the SCS from a forty- cent an hour trainee to a Junior Agronomist earning $1800.00 annually. After serving in the SCS Keathley moved to Lamesa, Texas, an outpost in West Central Texas, where he became Superintendent of SCS-16, a CCC camp, in September 1939. As Camp Superintendent, he oversaw the entire soil conservation effort in his immediate area and remained in this position until May 15, 1942, six weeks before the CCC was terminated.

Financially, the move to Lamesa was upwardly mobile as his pay increased by nearly $1000.00. This was especially fortuitous. He met and married Inez Edmonson while stationed at Lamesa. Inez brought into the marriage two young daughters whom George adopted. Overnight, George had an instant family.

MILITARY EXPERIENCE

When the CCC ended in at the end of June 1942, Keathley joined the United States Army and took his basic training at Camp Shelby, Mississippi. The next six months saw him on maneuvers in Louisiana and South Carolina with additional training in California. In January 1944 his unit, the 85th Infantry Division, went to North Africa for advanced training. Six months later, his outfit landed at Naples. His combat experience was about to begin.

The transfer from private life to the military was not difficult. At Texas A&M, a military school where he was in ROTC, George had already acquired a thorough military background. As a result, he rose quickly through the ranks, and by the time he had reached Italy, Keathley wore sergeant's stripes.

His unit was part of the offensive that broke the Gustav Line. Rome, however, had become General Clark's goal. As a result, Keathley's regiment joined forces with the Allied troops from the breakout at Anzio and raced toward Rome. Fighting every day en route, he replaced a wounded platoon leader and reorganized their platoon that had suffered significant casualties. For this action he received the Bronze Star.

By this time Keathley had been in combat nearly three months. He expressed his concerns to his brother in a letter: War is rough... It is not what it is cracked up to be. I personally don't care for the medals or the glory. I want to come home.

 By August the Germans had pulled back to the Gothic Line, the last major defense line designed by Field Marshal Kesselring. Extending nearly 120 miles from the Ligurian Sea, near Pisa, eastward toward Florence, it continued on a southeastern slant toward the Adriatic Sea, south of Rimiai. The Northern Apennines, a formidable mountain chain, anchored this heavily fortified line.

Consequently, the Fifth Army Command ordered the 338th Infantry Regiment to take the three-thousand-foot mountain, Mount Altuzzo. Company B, Keathley's unit was at the forefront of the attack that commenced September 13, 1944. After five days of vicious hand-to- hand combat, the Germans lost the mountain, and the Fifth Army had access to the North Central Apennines. But on the second day of battle, Keathley died when he led the remnants of his two platoons to a victory over a numerically superior German force of two companies.

Staff Sergeant Charles J. Dozier of Ellenville, Iowa, led his squad of the First Platoon into position to defend the right flank of Keathley's undermanned two platoons. Dozier said

> The enemy attacked from the front and both flanks, throwing "potato mashers" and were covered by intense automatic and small arms fire. They broke through on the right flank and we were fighting hand-to-hand with a desperate fanatical enemy...Sergeant Keathley was doing a wonderful job with the second and third platoons. I could hear him shouting orders and encouragement as he dashed from one position to another. I saw one of the hand grenades burst at his side. Yet he never stopped fighting. The fighting lasted another fifteen minutes. During that time Keathley jammed clip after clip into his rifle while shouting orders to his men. The Germans finally withdrew leaving their dead and wounded behind...When the enemy retreated Keathley fell to the ground. I rushed to his side and helped him to a sheltered spot on the hillside. He told me to write to his wife and tell her that I did everything for her and my

country. I had to turn away for I had witnessed the death of the bravest and most heroic man I had ever known.

After the battle, nearly two hundred Germans lay dead or wounded. Those who fought with Keathley that day agreed that he was the primary reason why they prevailed. Captain Maurice E. Peabody, B Company Commander, spoke in quiet reverence of Keathley's actions, "Only God will ever know what gave him the power to carry on those last fifteen minutes."

MEDAL OF HONOR CITATION

For conspicuous gallantry and intrepidity at risk of life above and beyond the call of duty, in action on the western ridge of Mount Altuzzo, Italy. After bitter fighting his company had advanced to within 50 yards of the objective, where it was held up due to intense enemy sniper, automatic, small arms, and mortar fire. The enemy launched 3 desperate counterattacks in an effort to regain their former positions, but all 3 were repulsed with heavy casualties on both sides. All officers and noncommissioned officers of the 2d and 3d platoons of Company B had become casualties, and S/Sgt. Keathley, guide of the 1st platoon, moved up and assumed command of both the 2d and 3d platoons, reduced to 20 men. The remnants of the 2 platoons were dangerously low on ammunition, so S/Sgt. Keathley, under deadly small arms and mortar fire, crawled from 1 casualty to another, collecting their ammunition and administering first aid. He then visited each man of his 2 platoons, issuing the precious ammunition he had collected from the dead and wounded, and giving them words of encouragement. The enemy now delivered their fourth counterattack, which was approximately 2 companies in strength. In a furious charge they attacked from the front and both flanks, throwing hand grenades, firing automatic weapons, and assisted by a terrific mortar barrage. So strong was the enemy counterattack that the company was given up for lost. The remnants of the 2d and 3d platoons of Company B were now looking to S/Sgt. Keathley for leadership. He shouted his orders precisely and with determination and the men responded with all that was in them. Time after time the enemy tried to drive a wedge into S/Sgt. Keathley's position and each time they were driven back, suffering huge casualties. Suddenly an enemy hand grenade hit and exploded near S/Sgt. Keathley, inflicting a mortal wound in his left side. However, hurling defiance at the enemy, he rose to his feet. Taking his left hand away from his wound and using it to steady his rifle, he fired and killed an attacking enemy soldier, and continued shouting orders to his men. His heroic and intrepid action so inspired his men that they fought with incomparable determination and viciousness. For 15 minutes S/Sgt. Keathley continued leading his men and effectively firing his rifle. He could have sought a sheltered spot and perhaps saved his life, but instead he elected to set an example for his men and make every possible effort to hold his position. Finally, friendly artillery fire helped to force the enemy to withdraw, leaving behind many of their number either dead or seriously wounded. S/Sgt. Keathley died a few moments later. Had it not been for his indomitable courage and incomparable heroism, the remnants of 3 rifle platoons of Company B might well have been annihilated by the overwhelming enemy attacking force. His actions were in keeping with the highest traditions of the military service.

MEDAL OF HONOR PRESENTATION

At Camp Walters, Texas, on April 11, 1945, Major General Bruce Magruder presented George D. Keathley's Medal of Honor posthumously to his wife, Inez Keathley.

HONORS

The United States Navy named a troop transport Sgt. George D. Keathley. It was used for troop transport and had spaces for troop hospital facilities.

Cameron University renamed its Department of Military Science the George D. Keathley Department of Military Science.

Texas A&M renamed a dormitory George D. Keathley Hall.

In February 1993 a bronze plaque commemorating George D. Keathley was placed at the Corps of Cadets Center at Texas A&M.

Keathley's Medal of Honor is on display at the Corps of Cadets Center at Texas A&M.

All incoming Texas A&M freshmen must memorize the names of the Medal of Honor recipients from World War II who had matriculated at Texas A&M.

BURIAL SITE

Keathley is buried at the American Cemetery at Florence, Italy.

HAROLD A. GARMAN

BIRTH DATE: February 26, 1918

BIRTH PLACE: Fairfield, Illinois

DEATH: August 13, 1992

MEDAL OF HONOR ACTION: Montereau, France. August 25, 1944.

RANK: Private, Medic/Litter Bearer

UNIT: Company B, 5th Medical Battalion, 5th Infantry Division

YEARS OF SERVICE: 1942 - 1946

AWARDS: Medal of Honor

CCC: D-3, Eldred, Illinois. October 1936 - March 1937. SP-25, Skokie Valley, Glenview, Illinois. April - July 1938.

HAROLD A. GARMAN

Harold's father, Alva Garman, and his mother, Phinia Lewis Garman, both from Illinois, had six children: four boys and two girls. Harold, their second child, was born on February 26, 1918. Census records from 1920 to 1940 reveal that Alva Garman was a self -employed farmer near Albion. It was in these formative years that Harold learned to love working on a farm.

It was a far simpler time but difficult economically for everyone in southern Illinois. That part of the state had severe erosion problems brought on by its proximity to the Illinois River. The river was a curse due to frequent flooding, but it was a blessing because of the rich bottom lands.

Harold quit school after he finished grade school. He was a healthy young man who was only five foot four inches tall and weighed 130 pounds. Harold worked with his Dad on the family farm. In 1936 he joined the CCC to help with the family's finances and designated his father to receive his allotment.

CCC EXPERIENCE

Garman served two different hitches in the CCC. From October 1936 to March 1937, he served at Camp D-3 near Eldred, Illinois. This camp was situated thirty miles north of the confluence of the Illinois and Mississippi Rivers. The priority of the camp dealt with erosion of the once fertile land in the immediate area. Since Eldred is located between huge limestone cliffs and farm areas, limestone quarries were utilized to make lime that could then be spread on the adjoining farmland to help revitalize the eroded land. Garman worked with teams that spread lime on farm land in the entire Eldred area. Because the task was not unlike working on a farm, he was satisfied with his work. At the end of Harold's first enlistment, he received an honorable discharge.

His second enlistment with the CCC was much less successful. He served at Camp SP-25 in Glenview, Illinois. The Skokie Valley CCC complex was a mega CCC camp consisting of ten separate camps all labeled SP or State Park camps. Harold, who loved the rural environment, could not acclimate himself to the urban surroundings at Camp Skokie Valley. The fact that he had a car certainly did not ingratiate himself with the CCC hierarchy for ownership of a car was forbidden for enrollees. Garman was brought before the company commander. At the hearing, Harold freely admitted ownership. The company commander then dismissed him from the CCC for administrative reasons.

MIILTARY EXPERIENCE

Garman returned home where he resumed working on the farm. A few months later, he joined the Army becoming a member of Company B, 5th Medical Battalion, 5th Infantry Division. His unit remained stateside until late 1943 and then shipped out to England as part of the plans for the invasion of France.

From the Forest to the Battlefield

His Military Occupational Specialty (MOS) was that of a litter bearer. He did not carry a weapon. His only forms of protection were the two Red Cross insignias he wore on each side of his helmet and the two Red Cross armbands on his fatigue jacket. It was not glamorous duty. As a matter of fact, a litter bearer's job often is very dirty and dangerous. His job was simple: to retrieve the wounded and take them to an aid station as quickly as possible, all the while through the din of combat.

Private Garman belonged to a litter-bearer platoon that consisted of an officer, a sergeant, a corporal, forty litter bearers, and five to seven ancillary personnel. Usually a medical platoon was attached to an infantry battalion. Their work began at an aid station, a short distance behind the front lines. It was not unusual for the litter bearers to be killed within eyesight of the aid station, especially if the front became fluid.

The rapid and efficient deployment of litter bearers was a crucial part of the medical chain stretching from the wounded lying on the killing field to the field hospital, perhaps ten miles away. Efficient movement of the wounded to an aid station increased survival rates dramatically.

The litter bearing scenarios were endless. In the desert, for example, the lack of cover and the relentless blinding wind made litter bearing an almost impossible task. The mountains of Italy were daunting. There litter bearers struggled mightily to transport the wounded down the steep paths that even goats found difficult to traverse. Litter bearers endured the perils of snakes, swamps, and vegetation in the jungles of the Pacific. At the Normandy invasion, these men lost most of their equipment but still saved lives often by holding the heads of their wounded comrades above water. At Bastogne, litter bearers not only carried the wounded through heavy enemy fire, but they had to cope with ten-foot snow drifts in subzero weather. One American ranking officer who survived the Battle of the Bulge said, "Litter- bearers should be enrolled among the unsung heroes of this war."

On June 6, 1944, the Fifth Division participated in the invasion of Normandy. Its target was Utah Beach. From there it fought daily, participating in the St. Lo breakout from Normandy into the interior of France. By August 25 the unit had crossed the Seine River. Casualties were ferried across the river to the southern bank near Montereau, France. When the Germans opened with deadly machine gun fire from across the river, Garman leaped into the river and swam out to help the wounded who were in danger of imminent death.

General Patton had witnessed Garman's action on the Seine River and decided to present him with the Medal of Honor immediately. Apparently, the general admired the plucky little hero, for they became friends. According to Garman, the two men "took a few days off from the war " for a fishing trip briefly after this action.

From the Forest to the Battlefield

MEDAL OF HONOR CITATION

For conspicuous gallantry and intrepidity at the risk of his life above and beyond the call of duty. On 25 August 1944, near Montereau, France, the enemy was sharply contesting any enlargement of the bridgehead which our forces had established on the northern bank of the Seine River in this sector. Casualties were being evacuated to the southern shore in assault boats paddled by litter bearers from a medical battalion. Pvt. Garman, also a litter bearer in this battalion, was working on the friendly shore carrying the wounded from the boats to waiting ambulances. As 1 boatload of wounded reached midstream, a German machinegun suddenly opened fire upon it from a commanding position on the northern bank 100 yards away. All the men in the boat immediately took to the water except 1 man who was so badly wounded he could not rise from his litter. Two other patients who were unable to swim because of their wounds clung to the sides of the boat. Seeing the extreme danger of these patients, Pvt. Garman without a moment's hesitation plunged into the Seine. Swimming directly into a hail of machinegun bullets, he rapidly reached the assault boat and then towed the boat with great effort to the southern shore. This soldier's moving heroism not only saved the lives of the three patients but so inspired his comrades that additional assault boats were immediately procured and the evacuation of the wounded resumed. Pvt. Garman's great courage and his heroic devotion to the highest tenets of the Medical Corps may be written with great pride in the annals of the corps.

THE MILITARY ROUTINE

As with most men who survived Medal of Honor action yet had not formally received the formal citation, Garman continued on the front line. He was wounded near Metz on March 8, 1945, when a shell exploded near him, giving him a severe concussion.

He was hospitalized in England. While recuperating, Garman received a direct call from General Patton, ordering him to fly to Paris. From Paris he traveled in General Patton's staff car to Division Headquarters at Lich, Germany. There he received the Medal of Honor.

When he got out of the car at Headquarters, Garman was greeted by colonels shaking his hands and slapping him on his back. He said, "This was something that had never happened to me before." Garman was overwhelmed by how fast everything was moving; for just hours earlier, he had been hospitalized. Additionally, he was anxious because he knew that becoming a Medal of Honor recipient meant that his combat days were over. Garman was elated. He was going home!

MEDAL OF HONOR PRESENTATION

Private Harold A. Garman received the Medal of Honor from General George Patton on March 29, 1945. Afterward, Patton asked, "Why did you do it?" Garman replied, "Well, someone had to do it."

Then Patton dropped a bomb. He said to Garman, "Soldier, we need men like you to stay in the Division-you're going to stay here."

"This lowered my morale about 100 percent," said Garman. True to Patton's words, Garman remained with the division until Germany surrendered six weeks later.

LIFE AFTER WORLD WAR II

Garman left the Army in 1945.On April 5, 1946, Chicago staged the largest parade in its history. President Harry Truman and General Dwight D. Eisenhower were present to celebrate the "GI Joe" who had slugged it out to victory. Sitting beside the two leaders was the red-headed young man from Albion: Harold A. Garman, their honored guest.

Harold Garman and Mary Louise Jones had married at Battle Creek, Michigan, in March 1942. They had two children, Steve and Sherry. Harold took a job with the Calvert Oil Company in Albion, Illinois. From that job he became a licensed inspector for the state of Illinois.

In the late 1940s, Garman had become friends with Audie Murphy, the famed Medal of Honor recipient, who had become a movie star in the 1950s. Murphy, who suffered from "battle fatigue," a condition presently known as post-traumatic stress disorder, spoke out about his problems and those of his wartime comrades. He did much to raise the public's level of awareness regarding the physical and mental health problems that plagued many World War II veterans.

Murphy had scheduled a business appointment for May 28, 1971, at Martinsville, Virginia. Garman was supposed to have been a passenger on that flight but could not make it. During a stormy flight, Murphy's plane crashed into Brush Mountain, twenty-five miles from Roanoke, Virginia, killing all aboard. Garman had escaped death again.

 According to his son, Steve, his father's pride and joy was his 225-acre farm near Albion. Harold died at his beloved farm on August 13, 1992. Mrs. Garman passed away in 2013 at the age of ninety-two. She left behind two children, four grandchildren, and one great-granddaughter.

Steve Garman remembers his dad as a "straight-arrow." He did not smoke or drink and was incorruptible. This latter trait certainly kept him in good stead while in public service in Illinois. Steve particularly remembered his dad's ability to tell remarkable stories.

HONORS

The US Army Medical Department Museum at Fort Sam Houston, San Antonio, Texas, has a museum dedicated to men of the Army Medical Corps. Within that complex there is a Medal of Honor Walk dedicated to the fifty men from the Medical Corps who became recipients of that award. The Walk has monument stations where each of these medics is honored. One is dedicated to Garman.

Private Garman is enshrined in the Pentagon's Hall of Heroes.

Harold Garman's story appeared in one segment of the historical series, *The World at War.*

BURIAL SITE

Harold Garman's remains rest at the Samara Baptist Church Cemetery in Albion, Edwards County, Illinois.

ALFRED L. WILSON

BIRTH DATE: September 18, 1919

BIRTH PLACE: Fairchance, Pennsylvania

DEATH: November 8, 1944. KIA.

MEDAL OF HONOR ACTION: Bezange la Petite, France. November 8, 1944.

RANK: Technician Fifth Grade

UNIT: Medical Detachment, 328th Infantry Regiment, 26th Infantry Division

YEARS OF SERVICE: March 1943 - November 8, 1944

AWARDS: Medal of Honor, Purple Heart

CCC: S-99. Somerset, Pennsylvania. April - September 1939.

From the Forest to the Battlefield

ALFRED L. WILSON

Author's Note:

Credit for the Alfred Wilson story is gratefully given to Carolyn McKinney, Alfred's niece. Her biography, THE GENTLE GIANT of the 20th DIVISION, is not only a tribute to her Uncle Alfred, but a major contribution to World War II history. Without McKinney's meticulous research, the account of Wilson's battlefield experience in France would be lost in the annuals of time.

George Wilson, Alfred's grandfather, was a miner who stood well over six feet tall and was as lean as a beanpole. He and his wife, Anna, had ten children. Jesse, Alfred's father, was their fourth child. When Jessie came of age, he went into the mines too. On December 24, 1912, he married Matilda "Tilly" Mitchell. Jesse was twenty-three and Tilly was twenty. From this union came eleven children. Alfred was their fourth born.

When Alfred was thirteen, his mother died after giving birth to her eleventh child. Sadly, the newborn infant also died. However, Tilly bequeathed a passion for love and goodness to Alfred; consequently, she remained his moral beacon.

Alfred's older brother, Harold, already married, started taking his family and Alfred to the Church of the Brethren. Alfred especially enjoyed Sunday school. On January 31, 1931, he was baptized into the church. As Alfred matured, the church became his moral foundation.

Alfred was impatient to do what he could for the family. Even though he tried his best in school, his heart wasn't in it. Alfred quit school after the ninth grade. It was the Depression and jobs were hard to find. At seventeen he worked for the WPA. The next year Alfred enrolled in the CCC.

CCC EXPERIENCE

Alfred signed up for six months. Alfred's father, Jesse, received his CCC allotment. The boy's duty station was S-99, Camp Kooser, near Somerset, Pennsylvania, which was forty miles east of his home. He was happiest whenever he made it home for the weekend. Consequently, Alfred hitched many rides from Somerset County to his home in Fairchance, a distance of one hundred miles round trip.

The CCC was good for Alfred. He grew in stature and matured as a man. Compared to the average CCC man, Alfred was a giant at six foot three inches in height and 197 pounds in weight. He worked hard and learned to get along with the other men. Alfred particularly liked the discipline of the camp life. In September 1939, after having served six months, he received an honorable discharge with no blemishes on his record. A job awaited him in the mines.

From the Forest to the Battlefield

HOME FROM THE CCC

Alfred was a man of simple tastes. Punjab, a nickname he had acquired from a character in *Little Orphan Annie,* would drop in at the Dairy Bar, a local coffee shop, to meet with his friends. He'd nurse a five-cent bottle of Coke and catch up on his friends' news. During tranquil times at home, he listened to music or hymns on the radio. His favorite hymn was "Onward Christian Soldiers," and his favorite book was the Bible. He never drank, smoked, or cursed, but he loved life.

After Pearl Harbor, Alfred continued working in the mine. He watched his buddies go off to war. At that time mining was an essential industry, making him ineligible for the draft. This reality caused him much mental turmoil. "You know," he told his sister Myrtle, "It don't feel right, me being here at home yet and working, while George Wilson and some of the other boys are either signing up or getting drafted. Just don't feel right." On the other hand, he was adamantly opposed to killing a human being.

MILITARY EXPERIENCE

In early 1943 Alfred was drafted. His letters home and his friends' recollections of him chronicle the "Gentle Giant's" odyssey which began at Fort Jackson and ended in a field at Bezange La Petite, France.

In one of his first letters home, he talked about his new life. "Boy! Is there a lot of card playing and playing of dice? There's a game going on right now. But I haven't played a game. They sell beer here, too." However, to assure his sister that he had not fallen prey to those vices, he said, "I went to church today and liked it."

His friend Paul recalled one of their after-hours pleasures. "We played football a lot. When I saw Alfred coming toward me it was wise to duck...or he would grab you and give you a big bear hug."

Alfred's faith never wavered. In a letter to his sister, he said, "Myrtle, I have gone to church every Sunday and am reading three chapters from the Bible every night."

Alfred remained a pacifist and was comfortable in his role of a medic. Although a few medics carried a concealed weapon, one of his friends said, "Alfred never did carry a weapon. He would not compromise his own ethics or a rule."

Alfred did not drink, but he told Myrtle how the boys had spiked his Red Pop. "I didn't know that they went and put whiskey in there. It sure made me cough, and I almost choked on the stuff. I wanted to laugh at the fellows, but figured I'd better be serious or they would do it again."

Bob Walls, his friend, said, "The boys always took him along whenever they went on a pass.... They called him Pappy because he was like a mother hen, always watching his chicks...One night the barrack door swung open and here comes Alfred with a soldier slung over his shoulder...He always got them back on time."

In another letter to his sister, Alfred said, "The biggest part of Army life is first aid classes, a lot of bandaging, and studying... It's worthwhile work and I like it better than the times with the rifle company."

One day Alfred went into town with a friend who bought flowers for his mother on Mother's Day. Alfred was saddened and wrote, "It nearly broke my heart because I sure wish I could have done the same, but I know that someday I will see her again On High."

On Mother's Day of 1943, Alfred got up early and dressed in his best uniform. A buddy asked, "What are you bucking for Pappy? There's no inspection today." Alfred replied, "I don't know about you fellows, but I'm going to church. It's Mother's Day." Later in the morning, his friend said, "The chapel was filled to capacity and I think it was worthy to note that Alfred's barracks was conspicuously devoid of soldiers."

On his voyage overseas in September 1944, Alfred had many long conversations with Frank Novichi, a sergeant in his unit. According to Novichi, Alfred expressed this premonition, "I have this feeling that I am going to be killed. I won't be coming back."

By October 1944 Alfred had seen a lot of death, but he still remembered the simple treasures that reminded him of home. In his last letter to his sister, he asked her to send him a few food items: stuffed olives, candy bars, pineapple juice, a fruit cake, and sweet pickles.

Alfred Wilson was severely wounded by a German artillery barrage. Despite numerous orders to go to the aid station, he remained on the field, tending to his wounded comrades. He worked feverously the rest of the day and into the evening before collapsing. When his friends finally got him to the aid station, it was too late. He died on November 8, 1944, at Bezange La Petit.

MEDAL OF HONOR CITATION

He volunteered to assist as an aid man in a company other than his own, which was suffering casualties from constant artillery fire. He administered to the wounded and returned to his own company when a shell burst injured a number of its men. While treating his comrades he was seriously wounded, but refused to be evacuated by litter bearers sent to relieve him. In spite of great pain and loss of blood, he continued to administer first aid until he was too weak to stand. Crawling from 1 patient to another, he continued his work until excessive loss of blood prevented him from moving. He then verbally directed unskilled enlisted men in continuing the first aid for the wounded. Still refusing assistance himself, he remained to instruct others in dressing the wounds of his comrades until he was unable to speak above a whisper and finally lapsed into unconsciousness. The effects of his injury later caused his death. By steadfastly remaining at the scene without regard for his own safety, Cpl. Wilson through distinguished devotion to duty and personal sacrifice helped to save the lives of at least 10 wounded men.

REACTION TO WILSON'S DEATH

When Alfred died, the whole 26th Division took it hard. Everyone knew about the Big Stoop or Pappy. He was the Gentle Giant. The medics took it hard. There just wasn't anyone like Alfred who symbolized something bigger and finer to his buddies. He had attained what they all wanted- respect, friendship, and a reputation for being the kind of guy everyone wanted to know. He did it just by being himself. As Captain Ed Kuligowski said, "We loved that boy."

Back in his hometown of Fairchance, the telegram arrived at his father's home in late morning on November 22, 1944. The kids came home from school and gathered in the big kitchen. They were all there when Jesse came from work. When he came through the door and saw the children together, no one had to hand him the telegram. With the anguished voice of a devoted father, he threw his arms into the air and screamed out, "Oh no! No, no! Not Alfred!"

A few days later, on a cold and dreary day, a group of infantrymen, with heads bowed, gathered in front of a flag-draped coffin beside a mound of earth at Limey, France. A Protestant chaplain committed to the ground one of their beloved comrades. When the service was over, they stoically climbed aboard their jeeps and headed in the direction of the ongoing war.

MEDAL OF HONOR PRESENTATION

On June 26, 1945, Brigadier General T. N. Cantron presented the Medal of Honor posthumously to Alfred's father, Jesse Wilson. Alfred's sisters and Melvin, a brother, also attended the proceedings. After Alfred's father accepted the medal, he made a poignant statement that has forever lingered in the memory of the Wilson family. He sadly commented, "I accept the honor, but the price was too high."

CAROLYN MCKINNEY'S QUEST

In the fall of 1990, Carolyn McKinney, Alfred's niece, traveled to France to learn more about his death. Armed with a map provided by Bob Marshall, she searched for the battlefield where her uncle had died. It was a quest; something that had to be done. Marshall had marked the spot in red where his friend died and the route the men took as they carried Alfred from the hill to the aid station.

Carolyn located the battlefield where Charlie Company, Wilson's outfit, had fought four decades previously. It was now a bucolic pasture with a small farmhouse nearby. In that pasture Alfred's niece envisioned the battle in her mind. Her search was over. She was at peace.

HONORS

All Medal of Honor recipients are remembered at the Medal of Honor Hall at the Pentagon in Washington, DC. Also, they are honored at Arlington National Cemetery on the second floor of the Amphitheater in front of the Tomb of the Unknown Soldier.

At Fort Riley, Kansas, and at Fort Belvoir, Virginia, barracks have been named in Wilson's honor. A firing range at Fort Benning, Georgia, bears Wilson's name.

Fort Sam Houston in San Antonio, Texas, has a Combat Medical Museum named Abel Hall. Located just inside the main foyer of the building is a small medical memorial. Lining a wall are the pictures and citations of every Medical Department Medal of Honor recipient. Alfred's citation is there too.

Alfred is remembered in Landstuhl, Germany. A school that was once used as Hitler's school for boys now bears the name of Wilson Barracks. It houses the medical personnel for Landstuhl Hospital. A large gray marble stone rests in front of the building and bears the words: Wilson Barracks, named in honor of T/5 Alfred L. Wilson, Medical Specialist 328th Infantry, 26th Division, Killed in Action 8 November 1944 near Bezange La Petite, France

BURIAL SITE

Alfred Wilson's remains were originally buried in a cemetery in France. Later his remains were reinterred at the Maple Grove Cemetery at Fairchance, Pennsylvania.

LLOYD G. McCARTER

BIRTH DATE: February 26, 1918

BIRTH PLACE: St. Maries, Idaho

DEATH: February 2, 1956

MEDAL OF HONOR ACTION: Corregidor, Philippine Islands. February 16, 1945.

RANK: Private/Paratrooper

UNIT: 503rd Parachute Infantry

YEARS OF SERVICE: October 17, 1942 - 1945

AWARDS: Medal of Honor, Purple Heart

CCC: F-44, Clarkia, Idaho. April - September 1940.

LLOYD G. McCARTER

Jerry McCarter (1875-1928) was a Canadian who came to the Idaho Panhandle before St. Maries and Benewah County were incorporated. By the turn of the century, he had become a bartender at a local saloon that catered to miners and lumberjacks. His future wife, Elizabeth Montandon (1880-1934), emigrated from Switzerland to the United States. She was fluent in German and French, valuable gifts in that emerging community. Jerry and Elizabeth were married on September 26, 1906. From this union came four children: William, Alice, and twins Lillie and Lloyd. Jerry worked in a sawmill and then as a contractor, eventually becoming the water commissioner at St. Maries. He suffered from deteriorating health problems. Some people maintained his health issues were caused by the Big Burn of 1910 that devastated much of the Idaho Panhandle. As his health declined, so did the fortunes of his family. He died in 1928, leaving his family destitute. The 1930 US Census reported Elizabeth as the head of the household. The twins were only twelve, but son William worked as a truck driver. Eighteen-year-old Alice was a telephone operator. Both provided some income for the family.

CCC EXPERIENCE

McCarter joined the CCC in April 1940. He was in the Corps six months, the standard enlisted requirement. Lloyd designated his mother as his allottee. His duty station was F-44 at Clarkia, Idaho, thirty-five miles southeast of St. Maries. During those six months, Lloyd worked on blister rust patrol, stoop labor at its worst that required crawling on his hands and knees eight hours a day. He had to pull out and then burn gooseberry and currant bushes; host plants to a fungus that threatened to destroy the western white pine tree, a valuable commodity in Idaho's economy. McCarter's work was always judged as satisfactory. He took a first aid course during his tour of duty and was honorably discharged in September 1940.

McCarter's early records show some discrepancies and contradictions. His CCC records indicated his birth date as May 11, 1915, and that he had quit school in tenth grade. It appears as if McCarter "fudged" his age to qualify for the CCC. His Army record, however, lists his birth date as February 26, 1918. That record indicated that he graduated from high school and had one year of college. All sources agree that he worked as a lumberjack prior to entering the service. Interestingly, McCarter was not listed in the 1940 US Census.

According to McCarter's sister-in-law, Mrs. Ida McCarter, Lloyd won a football scholarship to Gonzaga University in Spokane, Washington, and attended there for two semesters. She also said his nickname was "Muck." A young friend of his who stuttered could not say "Mac," hence that appellation stuck.

He enlisted in the Army on October 17, 1942, at Fort Lewis, Washington. He was five feet six inches tall and weighed 179 pounds. He listed his civilian occupation as a foreman in manufacturing.

BRAVEST WARRIOR I EVER KNEW

Lieutenant William Calhoun, McCarter's Company Commander, wrote an article, "The Bravest Warrior I Even Knew" for the 503rd Parachute Regiment. This account, along with an Army Press Release documenting McCarter's exploits are excellent firsthand accounts.

Calhoun's outfit was stationed at Oro Bay, New Guinea, when McCarter transferred into the unit. Calhoun was impressed with McCarter, who had taken a rate reduction from an artillery sergeant to an infantryman private just to get into the 503rd, a parachute outfit. After completing jump school, McCarter joined Lieutenant Calhoun's Company F of the 503rd. Impressed with McCarter's athletic build, Calhoun described him as "A heavily built man with powerful forearms that allowed him to fire a Thompson submachine gun from the hip with the gun on its side." Even though McCarter had not trained as an infantryman, Calhoun soon field tested the newcomer by sending him through a demanding jungle scout course. Lieutenant General Walter Krueger, Commander of the Seventh Army, ran an inspection that day. Everyone from the regiment down to the battalion and the company levels scrutinized this neophyte's work. At the end of the day, all agreed that they had found a talented, natural scout.

Calhoun claimed, "McCarter was so good that if it (the enemy) was there, he could find it. If he could not see it nor hear it, he could smell it." As a result he gained the trust of the company quickly. Calhoun continued to extol his virtues:

> McCarter loved a fire fight. He literally danced on the coral outcroppings somewhat like a ballet dancer...For example on July 19, 1944, we followed a trail through a forest of tall trees. A Japanese voice challenged us. I was behind Neville Powell and saw the entire action. McCarter answered in a guttural unintelligible voice and began to advance at his skipping, bouncing run. The puzzled Jap challenged again. Firing broke out but the enemy's hesitation was fatal. McCarter and Powell had killed the four Japs manning that position. McCarter was gleeful.

Calhoun made McCarter a scout after that incident.

As the 503rd began to stage for the invasion of Corregidor, McCarter went AWOL. Garrison life was not to his liking. Always looking for a scrap, he had gone to the mainland of New Guinea to fight more Japs. When discovered, he was tossed into the stockade. Eventually, Calhoun discovered where his prodigal son was and personally intervened with the authorities by vouching for McCarter who, according to Calhoun, was contrite and apologetic. Lieutenant Calhoun's pleas prevailed, and together they returned to the 503rd, ready to take on the Japanese.

CORREGIDOR

Corregidor, a small island of fewer than ten square miles and shaped like a tadpole, controlled access to Manila Bay and to the port of Manila. In his campaign to retake the Philippine Islands, General MacArthur

From the Forest to the Battlefield

deemed Corregidor's recapture as a military and a psychological necessity. On February 16, 1945, a coordinated parachute drop in tandem with an amphibious assault attacked. The 503rd Regimental Combat Team, comprised of over two thousand paratroopers, including Private Lloyd McCarter, made its jump onto Corregidor.

It was a difficult operation. Initially, the number of Japanese defenders was underestimated, and the enemy had prepared well. The island was honeycombed with tunnels, revetments, concrete bunkers, and fortifications. In addition, fallen trees and an encroaching jungle made movement very difficult. Yet on other parts of this tiny island, the American bombardment had eliminated all vegetation. One American officer said the ten-day battle was "Like being in an insane asylum."

Calhoun's trust in McCarter was redeemed quickly. On the second day of the invasion, two men from Company F became trapped inside an enemy concrete coastal battery. They had been cut off completely, and one man had already been killed in a rescue effort. McCarter and Sergeant John Phillips volunteered to save their friends. While the Japanese machine gunners dueled with American riflemen, the two men slipped from their position and moved to the rear of the enemy. First, they hurled hand grenades. Then they fired their submachine guns until exhausting their ammunition. Finding dead GI's weapons, the two men continued firing until running out of ammunition again. At that point, they stood up and threw rocks and verbal invectives at the Japanese emplacements. This caused enough diversion that the two trapped soldiers could slip out of the blockhouse and return safely. Lieutenant Calhoun called the two men's actions "outstanding."

The next day, February 18, 1945, Calhoun's unit occupied a strategic hill. By evening, McCarter had killed six enemy snipers even though he had never trained as a sniper. From dusk to dawn the following morning, McCarter was tested mightily when the enemy attempted to retake the hill. Here Private McCarter earned his sobriquet as the "One Man Army." The hill had been bombed heavily by the Americans prior to the invasion. As a result the entire area was devoid of trees, making the entrenched infantrymen exceedingly vulnerable. At dusk, the Japanese poured in heavy mortar and machine gun fire. When it became dark, the enemy attack began. It was relentless. They came from everywhere and swarmed the hill, attacking in waves.

TESTIMONY FROM THOSE WHO WERE THERE

Lieutenant Calhoun, Company Commander of F Company, was most effusive of McCarter's defense of that barren hill:

> When the enemy approached up the road he moved to an open position so that he could better cover the approach. In this position, he became a target for enemy machine guns, rifles, and hand grenades. Time and time again the enemy assaulted that position only to be turned back...By two A.M. all the men about him had been wounded; but shouting encouragement to his comrades

and defiance at the enemy, he continued to bear the brunt of the attack, fearlessly exposing himself to enemy soldiers to locate Japanese soldiers, and then pouring open fire upon them...He repeatedly crawled back to the American line to secure more ammunition. When his submachine gun would no longer operate, he grabbed an automatic rifle and continued the attack and continued to inflict many casualties. This weapon in turn became too hot; and discarding it, he continued with an M-1 rifle. At dawn the enemy attacked with renewed intensity. Completely exposing himself to hostile fire, he stood erect to locate the most dangerous enemy positions. He was wounded at about 7:30 in the morning when he was hit in the back and his shoulder...Around the road he defended we found 131 dead Nips, more than thirty around his position plus three enemy light machine guns, one .50 caliber machine gun, and about ten Molotov cocktails...We discovered his position was near a partially blocked enemy tunnel entrance. The tunnel was full of gasoline, potato masher hand grenades, shape charges, and TNT. Had the Japs taken his position, they could have blown up the whole hill. Certainly, I would not be here now.

First Lieutenant Daniel Lee said, "I am of the opinion that McCarter's acts of heroism prevented our position from being overrun and were far beyond the call of duty. His actions saved the lives of many of our troops."

Lieutenant John Mara, a battalion officer, testified, "His action was the most outstanding I have observed and in every way was well above and beyond the call of duty, done at extreme danger to his life."

Sergeant Chris Johnson, McCarter's squad leader, said, "I believe that if Private McCarter had not stayed in that dangerous position we would have more men killed and probably lost the hill. McCarter has always been a quick-thinking, bold and hard-working soldier."

Private John Bartlett opined, "McCarter's position in the squad is first scout and everyone who has seen him believes him to be the best in the entire Army."

Then McCarter's luck ran out. A piece of metal ripped through his chest about dawn of that morning. As he lay wounded, he identified the source of the enemy fire. Calhoun said, "We directed mortar fire as directed and we eliminated the enemy position."

It took six hours to evacuate McCarter to a battalion aid station. He had lost a lot of blood and the attending medic was out of plasma. When Calhoun first saw him, he was afraid that McCarter would lapse into shock and die. McCarter reassured his lieutenant that he would be okay. This prompted Calhoun to say, "He was tough. Complaint was not part of his vocabulary."

Calhoun wrote a narrative of the battle and recommended McCarter for the Medal of Honor. When Calhoun presented the recommendation to the Battalion Executive Officer, Lieutenant Colonel John Britten, he threatened to reduce the recommendation to a Distinguished Service Cross. Calhoun was ordered by Britten to leave the site immediately or else he would reduce the award to a Silver Cross!

From the Forest to the Battlefield

Much later Calhoun found out that the Regimental Commander, Colonel Jones, had said, "No man in my outfit with a record such as McCarter's is going to get the Congressional Medal of Honor."

Fortunately, a review board intervened. Upon its request, Calhoun sent the board "Two eyewitness affidavits, a hand-drawn sketch, and a weather and light description." Two months later, McCarter's company was notified that McCarter had been awarded the Medal of Honor.

MEDAL OF HONOR CITATION

He was a scout with the regiment which seized the fortress of Corregidor, Philippine Islands. Shortly after the initial parachute assault on 16 February 1945, he crossed 30 yards of open ground under intense enemy fire, and at pointblank range silenced a machinegun with hand grenades. On the afternoon of 18 February he killed 6 snipers. That evening, when a large force attempted to bypass his company, he voluntarily moved to an exposed area and opened fire. The enemy attacked his position repeatedly throughout the night and was each time repulsed. By 2 o'clock in the morning, all the men about him had been wounded; but shouting encouragement to his comrades and defiance at the enemy, he continued to bear the brunt of the attack, fearlessly exposing himself to locate enemy soldiers and then pouring heavy fire on them. He repeatedly crawled back to the American line to secure more ammunition. When his submachine gun would no longer operate, he seized an automatic rifle and continued to inflict heavy casualties. This weapon, in turn, became too hot to use and, discarding it, he continued with an M-1 rifle. At dawn the enemy attacked with renewed intensity. Completely exposing himself to hostile fire, he stood erect to locate the most dangerous enemy positions. He was seriously wounded; but, though he had already killed more than 30 of the enemy, he refused to evacuate until he had pointed out immediate objectives for attack. Through his sustained and outstanding heroism in the face of grave and obvious danger, Pvt. McCarter made outstanding contributions to the success of his company and to the recapture of Corregidor.

MEDAL OF HONOR PRESENTATION

Private Lloyd McCarter received the Medal of Honor from President Harry Truman in the East Room of the White House on August 23, 1945. He was one of twenty-four men honored that day. Skip Robinson, a close friend from St. Maries, Idaho, attended this historic occasion.

LIFE AFTER WORLD WAR II

Sadness and tragedy stalked McCarter after his return to civilian life. He suffered greatly from a bullet wound in his chest inflicted on his last day in combat. The bullet had lodged near his heart so the doctors would not remove it for fear of deadly consequences. As a result, pain became a constant factor in his life. According to multiple sources, he had difficulty adjusting to civilian life which was manifested chiefly as problems with alcoholism. But he went to work as a contact representative for the Veterans Administration, first in Sandpoint, Idaho, and then later in Boise. He remained close only with his twin sister, Lillie.

On February 18, 1948, he married Mable Dunnigan who provided a stability in his life that he had not enjoyed since his mother's death. Mable's nickname was Suzy. She was an attractive lady, slightly older than Lloyd. Unable to have children, they turned to adoption services. They were refused because of Lloyd's physical condition. Later, Suzy developed cancer. Her death was tragic: she shot herself. McCarter was devastated and never recovered emotionally. He killed himself at his home on February 2, 1956.

HONORS

American Legion Post 25 at St. Maries, Idaho, is named in McCarter's honor.

On October 19, 2013, a dedication ceremony was held at Benewah County Memorial Park, St. Maries, Idaho, for all those who served in the military. The county's three Medal of Honor recipients, Vernon Baker, Gregory Boyington, and Lloyd McCarter were cited. This memorial park was built from $60,000 in donations from the local people.

The United States Postal Service included Lloyd McCarter's name along with the other World War II recipients of the Medal of Honor on its Prestige Folio in June 2013.

A planted area at 893 North Government Way in Coeur D'Alene, Idaho, is dedicated to Pvt. Lloyd McCarter.

The BPOE (Elks) of Boise, Idaho, honored McCarter in the January 2013 *The Temple Chimes* by reprinting his Medal of Honor citation.

On July 25, 2015, 121 miles of Idaho State Highway 3 were dedicated to the thirteen Medal of Honor recipients from Idaho.

US Senator James McClure of Idaho dedicated a seven-foot obelisk at the Medal of Honor Grove in Valley Forge, Pennsylvania. McCarter's name was on the obelisk along with Idaho's other Medal of Honor recipients.

THOSE WHO REMEMBERED HIM

Lillie Glover, his twin sister, ordered his grave marker. Her thoughts of him were

> He always said he was no hero...The rest of the men were just as much a part of everything as he was...He never wore the Medal of Honor except the day President Truman hung it around his neck...He just didn't feel comfortable being a hero...He always said that he was just doing a

job...He told President Truman he was not a hero but was acting out of self-preservation.

Skip Robinson described him as "the kind of fellow who would never hurt anyone...We were so proud of him, and at heart he remained a St. Maries' boy."

Stanley "Sticks" Resor who had known McCarter as he was growing up, said, "He kept saying to Truman that he wasn't a god damn hero...He was just trying to save his own life...That's the kind of guy he was."

William McCarter, Lloyd's older brother and a veteran of World War II, remembered him as "An ordinary guy. A regular St. Maries' lumberjack."

BENEWAH COUNTY, IDAHO

Benewah County is in the Idaho Panhandle 150 miles south of the Canadian border. During the 1940s, St. Maries had about two thousand people; the entire county had less than 6,500 people. Presently the county has nine thousand inhabitants. Amazingly so, this tiny area was the home at one time or another to three Medal of Honor recipients.

Gregory "Pappy" Boyington was one of the country's greatest flying aces and spent much of his younger years in St. Maries. Vernon Baker came to Benewah County in 1986 after the death of his wife. There he lived in a cabin where he pursued his passion: hunting. While there the Army upgraded Baker's Distinguished Service Cross to the Medal of Honor in 1997. He died of cancer at his home in St. Maries in 2010. The third recipient was Lloyd McCarter whose parents were early settlers of St. Maries.

BURIAL SITE

Lloyd G. McCarter is buried at Woodlawn Cemetery, St. Maries, Idaho.

LUCIAN ADAMS

BIRTH DATE: October 22, 1922

BIRTH PLACE: Port Arthur, Texas

DEATH: March 31, 2003

MEDAL OF HONOR ACTION: Mortagne Forest near Saint-Die, France. October 28, 1944.

RANK: Staff Sergeant

UNIT: 3rd Battalion, 30th Infantry Regiment, 3rd Infantry Division

YEARS OF SERVICE: February 1943 - 1945

AWARDS: Medal of Honor, Bronze Star, Purple Heart, Others

CCC: MA-1, Beaumont, Texas. April 1940- June 1941. MA-3, Austin, Texas. July - October 1941. P-91, Humble, Texas. November 1941 - January 1942. MA-3, Austin, Texas. January - March 1942.

LUCIAN ADAMS

When Lucian Adams Sr. died, he left his wife Rosa, a native of Mexico, penniless with four children. The two older boys disappeared, leaving his twelve-year-old son, Lucian, as the titular man of the house along with his younger brother Joe. Later, Rosa remarried. Eight more children came from that union. Even though the children wore sackcloth, the family somehow survived. Rosa, who took in laundry to make ends meet, listed herself as the head of the household in the 1940 census.

Lucian was a bright young lad. One of his favorite subjects was arithmetic. As a youngster, he somehow persevered, making it through elementary and junior high school before dropping out in ninth grade to take a job delivering the local newspaper, the *Beaumont Enterprise*. At the same time, he also worked as a custodian at a local bakery before entering the CCC.

CCC EXPERIENCE

In April 1940 Lucian enrolled in the CCC, beginning a two-year odyssey that certainly had to have been a financial blessing for his mother as well as for her large family. Adams spent fourteen months at camp MA-1 located near Beaumont, Texas. He became an office orderly. It was a good job and certainly one that was not physical. It appears that the officers tipped him well for his CCC checking account reached nearly $100.00 before he transferred to camp MA-3 at Austin for four months. Next, Adams moved to P-91 at Humble, Texas, staying there for three months. His job at P-91 was listed as manual labor, that is, he pounded rocks for road building. He returned to Camp MA-3 for the final three months of his enlistment. During his tour of duty in the CCC, Lucian availed himself of the educational activities. He enrolled in some academic subjects including arithmetic, civics, history, and English. His ratings were always satisfactory. He was honorably discharged in March 1942.

Upon his return from the CCC, Adams immediately took a job in a ship building company. He built landing ships, the same kind that would carry him into battle at Anzio in Italy and then later to the invasion of Southern France.

When the Japanese launched their attack on Pearl Harbor on December 7, 1941, the Hispanic communities in the United States rallied around their country. According to Dr. Ricardo Romo, a Texas educator, "These folks, most of whom were first generation Americans, were patriotic people who loved their country. They responded to their country's needs from the barrios and the fields." Eventually, over 500,000 Hispanics entered the armed services, coming mostly from California, Arizona, New Mexico, Colorado, and Texas.

Historically, the Hispanics encountered less racial bias in the military than their black counterparts. Caucasians and Hispanics fought side-by-side, whereas the blacks were placed in segregated units.

Specifically, this discrimination was more obvious when one examines the awarding of the Medal of Honor. Thirteen Hispanics were awarded the Medal of Honor in World War II, while no black man received that coveted medal until decades later. One such Hispanic soldier who became a Medal of Honor recipient was Sergeant Lucian Adams who possessed an anglicized surname. He was proud of his origins and hailed from the tough streets of Port Arthur, Texas.

MILITARY EXPERIENCE

In February 1943 Adams joined the US Army. He took his basic training at Camp Butner, North Carolina, where he was assigned to the 3rd Infantry Division. Within a short time, he shipped out, en route to the Italian campaign at Anzio, Italy. Lucian remained at Anzio, enduring four months of continuous combat. There he destroyed an enemy machine gun nest, conduct that earned him a Bronze Star as well as a Purple Heart. When the Anzio breakout occurred in late May 1944, his unit fought its way to Rome before being pulled out to prepare for the amphibious assault on France via the Mediterranean Sea.

That invasion was quite successful, liberating much of southern France within the next four weeks. After capturing the massive port of Marseille, the 3rd Division continued northward up the Rhone Valley to the Vosages Mountains, where German resistance dramatically stiffened.

In late October, Sergeant Adams's company, a unit of the 30th Infantry Regiment, 3rd Infantry Division, had been ordered to reopen the supply lines that had been cut off by the troops of a crack German 201st Mountain Infantry Battalion.

According to an Army Press Release:

> The company had moved only a short distance when terrific fire from the enemy killed three men and wounded six more. Going like a whirlwind, Sergeant Adams, firing a borrowed Browning BAR from the hip, charged ahead, dodging behind trees, undeterred by intense machine gun fire from the enemy and rifle grenades. Approaching within ten yards of the nearest German machine gun position, he killed the enemy gunner with a grenade. When an enemy soldier ten yards away hurled a grenade at him, the sergeant quickly killed the enemy with a burst of his BAR fire. Resuming his charge, Sergeant Adams approached within fifteen yards of another machine gun, killed the gunner with a grenade and forced the two supporting infantrymen to surrender. Despite a concentrated fire from the remainder of the Germans, the Texas Doughboy continued his lone, gallant advance, locating and killing five more Germans. When, from a range of twenty yards, a third German machine gun opened on him, he killed the gunner with his BAR. Two remaining enemy troops fled in panic, and Sergeant Adams' comrades drove forward clearing the line of supply.

The Army Press Release quoted Lieutenant Frank Herrell who witnessed Adams's heroics:

> The opening fire killed our CO and our Executive Officer as well as three other men. The enemy

was dug in and had established a defense in depth. They were all specialists and carried automatic weapons, machine pistols, or grenade launchers. It was really rough. One Kraut had climbed into a knocked-out reconnaissance car and was operating his machine gun against us. Three others were raking my platoon front and our attack was momentarily halted. That's when Adams picked up a BAR and set off in a one-man wave of destruction. Firing his BAR from the hip, he dashed from tree to tree until he got within ten yards of the nearest machine gun emplacement. The Germans saw him coming and concentrated their fire upon him but he came through without a scratch. Standing there and with the machine gun firing straight at him, he calmly pulled the pin of the grenade, and as calmly, lobbed it into the machine gun position. Just as the grenade killed the gunner of the first machine gun, the Kraut who had been manning the machine gun in the reconnaissance car climbed out and threw several hand grenades at Sergeant Adams. He was only ten yards away and Sergeant Adams had moved outside the traversing arc of the machine gun. While these grenades were exploding about him Sergeant Adams killed the German with a burst from his BAR. All the enemy seemed to be firing at him now. Bullets clipped off branches of the evergreen trees inches within his body. Rifle grenades were exploding all about him. He refused to take cover. A second machine gun was firing at him ten to fifteen yards to his right. Sergeant Adams headed for this, threw a hand grenade and killed the gunner. As soon as this emplacement was put out of order two Krauts serving the gun came out of their foxholes alongside and surrendered. Into the thickest of fire directed at him, Sergeant Adams advanced with his BAR, spraying fire. He killed five more Germans in their protected positions. After fifty yards he came upon a third machine gun which was about twenty yards to his left and was firing right at him. With one long burst, he put the emplacement out of action. With the destruction of this third emplacement, the enemy took off in a complete rout. He drove us through completely clearing the line of supply.

Private First Class John Wood of Norwalk, Iowa, was another eyewitness. "I tried to get in a shot but before we could see the Krauts, he had killed them and moved on. It was a matter of seconds when he started in against those Kraut emplacements with his automatic weapon and left them behind, dead in their holes."

Staff Sergeant Russell Dunham, a future Medal of Honor recipient, immediately followed the swath cut by Adams. Dunham commented

Those Krauts were very rugged and had new equipment and an automatic weapon for each man. Sergeant Adams moved like a tornado and when he hit the first emplacement, the whole pit seemed to go up into the sky. The Kraut in the reconnaissance car kept the fire on him until he couldn't move his gun anymore. Then he let loose with potato mashers. It looked like the end. Sergeant Adams put a burst from his BAR through him. There were fire and explosives all around him as he went through the woods like a wild man. At the second machine gun nest, he stood as it fired twenty yards from him and for a second there was a violent duel between those two rapid fire weapons-the Kraut machine gun and the BAR in Adams' hands. All his bullets seemed to strike the German gunner. When those Krauts took off, they were in a panic.

From the Forest to the Battlefield

Years later, Adams had time for reflection. He told the *Dallas Morning News* in 1993: "I had seen all my buddies go down and calling for medics and I didn't want to go down with ammunition still on me. I kept firing and was lucky that I got them before they got me." Later, he told a *Los Angeles Times* reporter, "In combat, I had no fear. None, until the event was over and I began to realize how serious and dangerous it was."

Adams remained in combat six more months through the Siegfried Line, across the Rhine River, and then east into the heart of Germany. Fifteen days before V-E Day General Alexander Patch presented the Medal of Honor to five infantrymen, one of whom was Sergeant Lucian Adams. Another infantryman recipient was Sergeant Russell Dunham who had witnessed and benefited from Adams' one man attack. Coincidentally, Dunham, too, was a former CCC enrollee.

MEDAL OF HONOR CITATION

For conspicuous gallantry and intrepidity at risk of life above and beyond the call of duty on 28 October 1944, near St. Die, France. When his company was stopped in its effort to drive through the Mortagne Forest to reopen the supply line to the isolated third battalion, S/Sgt. Adams braved the concentrated fire of machineguns in a lone assault on a force of German troops. Although his company had progressed less than 10 yards and had lost 3 killed and 6 wounded, S/Sgt. Adams charged forward dodging from tree to tree firing a borrowed BAR from the hip. Despite intense machinegun fire which the enemy directed at him and rifle grenades which struck the trees over his head showering him with broken twigs and branches, S/Sgt. Adams made his way to within 10 yards of the closest machinegun and killed the gunner with a hand grenade. An enemy soldier threw hand grenades at him from a position only 10 yards distant; however, S/Sgt. Adams dispatched him with a single burst of BAR fire. Charging into the vortex of the enemy fire, he killed another machine gunner at 15 yards range with a hand grenade and forced the surrender of 2 supporting infantrymen. Although the remainder of the German group concentrated the full force of its automatic weapons fire in a desperate effort to knock him out, he proceeded through the woods to find and exterminate 5 more of the enemy. Finally, when the third German machinegun opened up on him at a range of 20 yards, S/Sgt. Adams killed the gunner with BAR fire. In the course of the action, he personally killed 9 Germans, eliminated 3 enemy machineguns, vanquished a specialized force which was armed with automatic weapons and grenade launchers, cleared the woods of hostile elements, and reopened the severed supply lines to the assault companies of his battalion.

MEDAL OF HONOR PRESENTATION

On April 22, 1945, the Medal of Honor presentations were made in a huge stadium in Nuremburg, Germany, a site where Hitler had spoken frequently. Overlooking the stadium was a huge German swastika that had been covered by an American flag. In an interview Sergeant Adams chuckled when he described the engineers blowing up the swastika immediately after the ceremonies.

From the Forest to the Battlefield

LIFE AFTER WORLD WAR II

In 1946 Lucian Adams took a job with the Veterans Administration as a counselor for veterans in San Antonio. He remained in that position for forty years until retirement in 1987. He said, "I never brought up the fact that I'd been in combat myself and had been awarded the Medal of Honor because I'm no hero. I'm just an ex-soldier."

Adams also was a veteran's consultant to United States Congressman Frank Tejeda from Texas.

HONORS

The Port Author, Texas, YMCA is named in Adams's honor.

The Lucian Adams Chapter of the American GI Forum is in Houston, Texas.

The Sergeant Lucian Adams Elementary School is part of the Port Arthur school system.

In 2002 the History Channel featured Adams in a television documentary, *Hispanics and the Medal of Honor.*

The Lucian Adams Freeway is part of Interstate Highway 37 in San Antonio, Texas.

On October 16, 2013, The Lutcher Theater of Orange, Texas, honored Sergeant Adams and First Lieutenant Douglas Fournet, a Medal of Honor recipient from the Viet Nam war, at a performance of *Beyond Glory*, a one-man show telling the stories of eight Medal of Honor recipients.

Aurora Park has been renamed Lucian Adams Field.

Museum of the Gulf Coast near Port Arthur, Texas, contains a bust of Lucian Adams.

A section of 61st Street in Port Arthur has been renamed in his honor.

DEATH OF LUCIAN ADAMS

Toward the end of his life, Adams was plagued with diabetes and a heart condition. He died on March 31, 2003, at age eighty-one. He was survived by three children, three brothers, three sisters, and two grandchildren.

Lucian's close friend, Jose Mendoza Lopez, also a recipient of the Medal of Honor, eulogized Adams as "A great, great man who did a terrific job."

His niece, Brenda Culver, wrote this about her famous uncle:

> Uncle Lucian will always be a hero to my family, the nation, and to the world. He was a wonderful example for his brothers, sisters, children, and all who knew him. A patriot and advocate for veterans for more than forty years, he carried the love of his family in his heart and in his day-to-day interactions. His legacy is one of courage, strength, and humility. Despite all his awards and commendations, he never lost sight of the soldiers who lost their lives during the War. He called them, "true heroes."

BURIAL SITE

Lucian Adams's remains were buried with full military honors at Fort Sam Houston Military Center in San Antonio, Texas.

STANLEY BENDER

BIRTH DATE: October 31, 1909

BIRTHPLACE: Carlisle, West Virginia

DEATH: June 22, 1994

MEDAL OF HONOR ACTION: La Londe, France. August 17, 1944.

RANK: Staff Sergeant

UNIT: Company E, 7th Infantry Regiment, 3rd Infantry Division

YEARS OF SERVICE: December 1939 - August 1945

AWARDS: Medal of Honor, Bronze Star, Purple Heart, 7 Battle Stars, Croix de Guerre (France)

CCC: SP-12, Cook County, Illinois. July 1934 - September 1935.

STANLEY BENDER

Stanley Bender's Russian father's last name was Bendorus. Ellis Island people anglicized it to Andrew Bender (1864-1923). He and his future wife Eva Sinkiewicz (1866-1945) arrived in New York in 1885. They married in 1894 and settled in southwestern Pennsylvania. He was a coal miner and she a housewife. The first four children, Johnny (1895), Toney (1900), Georgie (1902), and Maggie (1904) were born in a coal patch town near the Pennsylvania/West Virginia border. The remaining two children, Eva (1907) and Stanley (1910), were born in Carlisle, Fayette County, West Virginia. Andrew and Eva became citizens in 1916 just before Andrew became disabled because of a mine accident.

Stanley was a skinny young man who weighed about 140 pounds. He dropped out of school after seventh grade. Unlike his three brothers who remained in the mines, he moved to Chicago where he lived with his sister, Maggie, who had married Walter Cudziszewski. Unable to find work, he joined the Civilian Conservation Corps.

Bender served fourteen months at SP-12 in Cook County, Illinois, not too far from his sister's home. He worked at the usual CCC jobs such as tree planting and road building. His officers rated him as satisfactory even though he went AWOL three times. Apparently, the proximity to his sister's house was a mitigating factor. He was never docked for these absences, and he received an honorable discharge in September 1935.

He returned to live with his sister and eventually found work in a department store. Stanley drove a truck but doubled as a company chauffeur. Later, he joined the Illinois National Guard. He had worked thirty-five weeks in 1939, earning $750.00.

MILITARY EXPERIENCE

In December 1939 Bender joined the US Army and received his training near Clark, Washington, where he was assigned to Company E, 7th Infantry Regiment. This modest start marked the beginning of an illustrious service career.

He first saw combat in Tunisia from October 1943 to May 1944 against the vaunted Africa Corps. From there his unit, the 3rd Infantry Division, participated in the assault on Sicily (June - July 1943). Two months later he was on the mainland of Italy where he saw additional combat near Cassino and Anzio. After the breakout at Anzio in late May 1944, he participated in the liberation of Rome. At one point in the Italian campaign, Bender's battalion had fought for fifty-nine straight days without relief. Finally, his division was pulled out of the Italian mainland to prepare for the invasion of southern France via the Mediterranean Sea.

From the Forest to the Battlefield

Operation Dragoon was a massive operation involving 175,000 men, nearly one thousand airplanes, over 10,000 vehicles, and hundreds of ships. The target was the plush Cote d'Azure area in the southeastern corner of France, stretching from Cannes to twenty-five miles southeast of Saint-Tropez. The Allies made seven major assault landings in this zone. Bender's outfit hit the beach near Saint-Tropez. Within twenty-four hours the Allies had established a beachhead fifty miles wide and twenty miles deep and had repelled a major German counterattack. The race for the Rhone Valley had begun.

By this time the Germans conceded that the invasion could not be stopped. Therefore, their objective was to pull out the major part of their army before complete encirclement occurred. While the German main body of troops moved quickly toward the Rhone Valley, smaller battalion-sized units fought delaying actions.

The French terrain favored the German strategy. The inland town of La Londe was located on the Maravenne River and had three key bridges that led northwest to the Rhone Valley. The Germans established fortified road blocks to hold back the rapidly advancing troops.

Sergeant Bender's Easy Company hit the German roadblock first. They were stopped and driven back by intensive machine gun and anti-tank fire. Bender, however, jumped atop a demolished tank and stood a full two minutes while bullets whined and ricocheted, kicking up the dust about him. According to one witness, "This crazy man cupped his hand to head as if in a poor salute to shield his eyes so that he could see better." Finally, he jumped down after he had identified the enemy emplacements one hundred yards away.

First Lieutenant Joseph Franklin said, "Frankly, the reason I failed to take cover was because of Sergeant Bender's audacious conduct. I stood there, with my mouth wide open, wondering why he hadn't been killed."

The Army Press Release continued the narrative.

> Jumping off the tank, he (Bender) picked up a Thompson submachine gun...and ordering two squads to cover his advance, he led the squad along an irrigation ditch. When the Germans hurled hand grenades at him, he waited for his men to catch up, then as unperturbed as a soldier on a pass, he stalked toward the left flank of the enemy.

Lieutenant Franklin continued

> It was easy to see that he had the enemy in a sweat...The enemy turned one of the machine guns around and began to fire at Sergeant Bender. He moved within five yards and killed the gunner. Two Germans at the second machine gun turned their weapon upon the stalking sergeant who was boring in on them. He picked his way through enemy foxholes ignoring the bursting hand grenades about him...He stood on the edge of their emplacement with a blazing Tommy-gun

killing both.... He strode another thirty-five yards and killed another enemy rifleman. He methodically wiped out eight more riflemen.

At this point, according to Franklin, "The company went kill-happy and ran from their positions screaming and yelling like banshees. They were honestly inspired and ran into town and overpowered the enemy."

Bender's regimental commander said, "He easily performed an officer's task in locating the enemy and then worked out a tactical solution...Single-handedly, he performed at least a squad mission."

MEDAL OF HONOR CITATION

For conspicuous gallantry and intrepidity at risk of life above and beyond the call of duty. On 17 August 1944, near La Londe, France, he climbed on top of a knocked-out tank, in the face of withering machinegun fire which had halted the advance of his company, in an effort to locate the source of this fire. Although bullets ricocheted off the turret at his feet, he nevertheless remained standing upright in full view of the enemy for over 2 minutes. Locating the enemy machineguns on a knoll 200 yards away, he ordered 2 squads to cover him and led his men down an irrigation ditch, running a gauntlet of intense machinegun fire, which completely blanketed 50 yards of his advance and wounded 4 of his men. While the Germans hurled hand grenades at the ditch, he stood his ground until his squad caught up with him, then advanced alone, in a wide flanking approach, to the rear of the knoll. He walked deliberately a distance of 40 yards, without cover, in full view of the Germans and under a hail of both enemy and friendly fire, to the first machinegun and knocked it out with a single short burst. Then he made his way through the strong point, despite bursting hand grenades, toward the second machinegun, 25 yards distant, whose 2-man crew swung the machinegun around and fired two bursts at him, but he walked calmly through the fire and, reaching the edge of the emplacement, dispatched the crew. Signaling his men to rush the rifle pits, he then walked 35 yards further to kill an enemy rifleman and returned to lead his squad in the destruction of the 8 remaining Germans in the strong point. His audacity so inspired the remainder of the assault company that the men charged out of their positions, shouting and yelling, to overpower the enemy roadblock and sweep into town, knocking out two anti-tank guns, killing 37 Germans and capturing 26 others. He had sparked and led the assault company in an attack which overwhelmed the enemy, destroying a roadblock, taking a town, seizing intact 3 bridges over the Maravenne River, and capturing commanding terrain which dominated the area.

MEDAL OF HONOR PRESENTATION

On January 21, 1945, General Alexander Patch presented Sergeant Stanley Bender the Medal of Honor for his heroic action on August 17, 1944. During the presentation, General Patch asked whether he had been able to save any money since he had come to France. Bender responded, "General, I have had very little time to spend any of it." This was spoken like a seasoned infantryman who had waged war on two continents, participated in three amphibious landings, and lived to tell about it.

LIFE AFTER WORLD WAR II

Soon after his discharge Stanley Bender went to work as a counselor at a VA hospital in Chicago. He later took a similar position in Clarksburg, West Virginia. In 1949 he became the contact man for the Beckley, West Virginia, VA Hospital. In addition to representing the VA, he and his wife, Ethel, were active in the civic affairs of Beckley and belonged to several organizations. He also represented the Congressional Medal of Honor Society, traveling widely and speaking to many groups throughout the country. He retired at age sixty. When asked his plans for retirement, he said, "I'll do things that I have been putting off." Of course, he continued representing the Congressional Medal of Honor Society.

Stanley Bender died of cancer on June 22, 1994. He was survived by his wife, Ethel, two daughters, Shirley and Evelyn, and several grandchildren.

His wife didn't know for some time after they were married that he was a Medal of Honor recipient. "He was never one to talk about it," she said. "When someone asked him what he did to receive the Medal, he would always say that he did what anyone else would have done." She added, "He was modest, very much so. I think everyone admired him." At his funeral, his wife said, "He definitely will be missed by a lot of people, especially by me and my daughters. I loved him very much...I am so proud of him. I was back then, I still am, and I always will be."

Hershel Williams, also a Medal of Honor recipient from West Virginia, worked with Bender in the Veterans Administration. "It's almost like losing a brother," he said. "Stanley has been a long and very close friend for years."

United States Senator Robert C. Byrd of West Virginia said, "Bender is a true American hero." Byrd continued, "He answered the call for service during wartime and continued to answer that in his work with the Department of Veterans Affairs after his active duty service."

Perhaps, Stanley Bender had the last word. In an interview in 1990, he took a very dim view of war. He said, "Some big shot who knows the answer should make a way to stop this nonsense. That's all war is--a lot of unnecessary fireworks."

HONORS

Stanley Bender received the Croix de Guerre, the highest medal that France can bestow on a soldier.

In November 1954, the West Virginia Turnpike officially opened. The Turnpike Commission named a massive bridge in Stanley Bender's honor. There were speeches galore at the dedication, but the emotional high point occurred when Mrs. Bender cried as the Master of Ceremony read the dedication

From the Forest to the Battlefield

plaque commemorating her husband. Three decades later, the bridge was demolished as part of a turnpike modernization program. Mr. Bender seemed resigned to its fate. He said, "I will remember it. Memories cannot be destroyed."

In the mid-1990s, the Turnpike Commission named another bridge in his honor. Less spectacular, this bridge is in Fayette County near Bender's birthplace.

To commemorate the seventh anniversary of the Invasion of southern France, the citizens of La Londe renamed the Maravenne Bridge, the Stanley Bender Bridge. This bridge was one of the bridges saved by Bender's heroic actions.

Stanley Bender served one term as the Commander of the Disabled Veterans of America, the Beckley Chapter.

BURIAL SITE

Stanley Bender is buried at High Lawn Memorial Park at Oak Hill, West Virginia.

157

RUSSELL E. DUNHAM

BIRTH DATE: February 23, 1920

BIRTH PLACE: East Carondelet, Illinois

DEATH: April 6, 2009

MEDAL OF HONOR ACTION: Hill 616 near Keyserberg, France. January 8, 1945.

RANK: Technical Sergeant

UNIT: Company I, 3rd Battalion, 30th Infantry Regiment, 3rd Infantry Division

YEARS OF SERVICE: August 1940 - September 1945

AWARDS: Medal of Honor, Purple Heart, Distinguished Service Cross, Silver Star, Bronze Star, Croix de Guerre (France), Others

CCC: SCS-36, Carlinville, Illinois. January - June 1939.

RUSSELL E. DUNHAM

Russell E. Dunham was born in an old railroad boxcar in East Carondelet, Illinois, on February 20, 1920. He was the sixth child of Ola and Dorothy (Atwood) Dunham. His father had converted the boxcar into meager living quarters after the family had moved from St. Charles, Missouri, in 1915. At the time of Russell's birth, there were four boys: Ervin, Lester, Marvin, and Ralph. A girl, Gladys, was nine years old. Frieda was born in May 1922. Just after her birth, Dorothy became ill. "Dolly" suffered from a respiratory disease, and in the fall of 1924, the family moved to southwest Missouri where the air was cleaner and the weather warmer. They lived in a dilapidated farmhouse in the tiny village of Mountain Home.

The Dunham family moved many times before Russell was four years old. The moves tended to correlate with the date the rent was due. He had lived in East Carondelet, Hartford, and Fair Groves, Illinois, and Mountain Home and Willow Springs, Missouri. Each move was like a scene out of the Old West with horses pulling a farm wagon piled high with their belongings. Those that could do so walked. To young Russell it was like an ongoing picnic as he ran through the fields along the road and slept under the wagon at night. By this time another sister, Josephine, had been born, and Dolly was very sick. The older children, Ervin and Gladys, took over most of the household chores.

Although the country air in southwestern Missouri seemed to improve Dolly's health, the family missed their friends and family in the St. Louis area. In early 1926 they settled in an old farmhouse on eighty acres near Fosterburg, and "Pop" started a truck farming operation. Soon after the move, Dolly became bedridden, and a doctor made frequent calls to the farmhouse. In early fall of 1927, Dolly passed away due to tuberculosis. Russell was without a mother at age seven.

After Dolly's death there was speculation that the children would go to an orphanage, but the family stayed together. Within a few months, Ola was looking for a housekeeper. Housekeepers came and went. Gladys left home and was soon followed by Ervin. Pop made frequent trips to St. Louis to visit lady friends and would be gone for several days. The younger children soon learned how to survive on their own. Russell remembered harsh winters in the old, cold farmhouse. Their food consisted mostly of potatoes, beans, and a watery gravy. Russell walked two miles to school in the bitter cold. He was determined to stay in school even though his father refused to buy books or pencils.

In the fall of 1931, Pop brought home Thelma Murphy. Thelma and her three children moved into the Dunham farmhouse. The couple split up shortly after Christmas but were back together by May and were married in June 1932. Jim was born in August of that year. By then Marvin had left home but with eight in the household, food was scarce. Pop decided it was time to move again, and they relocated to a small farm near Woodburn. Floyd was born in December 1933. Pop and Thelma were constantly bickering or visiting St. Louis. Baby Floyd became Russell's responsibility.

From the Forest to the Battlefield

Russell's fondest memories are of hunting and trapping in the woods. Possum, squirrel, and rabbit were plentiful and kept food on the table. In the spring of 1934, Pop moved the family back to Fosterburg where he rented a small farm. Ralph and Russell worked as field hands for local farmers and sold hides from their trapping enterprise. In 1936 Florence was born, and once again food was scarce. Ralph left home that fall, and Thelma went to work in a shoe factory in St. Louis. Most of the time, Pop was in St. Louis, and Russell and his stepbrother, Leonard, enjoyed peace and quiet on the farm for a while.

Russell never got along with his stepmother, and his father blamed him for his rocky relationship with Thelma. Russell had enough and left home to work for a neighbor in the summer of 1937. He earned a dollar a day and saved his money to buy clothes. When the farm work ended in the fall, Russell moved to St. Louis to live with his older brother, Lester, whom he called "Pete." In the evenings, Russell sold hot tamales in the streets and peddled brooms and mops during the day. He filled in with other odd jobs and made thirty- five cents an hour distributing advertising circulars.

CCC EXPERIENCE

On January 12, 1939, Russell enrolled in the CCC. The eighteen-year-old was assigned to Camp Carlinville, SCS-36, Company 3677. The camp was located two miles south of Carlinville, Illinois, on the current site of the Macoupin County Fairgrounds. At the time of Russell's enrollment, he indicated he had been a general laborer for three years. At five foot seven inches tall and weighing 125 pounds, he was a typical enrollee. Russell had completed eighth grade at Fosterburg School in April 1934. Russell's reason to enroll was "to help the family." The twenty-two-dollar allotment was sent to his father, Ola, in Brighton, Illinois. His father promised to save the money for him. Dunham's occupational choice was welding. Other than going AWOL for one day just two weeks after his enrollment, Russell had a satisfactory experience in the CCC. He performed typical soil conservation work in an area that been impacted environmentally by coal mining. Dunham planted trees, built dams, and laid drain tile in fields. Russell took classes in safety and civics and enjoyed reading. The camp educational adviser, H. B. Diemer, reported that Russell was "courteous and willing." Dunham was honorably discharged at age nineteen on June 30, 1939.

After his CCC stint, Russell returned home and was disappointed to find out that Pop had spent the money he was supposed to be saving for him. In August 1939 Russell and his friend, Odell Warren, decided to go to California where Russell's brother, Marvin, was living. They hopped a freight train out of St. Louis and wound up in Fort Worth, Texas. With no work available, they continued on to Eloy, Arizona. After a few days of picking cotton in the brutal heat, they continued to California. Marvin was out of work in Stockton, California. He was married with a family and unable to help them. After picking cotton for a few days in Chowchilla, Russ and Odell decided to return to St. Louis and peddle brooms, mops, and advertising circulars again.

From the Forest to the Battlefield

In the spring of 1940, Russell and Odell thought things might be better in California and caught a Frisco freight train. This time they ended up in Tulsa, Oklahoma. They both found work with a carnival and traveled throughout the country for several weeks. By fall they were back in St. Louis.

MILITARY EXPERIENCE

With no jobs to be had, Russell, his brother, Ralph, and Odell Warren enlisted in the Army on August 16, 1940, in Peoria, Illinois. All three were assigned to the 30th Infantry Regiment, 3rd Infantry Division. Ralph and Russell were with Company I, and Odell was with Company B. They started out in Fort Ord, California, under General Stillwell. Russell had difficulty accepting Army discipline. He avoided the guardhouse but saw his share of KP duty.

In March 1941 Russell was transferred to the 3rd Infantry Division, 30th Infantry Regiment. Ralph stayed with the 7th Division because he was on the boxing team. When the war broke out in December 1941, Russ and Ralph were reunited at Fort Lewis, Washington. The brothers patrolled up and down the West coast guarding bridges and airports. They trained in amphibious operations with the Marines. Many evenings were filled with wine, women, and song!

In the fall of 1942, the division traveled by train to Camp Pickett, Virginia, a staging area for overseas duty. Russell shipped out to North Africa. Arriving on the coast of French Morocco on November 8, 1942, they were shot at as soon as they landed. The French surrendered in four days when Casablanca fell. Russell Dunham had been tested as a combat soldier and earned his first battle star.

After the fall of Casablanca, the company moved to Fedala and set up a camp known as Camp Johnson. Russell was bored with guard duty. He went into Fedala with another soldier in search of wine. They overstayed their passes and when they got back to camp, the outfit had been reassigned. They wandered back to town and were picked up by the company commander. Their wanderings resulted in seven days of hard labor.

The company welcomed in the New Year 1943 in Fedala. Martha Raye performed for the GIs. Guard duty and drills were incessant. When assigned to guard duty with his buddy, George Leach, they would cover for each other and run a card game. They would win a couple thousand dollars and quickly spend it in Casablanca. Finally Company I left Casablanca and was in Arzew, Algeria, by February 10, 1943. Company I's duty was to run demonstrations for troops being trained.

By April every GI at Arzew was physically fit and deeply tanned. On April 30 the 3rd Division assembled for a visit from General George Patton. Patton noticed several men in the stockade for drinking. He cursed and said, "Whoever heard of locking up a GI for drinking?" Then in a booming voice said, "Turn 'em loose!"

From the Forest to the Battlefield

On May 8, 1943, the 30th Infantry moved into the town of Jemmapes to begin training for the invasion of Sicily. They resumed amphibious training and had speed marches up to five miles per hour. When off duty, the GIs played cards and went to town in search of wine and women. Russ set up a black market and sold cigarettes and candy at a premium to the French and Arabs. Mattress covers sold for $32.00 and barracks bags went for $35.00. Morale was low and the company was hit by dysentery. They had to take tablets to prevent malaria. Finally, on July 7, 1943, the company left Africa for good.

Shortly after daybreak on July 10, 1943, Company I hit the beach at Licata, Sicily. Russ had barely cleared the ramp when a German artillery shell destroyed it. The temperature was well over 100 degrees and the ground was parched. German resistance was light. The company traveled 120 miles in five days leaving Patton's tank men behind. The heat took its toll and water was scarce. Russell's legs were raw, and blood seeped through his boots as they traveled across rough and hilly terrain. They finally arrived in Palermo on June 22 and recuperated in a lemon grove for eight days. On August 3 Company I received orders to take the town of San Fratello at the top of Hill 673. In the battle Dunham was knocked unconscious, but refused to see a medic.

Company I fought battle after battle as they moved up the coast of Sicily in the fall of 1943. Russ had seen too many of his buddies either killed or wounded. For him only prayer could deaden the misery of war. On November 6, 1943, the company was ordered to take Mount Rotundo in order to break the winter line at Cassino. The German shelling was endless in rain and fog. Russell was miserable in his foxhole. Eventually the unit was relieved by the 36th Division. In the 3rd Division only thirty-two men out of eight hundred walked off Mount Rotundo.

The company landed at Anzio on January 21, 1944, and moved toward the Mussolini Canal five miles away. Russell was in charge of the 2nd Squad in the 2nd Platoon. It was his first time to lead men into action. At first everything went according to plan, but then the battle turned into a blood bath. German artillery rained down on the GIs like hailstones. The dead and the dying were lying everywhere as the ground smoldered. On January 28 a piece of shrapnel from an exploding grenade hit Dunham in the leg. His face was hit with flying debris and a couple of teeth were knocked out. Company I had gone into battle with 202 men. Only twenty-two were left. Dunham spent his twenty-fourth birthday in the 300th General Hospital in Naples recovering from shrapnel wounds in the leg, mouth, and chin.

In early March Russell was released from the hospital and boarded a truck for Anzio. Once again American casualties were high. By mid-March the 3rd Division had suffered over one thousand killed, four thousand wounded, and one thousand were missing in action. A forty-eight-hour truce was declared to remove the dead and wounded. On March 28, 1944, the 3rd Division was relieved from front line duty. They had been fighting constantly for sixty-seven days.

From the Forest to the Battlefield

On June 2, 1944, Russ was in charge of a patrol in Labico, twenty miles southeast of Rome. They surprised a large group of Germans having a meeting in a building. The patrol had just disarmed the prisoners when a tank entered the town. Two of his men jumped up on the tank and captured two more Germans. Next an ambulance entered Labico with a German doctor. In later years, Dunham said, "We had to find all kinds of white cloth to show surrender so that our own artillery wouldn't come after us when we went back to camp. I was pretty proud of that tank!" Sergeant Dunham received a Silver Star for his part in the patrol. They had captured sixty Germans, a tank, and an ambulance!

On June 4 the battalion marched into Rome. Russ was tired, filthy, and the shrapnel wound in this foot was causing problems again. The Germans had evacuated the city without a fight. GIs filled the taverns. "Girlfriends" were usually ten cents, but within a week the price went up to $10.00. Dunham enjoyed a well-deserved eleven days of rest and relaxation.

In early August 1944, Company I sailed for France. Russ was still a platoon sergeant, and Ralph was a squad leader. Fighting was heavy as the troops moved deeper into France. At the battle of Bescancon, Russ lost his good friend, Millard Pierce. During a forty-eight-hour rest period, Russell learned the regiment had been awarded the Bronze Arrowhead, the last time this recognition was awarded to amphibious troops in Europe.

From September 13 until early December, Company I fought the stubborn Germans in the Vosges Mountains. In rain and snow, Russell saw many of his friends killed on the battlefield. Once again, Company I distinguished itself during this campaign. Sergeant Lucian Adams earned the Medal of Honor, and PFC Richard Sweet was awarded the Distinguished Service Cross. Six Silver Stars were awarded. One of them went to Ralph Dunham. Also, fourteen men in Company I were awarded the Bronze Star.

On December 13, 1944, orders came down to move to the Kayserberg area. By this time, Russ was in love with Helina who lived in Ezenheim. Her uncle had set up a still in his backyard and kept the company supplied with homemade schnapps made from potato peelings. Russ had spent as much time with Helina as possible. He said good-bye knowing that he would never see her again.

The company celebrated the Christmas holidays in Kayserberg. On New Year's Eve, Russell, Ralph, and several of his buddies had a wild time. In the course of the evening, Russ wrecked a civilian's bicycle. Ralph got in a fight over a girl. The group had been disrespectful to a lieutenant and a major. The next morning they were ordered to report to the commanding officer, Lieutenant Walker. He threatened to reduce them to the rank of private first class and break up the platoon. One man said "no way," and another said he would not fight in a unit without the Dunham brothers. On January 4 the CO asked another non-commissioned officer to take over the platoon. He replied, "Those are Dunham's men and I don't want any part of them." In the end, Walker reduced Dunham from technical sergeant to staff sergeant and allowed the platoon to stay together.

From the Forest to the Battlefield

On January 8, 1945, the company was ordered to attack Hill 616. The men were issued white mattress covers as camouflage in the deep snow. Russell Dunham was to lead the 2nd platoon attack. He was confident and said a quick prayer: "God give me this day." Dunham was armed with a carbine and hand grenades hanging from his belt, buttonholes, and suspenders. At 2:30 P.M. he heard the order, "On your feet." About forty-five yards up the hill, machine gun bullets started kicking up snow all around him. Dunham used a large tree for cover and inched forward. He spotted two machine gun nests. He threw a hand grenade at the closest nest. It hit a tree limb and rolled back down the hill. It exploded near the squad leader behind him. Dunham thought, "Oh, God! I've killed one of my own men."

A German sniper had Russell in his sights, and Dunham knew he had to keep moving. This time he advanced within a few yards of the nearest machine gun nest. He threw a grenade and killed two Germans. A lone survivor huddled in the bottom of the log emplacement. With his carbine empty, Dunham hauled him out by the collar and shoved him down the hill to his men.

Continuing to advance, Dunham raised to motion Ralph and his men forward. A bullet hit him in the back, tearing open a ten-inch gash. Russ felt a stinging sensation and rolled fifteen yards down the hill. As he sprang to his feet, a German egg grenade rolled beside him. He kicked it aside and furiously charged back up the hill.

With bullets flying around him, Dunham crawled to the second machine gun nest. He lobbed a grenade and killed the crew. Dunham continued and took out a third machine gun nest. By this time blood soaked his mattress cover, and a cold sweat ran off his forehead. He lay down in the snow for a few seconds to wait for his men.

As German infantrymen began scrambling out of their foxholes, Sergeant Dunham chased them down the back side of the hill. He and his brother encountered a fourth machine gun, and Ralph took it out. Suddenly, an enemy rifleman appeared out of the trees and shot point-blank at him. He missed Dunham, but killed a GI behind him. Russell immediately shot the German. The fighting was over by dark. Russ learned that he had not killed his squad leader with the grenade that bounced off the tree limb. Also, the company commander promoted Dunham to Technical Sergeant on the spot.

Second Lieutenant James M. Beck, platoon leader, was an eyewitness. He said, "Killing nine Germans, wounding seven, and capturing two, firing about 175 rounds of carbine ammunition and throwing eleven grenades, he carried out one of the most spectacular attacks ever seen."

The company had killed twenty-five German soldiers and captured ten prisoners. When they came off Hill 616, they were greeted by a number of GIs. Someone asked, "What was all the shooting about?" The company commander answered, "The Dunham brothers were on the loose again."

From the Forest to the Battlefield

On January 21 Russ returned from a Rest Center and rejoined Company I on the plains of Alsace Lorraine. His back wound had yet to fully heal. The next day the unit moved in on the little town of Holtzwihr. The Germans had command of the town with artillery as well as tanks. Some of the men from Company I had set up a command post in an old house with an attached barn. Russ was hunched up against a wall when a German tank stuck its "nose" in a window. He jumped out a back window, but the rest of the men were forced to surrender.

Dunham then crawled through a manure chute into the barn. He had lost his carbine in the getaway and needed a hiding place. He peeked out the front door and saw a large sauerkraut barrel to the right of the door. He crawled into the barrel and crouched down. This was possible only because Russ's weight had dropped down to 117 pounds from his usual 150 pounds. Dunham peeked out from time to time. By nightfall there were several hundred infantrymen in the town. It was bitterly cold in the barrel and snowing lightly. Russell was hungry and reached down for a handful of sauerkraut. At daylight Dunham knew he had to get out of the barrel. He slipped into the barn with a sigh of relief only to hear "Hands up!" Two German soldiers pointed a gun at his chest and led him into the house.

He was searched immediately, and they took two hand grenades. An officer ordered a body search, and they discovered cigarettes and candy. They argued over who would get the cigarettes. The search continued, and they took his billfold, dog tags, and a watch. Somehow they missed a Walther pistol in a shoulder holster under his arm. He was denied food and water and taken back to the barn.

Later in the day, his two captors transported him in a Jeep toward German lines. The driver was not familiar with the area and stopped frequently to ask directions. When the driver stopped at a bar, the second soldier wasn't paying attention and laid his rifle down on the floor of the Jeep. Dunham shot him twice in the head with his pistol. After jumping in a drainage ditch, he set off toward American lines in sub-zero temperatures. Dunham had a few close calls with German patrols, but thanks to his mattress cover camouflage, he was not spotted.

At dusk the next day, he crossed the Ill River in Alsace. His feet felt like two blocks of ice, and he could hardly walk. He was then discovered by American engineers working on a bridge. To his dismay they didn't believe he was an American! He was taken to a medical tent and heard a voice call out, "Dunham? What the hell happened to you?" A medic he had met in the Rest Center a few days before had recognized him. He was taken to a field hospital where doctors were able to save his feet from amputation. A battalion officer stopped by to tell Dunham he would be receiving the Medal of Honor instead of the Distinguished Service Cross. Russell was pleased!

Dunham had frost-bitten hands and ears, and both feet had been frozen. Also, he was suffering from battle fatigue and pneumonia. He was evacuated to a hospital in Meircourt, France. He began to mend but experienced severe pain in his left foot. An X-ray revealed a piece of shrapnel from Anzio was pinching a nerve. Surgery on the foot had Dunham on crutches again. The feet were slow to heal, and it was late March 1945 before Russ was released from the hospital.

MEDAL OF HONOR CITATION

For conspicuous gallantry and intrepidity at risk of life above and beyond the call of duty. At about 1430 hours on 8 January 1945, during an attack on Hill 616, near Kayserberg, France, T/Sgt. Dunham single-handedly assaulted 3 enemy machine guns. Wearing a white robe made of a mattress cover, carrying 12 carbine magazines and with a dozen hand grenades snagged in his belt, suspenders, and buttonholes, T/Sgt. Dunham advanced in the attack up a snow-covered hill under fire from 2 machine guns and supporting riflemen. His platoon 35 yards behind him, T/Sgt. Dunham crawled 75 yards under heavy direct fire toward the timbered emplacement shielding the left machine gun. As he jumped to his feet 10 yards from the gun and charged forward, machine gun fire tore through his camouflage robe and a rifle bullet seared a 10-inch gash across his back sending him spinning 15 yards downhill into the snow. When the indomitable sergeant sprang to his feet to renew his 1-man assault, a German egg grenade landed beside him. He kicked it aside, and as it exploded 5 yards away, shot and killed the German machine gunner and assistant gunner. His carbine empty, he jumped into the emplacement and hauled out the third member of the gun crew by the collar. Although his back wound was causing him excruciating pain and blood was seeping through his white coat, T/Sgt. Dunham proceeded 50 yards through a storm of automatic and rifle fire to attack the second machine gun. Twenty-five yards from the emplacement he hurled 2 grenades, destroying the gun and its crew; then fired down into the supporting foxholes with his carbine dispatching and dispersing the enemy riflemen. Although his coat was so thoroughly blood-soaked that he was a conspicuous target against the white landscape, T/Sgt. Dunham again advanced ahead of his platoon in an assault on enemy positions farther up the hill. Coming under machinegun fire from 65 yards to his front, while rifle grenades exploded 10 yards from his position, he hit the ground and crawled forward. At 15 yards range, he jumped to his feet, staggered a few paces toward the timbered machinegun emplacement and killed the crew with hand grenades. An enemy rifleman fired at pointblank range, but missed him. After killing the rifleman, T/Sgt. Dunham drove others from their foxholes with grenades and carbine fire. Killing 9 Germans—wounding 7 and capturing 2—firing about 175 rounds of carbine ammunition, and expending 11 grenades, T/Sgt. Dunham, despite a painful wound, spearheaded a spectacular and successful diversionary attack.

From the Forest to the Battlefield

MEDAL OF HONOR PRESENTATION

Technical Sergeant Russell E. Dunham was awarded the Medal of Honor on April 22, 1945, in Nuremberg's Zeppelin Stadium. The weather was cool, and Dunham and the four other men from the 3rd Infantry Division were anxious to get on with the ceremony. Russell was wearing an old leather jacket he picked up along the way after he had lost his regulation field jacket. The award officer was able to locate a jacket for him, but there was no time to sew on sergeant stripes. The men were to be decorated according to rank, so Russell would be the third man to receive his medal. The fourth man was his buddy, Staff Sergeant Lucian Adams. Adams had been at a Rest Center in Marseilles. At the last minute, a small observation plane was dispatched to pick him up. Lucian arrived with just a few minutes to spare.

Lieutenant General Alexander Patch, Commander of the 7th Army, saluted each man as he approached him. He then placed the Medal of Honor around each man's neck and shook his hand. General Patch said to Dunham, "Son, I've heard some great stories about you. After this day, you should never have to apologize to anyone."

At the end of the ceremony, a large concrete swastika at the end of the stadium was blown to bits by a dynamite charge. The blast rocked the stadium as pieces of the Nazi symbol flew through the air.

Russell Dunham returned to Company I and was assigned kitchen duty to prevent him from further combat. In early May Russ said his good-byes and caught a train for Marseilles. There he boarded an old transport ship and after twenty-two days at sea, arrived at Newport News, Virginia, on June 1, 1945. After eight major campaigns and credited with 407 days of combat, Technical Sergeant Russell E. Dunham was back on US soil!

THE DUNHAM BROTHERS

Russell and Ralph Dunham were good soldiers but were known as "hell raisers" especially early on in their military careers. They would sneak into town to visit girls and drink until early morning. Ralph and Russell were big gamblers, too. They would set up a gambling operation in the latrine on paydays. At times they made several hundred dollars. In February 1943 on an old French train in Algeria, they teamed up in a game of blackjack and won $1400.00. The money came easily and went just as easily.

It is written in the history of the 3rd Infantry Division that General Patton was ordered to take a town within twenty- four hours. An aide told him, "We took it yesterday." Patton then asked his aide, "How did we get it?" The reply was "The Dunham boys were out raising hell again!" Russell knew Patton fairly well. Patton told him, "If I had a million men like the Dunham brothers, I could whip the world."

From the Forest to the Battlefield

Marvin Dunham also served in World War II in the US Army Air Corps. Periodically, Marvin would cross paths with his brothers. In February 1942 Russ was hitchhiking back to the base from the town of Arzew in Algeria. A foreign car pulled up beside him, and he was surprised to see the driver was his brother, Marvin. The Dunham brothers spent a few days reminiscing about their boyhood days. When Russell was hospitalized in Naples with shrapnel in his leg after the battle along the Mussolini Canal in January 1944, he was happy when Marvin came to visit. After the episode on Hill 616, Russell was again hospitalized at a hospital in Meircourt. He got word that the regiment was having a big party in Nancy. He managed to get a pass and hitchhiked to Nancy to be reunited with Ralph and Marvin. They drank long and hard to block out the miseries of war.

Russell and Ralph Dunham came home as highly decorated soldiers. Between them they had twenty-six medals. Ralph had matched Russell medal for medal except for the Medal of Honor. He had been recommended for the Medal of Honor but received a lesser medal instead. Ralph had five Purple Hearts. Russell always said that Ralph was tougher than he was. Ralph was two years older than Russell and spent his entire life in the shadow of his younger brother. Sadly, Ralph was never at peace and died from alcoholism.

LIFE AFTER WORLD WAR II

After his discharge from the Army in September 1945, Russell Dunham briefly worked in a packing house and a steel mill. In 1946 he began a lengthy career as a benefits counselor with the Veterans Administration in St. Louis. He was pleased to serve as a counselor for short assignments in Korea, Viet Nam, and Germany. Russell retired in 1975.

Dunham married a woman named Mary shortly after coming home from the war. Their only child, Mary Lee, was born in 1947. Mary and Russell were divorced in 1950. Dunham made a home for Mary Lee in Jennings, Missouri. He was a loving, protective father. Mary Lee carried a case to school every year to show her classmates her father's medals. She became a good conversationalist and a self-assured hostess as Dunham had many visitors eager to talk to him about World War II.

Dunham married Wilda Long-Bazell on September 29, 1959, in Alton, Illinois. Russell and "Willy" lived on a forty-acre farm near Jerseyville, Illinois, for over thirty years. "We live quietly." Dunham said in 1999, "I plant a summer garden with lettuce, onions, and tomatoes." Russell enjoyed coon hunting and fishing in a nearby lake. He enjoyed parties, playing cards, and was a St. Louis Cardinals fan. Russ had sown his "wild oats" in his youth and never smoked or drank.

In 1981 D. Ray Wilson published a book titled, *Episode on Hill 616.* The book chronicles Russell Dunham's over four hundred days in combat during World War II. Dunham provided Wilson with a large, green binder containing 380 pages of neatly typed manuscript and almost two hundred tapes. Dunham had a story to tell!

Dunham spoke to children at area schools about the battle for Hill 616. Children would crowd around him to see his Medal of Honor and his other medals including the Purple Heart, Silver Star, Bronze Star, and the famous Croix de Guerre from the president of France. He would tell them about the piece of steel shrapnel from a German shell in his leg. "When the weather turns bad, I feel a numbness in my leg," he said. "The shrapnel is a reminder of the war we fought." He regularly attended a variety of functions honoring Medal of Honor recipients.

In 2008 a birthday party and bar-b-que was held at Dan Drainer's gun club in rural Jersey County, Illinois, to celebrate Dunham's eighty-eighth birthday. Russell brought his display case of medals with him and graciously answered questions. Dunham was described as being "sharp as a tack and still pretty spry." Forty-five days after his eighty-ninth birthday, Russell Dunham died of congestive heart failure.

HONORS

The Russell Dunham Outpost 17 erected a monument at the Jefferson Barracks Cemetery in St. Louis in honor of those who served with the 3rd Infantry Division. The monument was dedicated on May 20, 2000, and stands on the cemetery grounds near Flagstaff and Rostrum Drives.

Part of US Route 67 from the Jersey County line near Jerseyville and a portion of Illinois Route 255 is known as the Russell E. Dunham Memorial Highway.

The Indianapolis Medal of Honor Memorial was unveiled and dedicated on May 28, 1999, the last Memorial Day weekend of the twentieth century. Located in White River State Park in downtown Indianapolis, the site is adjacent to Military Park. The memorial was constructed with a fundraising campaign by the Indiana Power and Light Company. Dunham and all Medal of Honor recipients back to the Civil War were honored, and their names are engraved in the memorial. The next day Russell Dunham was one of the grand marshals at a big parade through the streets of Indianapolis and was a guest of honor at the Indianapolis 500 race.

BURIAL SITE

Russell E. Dunham died in his sleep on April 6, 2009, at age eighty-nine. He is buried at Valhalla Memorial Park in Godfrey, Illinois. He was predeceased by his wife, Wilda who died in 2002. Dunham was survived by a daughter from his first marriage, Mary Lee Neal. He was also survived by a step daughter, Annette Wilson, step son, David Bazell, three sisters, three brothers, three grandchildren, and nine great-grandchildren.

JOHN W. DUTKO

BIRTH DATE: October 24, 1917

BIRTH PLACE: Dilltown, Pennsylvania

DEATH: May 23, 1944. KIA.

MEDAL OF HONOR ACTION: Ponte Rotto, Italy. May 23, 1944.

RANK: Private First Class

UNIT: 30th Infantry Regiment, 3rd Infantry Division

YEARS OF SERVICE: February 1941 - May 23, 1944

AWARDS: Medal of Honor, Purple Heart, Combat Infantryman Badge, Others

CCC: S-97, Salisbury, Pennsylvania. April 1933. F-37, Carlsbad, New Mexico. January - March 1939.

JOHN W. DUTKO

John D. Dutko and his wife, Anna Cilip, immigrants from Slovenia, lived the American dream. Both came from Slovenia to Scranton, Pennsylvania, where each became citizens of the United States. By chance, each moved again, only this time, a few hundred miles west across the state. They had met by this time and were married at Beaverdale, Pennsylvania. The couple settled at Wehrum, a coal patch town in Indiana County.

The elder Dutko worked in the mines of Wehrum as a motorman. During this time, the couple had two children: Anne, born February 17, 1915, and John, born October 24, 1917. After the birth of his children, the elder Dutko left the mines and bought a small farm that he worked for a decade. Then using the money derived from the sale of this smaller farm, he bought a larger 102-acre farm in 1931.

Their children received grammar school education in the Wehrum public school. A typical company-owned town, Wehrum was a harsh place to grow up, even in good times. The Great Depression made matters worse. The mining industry, the mainstay of Indiana County's economy, drastically cut jobs, helping to push the county's unemployment rate to 30 percent.

There were no jobs available to young adults like John. Because of this hardscrabble life, he developed the toughness necessary for survival. According to articles from the *Indiana Evening Gazette* during the mid-1930s, he and his friends were involved in a couple of altercations with the law that ultimately led to little more than stern warnings by the county police.

John was a good son, helping his father to work the new farm. He took a correspondence course in taxidermy and learned the rudiments of veterinary work. As a result, surrounding farmers brought their sick animals to him for treatment. At the same time, he became an avid hunter and trapper. Hunting was recreational as food was never a problem for the family. Hard cash, however, was always an issue, so he used trapping to supplement his meager income.

CCC EXPERIENCE

Dutko joined the Civilian Conservation Corps first in 1935 and again in 1939. His first duty station was S-97 at Salisbury, Pennsylvania, where he served only three weeks. There he received an honorable discharge to seek work in the private sector with a stipulation that he could not reenroll in the CCC. Four years later, however, he signed up again and was assigned to F-37 at Carlsbad, New Mexico. Although his work was judged as satisfactory, the educational adviser wrote that Dutko was "...a maladjusted person probably due to his home condition." He lasted two months (January - March) before going AWOL.

From the Forest to the Battlefield

Because a CCC enrollee was not bound by the Uniform Code of Military Justice, Dutko's desertion was not a criminal act. In fact, desertion was common, as nationally the CCC averaged a 20 percent desertion rate. The only consequence of his action was that CCC officials removed his name from its ranks, took away his parent's allotment, and dishonorably discharged him.

When asked why he left the CCC, John said, "I wanted to enlist in the Army but the officers held me to my initial enlistment time in the CCC." Upon his leaving the CCC, he did not immediately join the Army. He stayed in New Mexico, working as a lineman for an electric company.

MILITARY CAREER

Dutko joined the Medical Corps of the US Army in February 1941 at Harrisburg, Pennsylvania, and took his basic training at Walter Reed Hospital. From there he transferred to Tilton Hospital at Fort Dix, New Jersey, where he became Ward Master of the hospital while also serving in the Military Police. Promoted to Sergeant, John married Ethel Costello while at Fort Dix.

Dutko's antipathy toward the Germans grew stronger, as he treated American servicemen maimed and wounded in military action. Outraged and frustrated, he felt helpless, watching his patients suffer and die. He blamed their deaths on the Axis. Wallace McGaughey, his brother-in-law, said, "He had seen enough and joined the infantry where he could do the most good."

Dutko requested transfer from the Medical Corps to the US Infantry, but in doing so, he paid a price: reduction in rank. Private Dutko's next duty post was at Camp McCain, Mississippi, where he received his combat training. From there he joined the Third Infantry Division as it moved from North Africa to Sicily.

INVASION OF ITALY SEPTEMBER 1943

Winston Churchill pushed for an Italian Front while the United States emphasized the forthcoming invasion of France. Ultimately the Allies agreed to a smaller-scaled Italian offensive, and plans for the invasion, scheduled for early September 1943, moved ahead.

Unbeknownst to the Allies, Field Marshall Albert Kesselring had convinced Hitler that the defense of Italy was strategically important to Germany. He argued that if the Allies won a quick victory, they would invade the Balkans to gain control of the rich oil fields and then use the many Italian air fields as bases to bomb the German homeland.

The Allied plan chose the toughest route to defeat the Germans in Italy. Forgoing the more conventional invasion via the "top" of Italy, Allied troops were to move northward from the boot of Italy through the Apennine Mountains, the spine of Italy.

From the Forest to the Battlefield

On the other hand, Kesselring utilized Italy's geography. He implemented a series of defensive lines stretching the width of the country, thereby using the region's mountains and innumerable narrow valleys, and making every peak, valley, or river a potential battle site.

By December, Kesselring's Gustav Line (Winter Line) brought the Allies' Italian Campaign to a halt. Monte Cassino, the lynchpin of the Gustav Line, was impenetrable. From this quagmire came an Allied plan to relieve the pressures on the American and British forces stalled on the Winter Line: invasion of the Anzio-Nettuno areas that lay thirty-five miles south of Rome and fifty-five miles north of the German Winter Line.

The invasion occurred on January 22, 1944. It took the Germans by complete surprise. Unfortunately, the Allied Army chose to consolidate their forces within the Anzio perimeter rather than racing into the Italian interior. This indecisiveness allowed the Germans sufficient time to send in massive reinforcements setting the stage for a brutal four- month stalemate.

Anzio quickly became an Allied general's worst nightmare. The entire beachhead was approximately sixteen miles wide and ten miles at its deepest point. With the Mediterranean Sea at their back, the Allies were hemmed in. There was no front line, for the Germans commanded the higher positions, enabling them to shell the entire area with impunity. Early on, when the first breakout occurred, the Germans were fully prepared and stopped the Allied offensive. As a result, the next six weeks saw a bloody dance of death. Both sides repeatedly attacked, were repulsed, only to regroup and attack again. No land was exchanged but the casualty rate sky-rocketed. The entire area resembled World War One trench warfare. Sergeant Russell Dunham, a Medal of Honor recipient, said of Anzio, "It was a real blood bath. We went in with 202 men and the next morning we were only twenty-two."

Bogged down in mud and exhausted by intense combat, both sides were content to wait until spring before resuming major action. In the meantime German artillery played havoc with the Allies, accounting for a steady stream of casualties as well as taking a significant psychological toll on the zeroed-in troops. Every day, men hunkered down as artillery duels continued. Both sides used planes to strafe and bomb. The crack of rifle fire and the chatter of machine guns were commonplace as were the soft "whumps" of mortars firing close by. Night patrols were common.

DUTKO TAKES THE WAR TO THE GERMANS

John Dutko had become a seasoned veteran of these activities. The men respectfully called him "mad-man" because of his hatred of the Germans. His weapon of choice was a Browning automatic rifle (BAR) that he called his "heater," and he scoffed at statistics that showed a BAR man's life in combat was less than thirty minutes. Using this weapon as if it were an appendage of his body, Dutko was a fearsome foe.

From the Forest to the Battlefield

An unnamed Associated Press reporter filed this report from Anzio in early April 1944:

John Dutko and his buddies crossed over into German lines near Cisterna, Italy. It was a black moonless night, and from his past experience, he knew the job that lay before him, would be no picnic. Assigned to a small patrol that was to go out and bring Germans back for questioning, the young infantryman was prepared for the worst. He explained, "Germans don't like to be taken anywhere, especially by Americans."

His patrol decided to travel light--some without a cartridge belt and some with only a pistol with extra clips. Others brought rifles with bandoliers draped over their shoulders. Dutko carried his "heater."

The no-man's land that lay between the two sides was less than 1,000 yards and had been heavily mined by the Third Division Combat Engineers. With the assistance of a combat engineer, the patrol made it through the danger zone. Once through, the engineer turned back, warning the patrol leaders to return exactly by the same path.

Deploying in a skirmish line and advancing under cover of their own artillery, the men peered into foxholes and slit trenches to capture at least five Germans and then return to their own lines with the prisoners.

The officer in charge, Lieutenant John Hewitt along with Sergeant William Schneider drew first blood. Sneaking up on a slit trench that had a sheet of tin covering it, Schneider poked his rifle under the tin roof, demanding those inside to surrender. Quickly a Nazi Oberleutnant and a corporal scrambled to their feet and were quickly hastened back to the rear. After eight Nazis had been captured that way a green flare went up signaling the patrol to assemble for the trek back to safety.

At this point, Dutko said, "Things began to happen."

Private Carl Callister shot and killed two prisoners who had bolted. "After ignoring my order to halt, I let them have it," he said. "I shot them point blank, about ten feet away." The shots aroused the Germans. Suddenly machine guns opened up on the left flank. Dutko and another patrol member were deployed to assess the situation. By that time the Germans put up their flares, another machine gun chattered from their right flank. Soon another machine gun fired directly into the patrol's center position, putting the entire patrol under a withering cross-fire. The patrol chose not to make a fight of it and moved back to the edge of the mine field with two dead, four injured, and six prisoners."

Dutko said "We were all dispersed running back to the mine field and when we got there, we could not find the path. We decided to walk across it and how we made it without setting off a single mine was a miracle. We got those six Krauts back alive all right but I was sure that every step I took in that mine field was going to be my very last."

From the Forest to the Battlefield

In mid-May, four months after the Anzio invasion, the Allies finally breached the Gustav Line, making the Nazi perimeter at Anzio untenable. In less than two weeks, the Allies broke out of Anzio. Even so, that Allied offensive cost one hundred armored vehicles and incurred another 4,500 casualties.

The Anzio breakout cost John W. Dutko his life.

On the early morning of May 23, 1944, an intensive artillery bombardment on German positions signaled the beginning of the Allied offensive. While planes flew overhead, hundreds of tanks rolled forward followed by foot soldiers, most of whom had been brought in under the cover of darkness.

Dutko's battalion was near Ponte Rotta, a mile east of Cisterna. His outfit had to hold up as it had advanced farther than expected and was endangered by "friendly fire." Somehow, a German 88mm canon and three machine gun positions had survived the shelling and blocked any movement forward.

Pinned down, Dutko's unit found temporary shelter in a trench. At this point, he jumped out of the trench and shouted, "I'm gonna get them with my heater." He then proceeded to run into the open toward the German gun emplacement.

Private Anatole J. Simon recounted later, "He must have known that he would be killed when he left the cover of the trench. But he did it...that was his thing. The Germans stopped firing on the American position. They turned their machine guns on Dutko."

According to an official Army Report:

> The infantrymen in the trench watched in utter fascination. It was safe to watch. For the time being no bullets were coming in their direction. Even the .88 turned its muzzle toward the running figure...tracer bullets formed a solid white streak behind Dutko. He ran another 100 yards before the enemy could traverse their machine guns. An 88mm shell exploded within thirty yards of him.

Sergeant Cleo Toothman, another eyewitness, testified

> He jumped into a shell crater and only stayed there long enough to catch his breath and then he took off again. He knocked out one machine nest with a hand grenade. Although wounded, he continued to move on and caught the German 88mm gun emplacement unaware and killed all five Germans. Suddenly another machine gun opened up on him. He turned and blazed away while advancing toward the machine gun nest. Later, his body was found sprawled over a handful of dead Germans in a machine gun pit.

Colonel Lionel C. McCarr, the Commanding Officer of Dutko's regiment, said, "I am proud to command a regiment that has such men as PFC Dutko. The spectacular courage of this lone man enabled his division to retain the original impetus of its advance."

MEDAL OF HONOR CITATION

For conspicuous gallantry and intrepidity at risk of life above and beyond the call of duty, on 23 May 1944, near Ponte Rotta, Italy, PFC. Dutko left the cover of an abandoned enemy trench at the height of an artillery concentration in a single handed attack upon three machine guns and an 88mm mobile gun. Despite the intense fire of these four weapons which were aimed directly at him, PFC. Dutko ran 100 yards through the impact area, paused momentarily at a shell crater, and then continued his one-man assault. Although the machine gun bullets kicked up dirt at his heels and 88mm shells exploded within thirty yards of him, PFC Dutko nevertheless made his way to a point within thirty yards of the first enemy machine gunner and killed both gunners with a hand grenade. Although the second machine gun wounded him, knocking him to the ground, PFC Dutko got up and advanced on the 88mm gun, firing his Browning automatic rifle from his hip. When he came within ten yards of the weapon, he killed the five man crew with a long burst of fire. Wheeling on the machine gun that wounded him, PFC Dutko killed the gunner and his assistant. The third machine gun fired at him from twenty yards distant wounding him a second time as he proceeded toward the weapon at a half run He killed both members of its crew with a single burst from his Browning automatic rifle and continued toward the gun and died, his body falling across the dead German crew.

MEDAL OF HONOR PRESENTATION

On October 17, 1944, Major General Henry Tevret, the Commanding Officer of the 22rd Corps, presented the Medal of Honor posthumously to John W. Dutko. His wife Ethel Dutko accepted the medal in her husband's name.

NEW JERSEY: DUTKO'S HOME STATE?

There was confusion over Dutko's home state for almost fifty years after his death. Official records listed New Jersey as his home. As a matter of fact, Riverside, New Jersey, claimed him as one of its own. Wallace McGaughey, a hero in his own right, Distinguished Flying Cross with two Oak Leaf Clusters and the brother-in-law of John Dutko, waged a lengthy battle to change this error. He lobbied intensively and wrote countless letters to the government and to the Purple Heart Society to rectify this mistake. Finally, in 1991, the error had been recognized. When the good news reached Anne McGaughey, Dutko's only sister, she said, "I feel my brother finally has come home to Pennsylvania in spirit."

JOHN DUTKO'S FUNERAL

John W. Dutko was laid to rest with appropriate military ceremonies at Beverly National Cemetery in Burlington County, New Jersey, on August 3, 1947. Two recipients of the Medal of Honor served as his honor guard. While his wife, Ethel, of nearby Delanco, New Jersey, looked on, their four-year-old daughter, who had never seen her father, was given her father's flag. She said, "My daddy's come home."

HONORS

The Homer City, Pennsylvania, VFW was named the John W. Dutko Post. Later the Post disbanded; the American Legion Post 493 in Homer City, however, has memorialized John and other local heroes.

The US Army promoted Dutko posthumously to Sergeant.

Dutko's name is listed on a plaque honoring all of Indiana County's veterans.

John W. Dutko was enshrined at the Soldiers and Sailors Memorial Hall and Museum in Pittsburgh, Pennsylvania.

In 1995, Pennsylvania sponsored a fiftieth anniversary of the end of World War II. Included within this tribute was a special ceremony to honor Pennsylvanians who had been recipients of the Medal of Honor. The event was held on the Soldiers Garden section of the Capitol grounds. In attendance were national, state, and local dignitaries as well as military representatives. Included as honored guests were Mr. and Mrs. Wallace McGaughey. They witnessed Sergeant Dutko's induction into the Soldiers' Garden, a special place of honor for Medal of Honor recipients.

This heartfelt letter might be Dutko's most significant memorial. Mrs. Mary Leidel wrote this to a Lima, Ohio, newspaper for Veterans Day 2007, sixty-three years after Dutko's death!

> I want to take time to thank all veterans for their service to our country. My husband, Paul Leidel was a World War II veteran. I have heard many war stories about him and his friend John W. Dutko, a hero who died in a war fighting for freedom of others.
>
> Dutko ran over 100 yards through an impact area in a one-man assault. He made his way within thirty yards of the first machine gun nest and killed both men with a hand grenade. He was knocked to the ground when wounded but he arose and advanced on a German 88mm weapon. Shooting his Browning automatic rifle from his hip, he got within ten yards of the gun site and killed the whole crew. He then moved against another machine gun position that had wounded him. He killed the gunner before dying.
>
> No one can understand what goes on in a soldier's mind during combat. So, I praise all military men and also pray for them. I think we all should do the same. I am proud to be the wife of a wounded veteran. He was a good and loyal soldier as well as a father and husband and is greatly appreciated by many. He is my hero just as John Dutko was a hero to my husband. Where would all of us be now and what condition would the world be in if it were not for soldiers who gave themselves for our country? God bless all of you.

CARLTON W. BARRETT

BIRTH DATE: November 24, 1919

BIRTH PLACE: Fulton, New York

DEATH: May 3, 1986

MEDAL OF HONOR ACTION: St. Laurent-sur-Mer, France (Omaha Beach). June 6, 1944.

RANK: Private First Class

UNIT: 18th Infantry Regiment, 1st Infantry Division

YEARS OF SERVICE: October 29, 1940 - 1963

AWARDS: Medal of Honor, Bronze Star, Purple Heart, Combat Infantryman Badge

CCC: S-79, Fort Bryon, New York. March - September 1936. F-180, Coeur d'Alene, Idaho. October 1936 - September 1938. P-99, Long Island, New York. October 1938.

CARLTON W. BARRETT

Lester Barrett (1894-1964) and his wife, Olive, (1896-1967) were married in 1916 and had three children; a girl, Madeline Olive, and two boys, Roland and Carlton. Lester was drafted in 1918 and served less than a year in the military before being honorably discharged. A barber by trade, he had a shop in his home. According to the US Census reports of 1920-30-40, his income was meager, barely enough to support a family. In 1940 he ran a confectionery shop in Luzern Springs, New York, where his son, Carlton, worked occasionally. After his sons went into the service during World War II, he was hospitalized in West Mountain Sanatorium at Glen Falls, New York, for an undisclosed illness.

In examining various public records, it appears as if Lester and Olive suffered marital problems that resulted in an eventual divorce. Early on, Olive lived with her mother and step-father in Caramel, New York, while the children remained with their father. There appears to have been one attempt at reconciliation, but by 1940, Lester and his son lived in a rented home with their housekeeper, Ethel Prathaw, age forty-eight. In an earlier Army record, Carlton listed his father's wife as Mrs. Lester Barrett. Apparently, he could not, or would not, call her by her first name. A 1944 US Army Press Release announcing Carlton's Medal of Honor referred to a woman as Carlton's step-mother. Still another Army Press Release specifically mentioned his mother, Mrs. Olive Barrett, who resided with her daughter, Mrs. Madeline Battreal, in Saratoga Springs, New York. Mrs. Barrett died in Winchester, New York, in 1967.

Lester Barrett, on the other hand, moved west. He received his Social Security card while in Nevada. Then he moved to San Diego, California, where he passed away in 1964. There is no evidence that he saw his children before his death.

CCC EXPERIENCE

As a CCC enrollee, Carlton Barrett had an unusual CCC record. He enlisted three different times. His first hitch was at a CCC camp in New York, while the second enlistment took him to Idaho. The third enlistment was also at a New York camp but was a disaster. He received honorable discharges from the first two CCC stints but only lasted a few days in the latter assignment before receiving a dishonorable discharge.

His first duty station was S-79 at Fort Bryon, New York. For his six-month term from March to September 1936, Barrett worked at an entry level position. His second enlistment saw him stationed at F-180 near Coeur d'Alene, Idaho, where he served two years. There he did timber survey work, fought forest fires, and worked on the blister rust crew, acknowledged as one of the most onerous jobs in the CCC. His superiors rated his work as satisfactory, and he even had time to take a safety and a typing course. Carlton received an honorable discharge.

Barrett reenlisted again and, this time his duty station was P-99 on Long island. Unfortunately, New York had blister rust problems, too. Barrett's duty was disease control; therefore, he faced six more months of tedious, familiar work. Barrett had an innate stubborn streak, and this trait soon manifested itself when he told his foreman, "I won't work. I want out."

Barrett was brought before his company commander at an official hearing. There, William Opffenbaker, his foreman, testified

> On October 18, 1938, Carlton Barrett handed me his bark-knife stating he did not like the work and he wanted his discharge. He had been previously caught in a lie when he put an artificial egg cluster in his pocket stating to me that he had not found it. When I instructed the men in the methods of scouting, Barrett refused to do anything explained to him. During the time he was with the crew he maintained a dilatory, nonchalant attitude and was a detriment to the crew. Therefore, with this in mind, I turned him over to Army authorities.

The company commander agreed and so did Barrett. He was dishonorably discharged, but he had served his country honorably for the previous eighteen months. At age twenty his future lay in the military.

MILITARY EXPERIENCE

Upon returning home, he worked sporadically, first as a cook and then at his dad's candy shop. On October 29, 1940, Barrett enlisted in the US Army at Albany, New York, thus beginning a twenty-three-year military career. He took his basic training at Fort Hancock, New Jersey, and after completion, Barrett was immediately assigned to the 18th Infantry Regiment, First Infantry Division- the Big Red One.

The division was quite active before Pearl Harbor, participating in War Games in Louisiana as well as in North Carolina. It settled in at Indiantown Gap, Pennsylvania, prior to embarkation to England. In October 1942, the division participated in the invasion of North Africa at Orin, Algeria. The Division took heavy casualties in a half dozen major battles as it pushed through Tunisia northward to the Mediterranean.

At El Guettar, in South Central Tunisia, an epic tank/infantry battle occurred during the last few days of March and into early April 1943. The initial stages of the battle were depicted in the movie *Patton*. Here Private Barrett was in advance of his unit laying mines and was struck by a German machine gun bullet. After completing his assignment, he then reported to a battalion aid station where he was treated and released. Carlton immediately reported back to his unit. In Africa and later in Sicily, Barrett's weapon of choice was a 1903 Springfield rifle which he used to kill Germans. He said in 1945, "El Guettar was tougher than Normandy."

General Patton chose the Big Red One to spearhead the invasion of Sicily in July 1943. Again, the division took heavy losses, but by the end of July, the Germans were pushed off that island, thus setting the stage for the invasion of Italy two months later. The First Division, however, was pulled out of the upcoming Italian campaign and sent to England where it trained another ten months prior to the invasion of France.

180

From the Forest to the Battlefield

In the early hours of June 6, 1944, Operation Overlord plans met the ultimate test: the opening of the Western Front. The attack occurred over a sixty mile stretch of the Normandy coast, involving five Allied assault points: Sword, Juno, Gold, Omaha, and Utah beaches. Of the five beaches, Omaha Beach was the pivotal objective.

Thirty minutes after the first wave hit the beach, Barrett waded ashore in neck-deep water, two hundred yards from the shore amid indescribable confusion, terror, horror, and death. Zeroed-in German small arms, mortar, and cannon fire decimated the incoming troops. Barrett dressed wounds, calmed the dying, and gave aid wherever it was needed. He dragged men ashore, keeping them from drowning. Then he sought cover for the wounded before plunging back into the surf to save more floundering infantrymen. Barrett collected litters strewn about and placed the wounded on each litter before half-carrying and half-swimming to a waiting evacuation boat. At times he walked upright as if on a stroll at the beach while bullets tore up the sand. He did all this while carrying out his primary mission which was to guide the landing ships onto the beach and then supervise the unloading of the boats. At one point Barrett saw a group of men huddled onto the surfside of an anti-tank ditch. He shouted, "Follow me, men," and stepped into the ditch showing the frightened men that it was possible to cross. He relayed important messages to the scattered remnants of his unit while always maintaining a calm demeanor. By 11:00 P.M., Barrett had been wounded in both hips, legs, and in his left foot.

MEDAL OF HONOR CITATION

For gallantry and intrepidity at the risk of his life above and beyond the call of duty on 6 June 1944, in the vicinity of St. Laurent-sur-Mer, France. On the morning of D-day Pvt. Barrett, landing in the face of extremely heavy enemy fire, was forced to wade ashore through neck-deep water. Disregarding the personal danger, he returned to the surf again and again to assist his floundering comrades and save them from drowning. Refusing to remain pinned down by the intense barrage of small-arms and mortar fire poured at the landing points, Pvt. Barrett, working with fierce determination, saved many lives by carrying casualties to an evacuation boat lying offshore. In addition to his assigned mission as guide, he carried dispatches the length of the fire-swept beach; he assisted the wounded; he calmed the shocked; he arose as a leader in the stress of the occasion. His coolness and his dauntless daring courage while constantly risking his life during a period of many hours had an inestimable effect on his comrades and is in keeping with the highest traditions of the U.S. Army.

MEDAL OF HONOR PRESENTATION

After evacuation from Normandy, Barrett transferred to a hospital near Cardiff, Wales, where he recovered from his wounds. From there he transferred to a replacement center in England. On November 17, 1944, Barrett was summoned to the Hotel Majestic, Paris, France, where Lieutenant General C. H. Lee, a member of General Eisenhower's staff, made the Medal of Honor presentation.

After the ceremony he modestly said

> I don't think I deserve any more credit than anyone else who was on the beach that day. I acted instinctively, I didn't think things out because there wasn't any time. Jerry was making it too hot for us on the beach for anyone to do anything but act. I did what I'd been taught. The infantry is a team, you know, and I was just doing my job as part of the team.

Later he was transferred to Washington, DC, where he served on temporary duty to Army Ground Forces headquarters. There he had photo opportunities with General Joseph W. Stilwell, Commanding Officer, and Major General James G. Christianson, Chief of Staff, both of Army Ground Forces. The generals questioned Barrett at length, and he answered them easily.

> I enlisted in the Army more than four years ago and being an infantryman is what I know best. I learned how to fight and I'd like to keep doing my share of fighting. As soon as I have sufficiently recovered from my wounds, I hope the Army sends me back to combat.

When told that his next assignment would be at an Infantry Training Center as an instructor, he said

> I expect to tell the men training for combat that we have the best infantry leaders in the world. I'll tell them to master their weapons because a doughboy must know how to take care of himself in battle and must be familiar with all the weapons he may be called to use...I'll tell them to obey orders unquestionably. I always did that and never regretted it. The officers and noncoms have earned their bars and stripes and I never knew an order to be given without good reason.

When Barrett returned to the United States, he wrote to his former company commander, Captain John Brownlee, to ask whether he was eligible for the Combat Infantryman Badge. Brownlee responded with the badge and the regimental orders that awarded it to Barrett. Barrett said, "That badge means as much to me as the Medal of Honor, for I know the best fighting men in the world are wearing it."

LIFE AFTER WORLD WAR II

Carlton Barrett married Josephine George from Wilkes Barre, Pennsylvania, on June 6, 1947, in Grand Rapids, Michigan. They had three children, one of whom died in infancy. The marriage ended in a divorce.

Barrett retired in 1963 after twenty-three years in the service. According to one source, his post-war life was troubled. John McManus, a historian of the Big Red One Division, said that Barrett had been estranged from his family but reconciled with them prior to his death.

BURIAL SITE

Carlton W. Barrett died on May 3, 1986. His remains were interred at the Chapel of the Chimes Cemetery, in Napa, California.

THOMAS A. BAKER

BIRTH DATE: June 25, 1916

BIRTH PLACE: Troy, New York

DEATH: July 7, 1944. KIA.

MEDAL OF HONOR ACTION: Saipan. July 7, 1944.

RANK: Sergeant

UNIT: Company A, 105th Infantry Regiment, 27th Infantry Division

YEARS OF SERVICE: October 15, 1940 - July 7, 1944

AWARDS: Medal of Honor, Purple Heart, Combat Infantryman Badge

CCC: S-77, Cherry Plain, New York. August 1934 - September 1935. P-121, Port Ann, New York. October-December 1935.

From the Forest to the Battlefield

THOMAS A. BAKER

Thomas Baker Sr. (1874-1935) and Emma Baker (1886-1955) were the parents of two boys, Thomas and Joseph. They lived on 10th Street in Troy, New York. Thomas Sr. worked in a shirt factory while the mother tended the two boys at home. The Bakers were poor. When Thomas Sr. passed away, the family was financially bereft. However, Emma Baker did not equate poverty with strong family values. As a result, young Thomas always hustled for jobs.

CCC EXPERIENCE

Shortly after high school graduation in 1934, Thomas Baker enlisted in the CCC. His first posting was at S-77 at Cherry Plain, New York, less than ten miles from his home. He worked as a laborer on the development of a four-county park system that surrounded historic Albany, New York. Baker remained there for a year. From there he transferred to P-121 for the last few months of his enlistment. At Fort Anne, New York, he participated in a region-wide effort to control gypsy moth infestation.

Baker's CCC tours of duty were unremarkable. His ratings were satisfactory, and he got along well with his peers. He went AWOL on the first weekend of December 1935 but returned for duty the following Monday morning. The company commander addressed the infraction by placing a letter in his personnel jacket. A few weeks later, he was discharged honorably after having served fifteen months.

After his CCC experience, he enlisted in the New York National Guard where he served for three years (1935-1938). At the same time, he worked for the YMCA in Troy, New York. He then became a fireman, and later took up automobile mechanics. According to the census of 1940, his income for the previous year was $720.00.

MILITARY EXPERIENCE

Baker rejoined the New York National Guard when it was activated in 1940. He received his basic training at Fort McClellan, Alabama, and participated later in the Louisiana War Games. After Pearl Harbor, Baker's division, the 27th Infantry, moved cross-country to California, where it guarded the California coastline against a possible Japanese landing. By March 1942, the 27th Division was on the move again to Hawaii where the division guarded the Islands from possible Japanese assault. Although some segments of the division were used in scattered amphibious operations at Makin Atoll and Eniwetok Atoll, Baker's battalion remained in Hawaii. It was not until 1944 that the entire 27th Division saw combat at Saipan.

JAPANESE BANZAI CHARGE JULY 7, 1944

General William T. Sherman's statement "War is hell" was never more telling than with the Americans during the Battle of Saipan. Although the island was secured in less than a month, both sides suffered

184

huge losses. Cut off and without any possible hope from the Japanese Navy, the Japanese defenders at Saipan engaged in a fanatical campaign that presaged Iwo Jima eight months later. Almost all the Japanese garrison of thirty thousand men died. The American losses numbered one in six men killed or wounded (14,000), the nation's greatest loss in the Pacific to that date.

Japanese capitulation was not an option to General Saito who commanded the Japanese forces. He gave this final order to his men:

> Whether we attack or whether we stay where we are, there is only death. However, in death there is life. We must utilize this event to exalt Japanese manhood. I will advance with those who remain to still deliver another blow to the American Devils, and leave my body on Saipan as a bulwark of the Pacific.

This triggered the largest Japanese banzai attack in the war. Before the attack the Japanese killed their wounded men who were unable to walk. The remaining troops fully understood their mission: to take at least seven Americans with them to their deaths.

At 4:45 A.M. on July 7, 1944, over four thousand "wildly screaming" Japanese soldiers, including the walking-wounded and near-dying, penetrated nearly a half mile into the American lines. Their motivation was fanaticism. Their weapons of choice were guns, rocks, pointed sticks, or anything they could carry. This epic battle was primordial: hand-to-hand and foxhole-to-foxhole at point blank range.

Major Edward McCarthy, the Commander of the 2nd Battalion of the 105th Division, described the attack, "It was like one of those old cattle stampede movies where the camera is in a hole in the ground and the herd keeps coming and coming and they leap up and jump over you. Only this time it wasn't cattle, the Japs kept coming and coming."

The battle continued into the night. The Japanese lost everyone, but succeeded in killing over one thousand men, mostly from the 1st and 2nd Battalions of the 105th Infantry Regiment, 27th Infantry Division.

EYEWITNESS ACCOUNTS OF THOMAS A. BAKER'S HEROISM

Technical Sergeant Dominick Dourio of Valley Falls, New York, testified

> On June 19 when our company ran into heavy automatic weapons fire, I saw Baker pick up a bazooka and move out alone against the enemy fortifications. They saw him coming with the bazooka and the Japs let him have it with every weapon they had. He moved within 100 yards of the position and calmly fired four rounds into the strong point. Then, out of ammunition, he rushed the strong point and with his bayonet finished off the remaining Japs.

From the Forest to the Battlefield

Added Technical Sergeant Richard Hoffney of West Sand Lake, New York, "The Japs couldn't hit him with their automatic weapons fire, and they couldn't stop him with steel in the close fighting."

"Those were two heavily fortified positions behind our lines," said Sergeant Marion Occhinero. "Baker set out to destroy them. During the attack, he killed two Jap officers and ten enlisted men."

Heavy fighting continued. Eighteen days later, July 7, 1944, Baker's battalion was hit hard and quickly by the Japanese onrushing suicide troops. According to the US Army Press Release:

> Sergeant Baker was gravely wounded in the initial wave. Despite his wound he insisted in staying on line. Until his ammunition was expended he fired at the Japanese sometimes at ranges of less than five yards. He then engaged the enemy in hand-to-hand combat. Finally his rifle was battered into uselessness, and Baker fell exhausted. A comrade carried him about fifty yards but the rescuing infantryman was shot by enemy fire.

Technician Fifth Grade Carlo Petriocelli of Troy, was the last man to see Baker alive.

> I saw Baker sitting against a tree and tried to pick him up as we withdrew to the beach. He wouldn't let anyone help him. 'It's no use, Pat, I'm done for and there's no use of anyone else getting hit." He was badly hurt. He asked me for a cigarette and acted as if nothing had happened. He said he'd like the pistol I was carrying. When I gave it to him I was carrying only eight rounds. "Thanks, now I can take some more of those Japs," he said. We heard another wave of Japs coming, and he ordered me to leave. He said, "It's better to get out now. Thanks and give my regards to everyone." I helped him sit up against a tree with a pistol in one hand and a cigarette in the other, calmly waiting for them to come.

It took all evening and into the next day for the Americans to secure the field. It required a few more days to clear the battlefield of the dead. This was particularly risky, as a few Japanese soldiers lying among their dead comrades would jump up and throw grenades at the unsuspecting Americans.

Sergeant Occhinero searched the area where Baker was last seen. "I finally found Baker's body alongside a tree. Still tightly held in his hand was the .45 caliber automatic pistol he had borrowed. He was lying on his side. Scattered in front of him were eight dead Japs. His pistol was empty."

MEDAL OF HONOR CITATION

For conspicuous gallantry and intrepidity at the risk of his life above and beyond the call of duty at Saipan, Mariana Islands, 19 June to 7 July 1944. When his entire company was held up by fire from automatic weapons and small-arms fire from strongly fortified enemy positions that commanded the view of the company, Sgt. (then Pvt.) Baker voluntarily took a bazooka and dashed alone to within 100 yards of the enemy. Through heavy rifle and machinegun fire that was directed at him by the enemy, he knocked out the strong point, enabling his company to assault the ridge. Some days later while his company advanced across the open field flanked with obstructions and places of concealment for the enemy, Sgt. Baker again voluntarily took up a position in the rear to protect the company against surprise attack and came upon 2 heavily fortified enemy pockets manned by 2 officers and 10 enlisted men which had been bypassed. Without regard for such superior numbers, he unhesitatingly attacked and killed all of them. Five hundred yards farther, he discovered 6 men of the enemy who had concealed themselves behind our lines and destroyed all of them. On 7 July 1944, the perimeter of which Sgt. Baker was a part was attacked from 3 sides by from 3,000 to 5,000 Japanese. During the early stages of this attack, Sgt. Baker was seriously wounded but he insisted on remaining in the line and fired at the enemy at ranges sometimes as close as 5 yards until his ammunition ran out. Without ammunition and with his own weapon battered to uselessness from hand-to-hand combat, he was carried about 50 yards to the rear by a comrade, who was then himself wounded. At this point Sgt. Baker refused to be moved any farther stating that he preferred to be left to die rather than risk the lives of any more of his friends. A short time later, at his request, he was placed in a sitting position against a small tree. Another comrade, withdrawing, offered assistance. Sgt. Baker refused, insisting that he be left alone and be given a soldier's pistol with its remaining 8 rounds of ammunition. When last seen alive, Sgt. Baker was propped against a tree, pistol in hand, calmly facing the foe. Later Sgt. Baker's body was found in the same position, gun empty, with 8 Japanese lying dead before him. His deeds were in keeping with the highest traditions of the U.S. Army.

A POSTCRIPT TO THAT TERRIBLE DAY

On the day of the Japanese banzai attack on Saipan, the 27th Infantry Division suffered major losses. Among the dead were Thomas A. Baker and Lt. Colonel William J. O'Brien, both from Troy, New York. Each died within hours of the other. Both men became Medal of Honor recipients.

Those two men left indelible visual impressions that stand out among the annals of heroism. O'Brien, surrounded by sword-wielding Japanese, remained on the top of his jeep blasting away until his ammunition ran out. Not too far away, Baker, mortally wounded, leaned against a tree, calmly smoking his cigarette, as he waited for the final onslaught.

The Medals of Honor were awarded on May 27, 1945, at RPI Field (Rensselaer Polytechnic Institute) by General of the Armies J. Lawton Collins.

HONORS

Thomas Baker received the rank of sergeant posthumously.

The Fort Drum military base in New York renamed two buildings in honor of Lt. Colonel William J. O'Brien and Sergeant Thomas A. Baker. Building 50001 was rechristened the O'Brien Readiness Center, while the former Engagement Skills Trainer Weapons Simulator's name became the Baker Weapons Training Facility.

The Rensselaer County Legislature created a memorial to Lt. Colonel William O'Brien and Sergeant Thomas Baker on the third-floor lobby of the county office building on Seventh Avenue. The memorial features replicas of the Medal of Honor as well as portraits of each man.

BURIAL SITE

Originally, Thomas A. Baker's burial site was at the National Memorial Cemetery of the Pacific. Later, he was reinterred at the Gerald B. H. Solomon Saratoga National Cemetery at Schuylerville, Saratoga County, New York. Baker left behind his wife, Constance Cecelia Coyne Baker, his mother, Mrs. Emma Baker, and a brother and a sister.

VERNON MCGARITY

BIRTH DATE: December 1, 1921

BIRTH PLACE: Right, Tennessee

DEATH: May 21, 2013

MEDAL OF HONOR ACTION: Krinkelt, Belgium. December 16, 1944.

RANK: Technical Sergeant

UNIT: Company L, 3rd Battalion, 393rd Infantry Regiment, 99th Infantry Division

YEARS OF SERVICE: November 1942 - 1973. Served twenty-eight years in the Tennessee National Guard and retired as a Lieutenant Colonel.

AWARDS: Medal of Honor, Purple Heart, Bronze Star

CCC: TVA-36, Paris, Tennessee. April 1939 - June 1940. TVA-48, Camden, Tennessee. June 1940 - March 1941.

VERNON McGARITY

Vernon McGarity's early childhood was not an easy one. During the early 1930s, his mother, Anne McGarity, lived with her grandparents, William and Nancy McGarity. William was the head of a household that included an extended family, usually relatives. Vilius and Rosie McGarity were listed as his son and daughter-in-law. The eight remaining people, between the ages of six to twenty-nine, were listed as William and Nancy's grandchildren. The family income was little or nothing.

By 1940 things had not improved much for Anne McGarity. In that census she listed herself as a widow who lived with her cousin James and Amanda McPeake. Once again the income of the family was negligible.

Vernon McGarity was the eldest of three children, two boys and a girl. He was born December 1, 1921, in Harden County, Tennessee. He attended Morris Chapel School and dropped out when he was in tenth grade to help work on the farm. Economically, things remained difficult for his family. Consequently, he enrolled in the CCC in 1939 to help his mother.

CCC EXPERIENCE

From April 1939 to June the following year, Vernon was stationed at Camp TVA- 36 at Paris, Tennessee, not far from his home. Later he reenrolled and transferred to Camp TVA-48 near Camden, Tennessee, fewer than twenty-five miles from Paris. There he served another nine months before his honorable discharge on March 29, 1941.

About 30 percent of the CCC camps in Tennessee were listed as TVA/CCC camps. The CCC worked in close conjunction with the Tennessee Valley Authority regarding recreational possibilities. The dams created huge lakes such as Kentucky Lake situated near Paris and Camden, Tennessee, where Vernon McGarity worked for two years. Initially, he worked on mosquito eradication. Later Vernon worked at erosion control that included the building of check-dams, ditching, and extensive stone work. When not engaging in those projects, he planted trees.

In his two years of service, Vernon had no unauthorized leaves. He did have three furloughs home, each for five days. His work was deemed satisfactory by his superiors. He took two classes: music and first aid. He scored well in each course, and his educational adviser judged him to have a strong character. Vernon's mother, Anne McGarity, received his allotment. Later, when she remarried, her allotment was reduced by ten dollars a month.

A few days before his entering the Army on November 24, 1942, Vernon married Ethel Nunn. After a brief honeymoon, McGarity shipped out to Fort Oglethorpe, Georgia, where he began his military career. From there Vernon went to Camp Van Dorn, Mississippi, for his basic training. He participated in the Louisiana War Games before being stationed at Camp Maxey, Texas. His stateside training lasted twenty-two months before he shipped out to England in September 1944. For almost a month, his unit participated in more training before crossing the Channel to France. In late November 1944, his outfit saw combat near the Siegfried Line before settling in at a supposedly safe area of the Ardennes.

THE BATTLE OF THE BULGE

In the early morning hours of December 16, 1944, the German Army struck decisively in a massive counterattack aimed at taking the Dutch seaport of Antwerp. Hitler hoped that by splitting the American and English lines he could negotiate separate treaties with the two countries before stopping the Russians who were marching relentlessly toward Berlin. It was a grandiose plan that almost worked. The whole plan hinged on four intangibles: absolute surprise, the continuation of the traditionally bad December weather in the region, the inability of the American forces to fight, and the need for the Germans to capture enough fuel from supply depots deep within the American lines.

Although the attack did achieve its first objective of surprise, the Germans were stymied elsewhere. The German high command viewed the American soldiers as weak, especially when compared to the Russian troops. Therefore, they did not expect to encounter the incredible American resistance that slowed down the German time table, especially around the Belgium town of Bastogne. The severe weather that had covered much of the Ardennes also worked against the German mechanized forces, causing tremendous delays on the narrow and slippery Belgium roads. When the weather improved the day before Christmas, the US Air Force resupplied the ground troops, as well as playing havoc on the German tanks and troops. The day after Christmas, elements of Patton's 3rd Army arrived after an impressive northward drive to relieve the beleaguered forces around Bastogne. The very next day Patton threw three divisions against the Germans, breaking the siege of Bastogne.

By January 26, 1945, one month after the German offensive had begun, the Battle of the Bulge was over. Within weeks the Bulge no longer existed. While the German losses were unsustainable, the Allies were poised to make their final assault on Fortress Germany.

McGARITY BECOMES A HERO

The American GI was not privy, of course, to the grand plans of the generals. McGarity's outfit, the men of Company L of the 393rd Regiment, tried to find as much comfort as possible in their foxholes in the Ardennes on the very cold, snowy night of December 15. The high command felt that this sector was safe from combat many miles away. At 4:00 A.M. the next morning, the men of Company L were awakened by thundering artillery coming from the enemy lines. The men had never heard anything like this and it caused them to hunch deeper in their foxholes. The artillery shells sheared off tops of seventy foot trees, turning them into lethal weapons as they fell into the foxholes. What was considered a safe haven had become one of the major points of the enemy attack. During the relentless barrage, Staff Sergeant Vernon McGarity suffered serious wounds and was sent to an aid station to receive treatment. There the medics told him he had a "million dollar wound" and would be evacuated. McGarity ignored that possibility.

Second Lieutenant Kenneth Juhl said, "Sergeant McGarity's wounds to his cheek and legs were serious and painful and I ordered him back. He was to be evacuated but refused. Under heavy fire he returned to his unit bandaged up because he knew the situation was grave."

As the fighting continued, one man in a forward position was wounded. Juhl said, "I saw Sergeant McGarity, immediately and without any hesitation, leave his sheltered position to go to the side of this man. In the face of heavy fire, he brought his comrade back to a safe position where he could be evacuated."

Sergeant Tommie G.V. Prendergast continued the story of McGarity's heroism.

> Fighting was at an unprecedented height during the entire day, but due to McGarity's superior tact and ability to lead his men, the squad suffered only one casualty. The next morning he took a bazooka from a man in his squad and crawled out to meet a German tank that was attacking with a large number of German infantrymen following it. He knocked the tank out of action with one shot and dispersed the infantrymen. Immediately after this, the Germans attempted to bring up a light cannon into action. He called in for rifle grenades to be directed at the cannon as well as concentrated small arms fire, and we knocked it out. Then under a hail of bullets McGarity rescued another wounded American.

Sergeant Jacob Yohe observed McGarity's ability to inspire and encourage other soldiers around him. "The unit had been under attack for almost a full day and the morale was declining because of exhaustion and lack of food. But the sergeant's encouraging words and his fearless actions inspired everyone around him."

Sergeant Lloyd Hoff told how McGarity solved the ammunition problem in the height of the battle:

> Ammunition was running low so he assured his men he would get more. He ran boldly toward a hole 100 yards away where ammunition had been stored. Heavy fire didn't bother him. The enemy redoubled its efforts to get him... But by some miracle he got through and issued us much needed ammunition...Then he had presence of mind to remember the location of two snipers who had shot at him while getting the ammunition. He killed both with his accurate rifle fire. When the Germans cut off the squad's escape route he left his cover and killed or wounded a machine gun nest that threatened his position.

"His fearlessness in the face of superior enemy fire," reported Staff Sergeant Robert Ortalda, "made for complete coordination and effective fire with the use of a minimum amount of ammunition. All during the time that I was able to observe him before being blown out of my foxhole, Sergeant McGarity's actions were superb."

Sergeant McGarity's position was eventually overrun by the Germans, and he became their prisoner. Later he said, "I was still holding and did hold until such time that we ran out of ammunition and had to surrender."

McGARITY'S STATUS AS A POW

On January 25, 1945, Mrs. Ethel McGarity was informed by the War Department that her husband had been missing in action since December 16, 1944. Mrs. McGarity and her daughter, Sharon Jean, made their home with her parents, Mr. and Mrs. C.B. Nunn of Model, Tennessee.

Mrs. McGarity was informed on April 12, 1945, that her husband was a prisoner of war somewhere in Germany.

One month after V-E Day, the government notified Mrs. McGarity that her husband had been liberated from a German POW camp. This news was shared with Sergeant McGarity's mother, Mrs. Anne Turner, of Paris, Tennessee.

MEDAL OF HONOR CITATION

He was painfully wounded in an artillery barrage that preceded the powerful counteroffensive launched by the Germans near Krinkelt, Belgium, on the morning of 16 December 1944. He made his way to an aid station, received treatment, and then refused to be evacuated, choosing to return to his hard-pressed men instead. The fury of the enemy's great Western Front offensive swirled about the position held by T/Sgt. McGarity's small force, but so tenaciously did these men fight on orders to stand firm at all costs that they could not be dislodged despite murderous enemy fire and the breakdown of their communications. During the day the heroic squad leader rescued 1 of his friends who had been wounded in a forward position, and throughout the night he exhorted his comrades to repulse the enemy's attempts at infiltration. When morning came and the Germans attacked with tanks and infantry, he braved heavy fire to run to an advantageous position where he immobilized the enemy's lead tank with a round from a rocket launcher. Fire from his squad drove the attacking infantrymen back, and 3 supporting tanks withdrew. He rescued, under heavy fire, another wounded American, and then directed devastating fire on a light cannon which had been brought up by the hostile troops to clear resistance from the area. When ammunition began to run low, T/Sgt. McGarity, remembering an old ammunition hole about 100 yards distant in the general direction of the enemy, braved a concentration of hostile fire to replenish his unit's supply. By circuitous route the enemy managed to emplace a machinegun to the rear and flank of the squad's position, cutting off the only escape route. Unhesitatingly, the gallant soldier took it upon himself to destroy this menace single-handedly. He left cover, and while under steady fire from the enemy, killed or wounded all the hostile gunners with deadly accurate rifle fire and prevented all attempts to re-man the gun. Only when the squad's last round had been fired was the enemy able to advance and capture the intrepid leader and his men. The extraordinary bravery and extreme devotion to duty of T/Sgt. McGarity supported a remarkable delaying action which provided the time necessary for assembling reserves and forming a line against which the German striking power was shattered.

MEDAL OF HONOR PRESENTATION

President Harry Truman presented Vernon McGarity with the Medal of Honor on October 12, 1945, in Washington, DC.

LIFE AFTER WORLD WAR II

Vernon McGarity served in the Tennessee National Guard for twenty-eight years before retiring as a Lieutenant Colonel. Also, he was a counselor for the Veterans Administration for three decades before retirement.

HONORS

The Harrison-McGarity Bridge at Savannah, Tennessee, was named in honor of two Medal of Honor recipients: Bolden Harrison and Vernon McGarity.

McGarity's name is on a plaque at the Medal of Honor alcove inside the National Guard Memorial in Washington, DC.

In 2003 the Veterans of Foreign Wars named the 99th Regional Support Command in McGarity's honor.

The United States Postal Service honored Vernon McGarity by including him as one of the twelve Medal of Honor recipients on the Medal of Honor Forever stamps.

There is a plaque of Vernon McGarity in Bartlett, Tennessee, at Veterans Park.

The National Guard Armory in Paris, Tennessee, was named the Vernon McGarity National Guard Armory.

McGARITY'S DEATH

According to his daughter-in-law, Lee McGarity, Vernon McGarity died of cancer on May 21, 2013. He was survived by his son Vernon Roy McGarity and his wife, Lee McGarity. Vernon McGarity's wife of fifty-six years, Ethel, died in 1998, and their daughter Sharon also had predeceased him. His son, Roy, said his father did not like to talk about his war exploits. He eulogized his father by saying, "Daddy was quiet and strong. A father's love never dies nor does a family and son's love for him...He certainly was what I would call a true American hero."

Vernon McGarity's obituary was carried in at least thirty national, state, and local newspapers throughout the nation. Both CNN-TV and NBC-TV aired a two- minute piece about his life.

BURIAL SITE

Vernon McGarity was buried at the National Park Cemetery in Memphis, Tennessee.

TROY A. McGILL

BIRTH DATE: July 15, 1914

BIRTH PLACE: Knoxville, Tennessee

DEATH: March 4, 1944. KIA.

MEDAL OF HONOR ACTION: Los Negros, Admiralty Islands. March 4, 1944.

RANK: Sergeant

UNIT: Troop G, 5th Calvary Regiment, 1st Calvary Division

YEARS OF SERVICE: November 1940 - March 4, 1944

AWARDS: Medal of Honor, Purple Heart

CCC: S-54T, Maydelle, Texas. 1934. Three months.

TROY A. MCGILL

Troy McGill's parents, James H. McGill (1870-1936) and his wife, Pearl Pittman McGill (1886-1940), were native born Tennesseans who lived in the Mount Olive community of South Knoxville. Born in 1914, Troy was the third of six children. James was a poor farm worker. When he died in 1936, he left the family penniless. Pearl took various menial jobs just to keep the family intact.

Troy moved with his family to El Dorado, Arkansas, where he received eight years of education at the Rosehill Public School in Logan County. After leaving school in 1931, he worked at whatever job was available. In 1934 he enrolled in the CCC at Long View, Texas. He designated his father to receive his allotment.

Troy's CCC tour of duty was unremarkable. He served three months at Camp S -54T, a reforestation camp in Maydelle, Texas, before opting out of the C's to seek employment in the private sector. He received an honorable discharge. By this time young Troy, four inches short of six feet and weighing 140 pounds, had matured into an assured young man who wanted to work in the oil fields of Texas.

He took up residence in Kilgore, Texas, where he soon secured work as a driller's helper. He married a young lady, Jennie, from Kilgore, and he worked there until his entry into the military at Ada, Oklahoma, in November 1940. At the time of his enlistment, he was making $1800.00 a year.

EARLY MILITARY EXPERIENCE

After basic training Troy became part of the 5th Calvary Regiment, 1st Calvary Division of the US Army. His outfit remained in the United States until 1944 when it shipped out to Australia. Later, the Division embarked for the Los Negros invasion where it became engaged in combat for the first time.

ON TO THE PHILIPPINES

General MacArthur's return to the Philippines depended upon the capture and control of the Admiralty Islands for two reasons: to complete the isolation of two huge Japanese strongholds, Rabaul and Truk, and to acquire Steedler Harbor, an excellent shelter capable of supporting future operations in New Guinea and the Philippines.

During the period from late January through early March 1944, the Americans secured Manus and Los Negros Island but not without a significant cost. On February 29, 1944, the 1st Cavalry Division invaded Los Negros. After capturing an important airfield, the division soon found itself unexpectedly surrounded. Fortunately, the superior American naval and air force maintained withering pressure upon the Japanese which saved the day. By March 3 the starving Japanese garrison began its desperate banzai charges.

From the Forest to the Battlefield

A VIEW OF A JAPANESE BANZI ATTACK

Eyewitness accounts of a Japanese banzai attack dredge up horrible nightmares of a world gone mad. One survivor likened this mass attack to standing on a beach while in bare feet, "The water rolls in straight at you, but it also spills around your feet and then reconnects behind you, gaining renewed momentum as it again rushes past you toward the sea. It is uncontrollable." Still another survivor said, "It goes counter against everything I have learned religiously and militarily." John Basilone, a Medal of Honor recipient at Guadalcanal, killed so many advancing enemy troops in one such battle near Henderson Field that his assistant gunner had to remove piles of bodies, allowing Basilone a clear field of fire again. "The suicide charge was like a horde of ants," said another veteran, "madly crawling over its own dead to reach its objective."

Although banzai attacks remained a strong psychological threat, they were tactically futile and were negated by superior firepower such as the M1 semi-automatic rifle, the BAR, Thompson submachine guns, and machine gun emplacements. During such an insane charge, however, most defensive positions suffered unusually high casualties. Everyone agreed that the mass slaughter inflicted during these senseless attacks psychologically overwhelmed even the most hardened combat veteran.

Before the first light on March 4, 1944, nearly two hundred besieged Japanese troops charged a defensive position occupied by Sergeant McGill and eight of his squad members. Six men fell immediately. McGill and one other squad member survived. Ordering his comrade to the rear, McGill then single-handedly attacked the enemy armed only with his rifle, a combat knife, and 250 rounds of ammunition. After blasting his way through the enemy lines with his rifle, he then attacked the enemy with his knife, stabbing and slashing, while simultaneously using his rifle as a club. Along with McGill's body, Army investigators found 105 dead Japanese soldiers, many of whom had died of blunt force attack.

MEDAL OF HONOR CITATION

For conspicuous gallantry and intrepidity above and beyond the call of duty in action with the enemy at Los Negros Island, Admiralty Group, on 4 March 1944. In the early morning hours Sgt. McGill, with a squad of 8 men, occupied a revetment which bore the brunt of a furious attack by approximately 200 drink-crazed enemy troops. Although covered by crossfire from machine-guns on the right and left flank he could receive no support from the remainder of our troops stationed at his rear. All members of the squad were killed or wounded except Sgt. McGill and another man, whom he ordered to return to the next revetment. Courageously resolved to hold his position at all cost, he fired his weapon until it ceased to function. Then, with the enemy only 5 yards away, he charged from his foxhole in the face of certain death and clubbed the enemy with his rifle in hand-to-hand combat until he was killed. At dawn 105 enemy dead were found around his position. Sgt. McGill's intrepid stand was an inspiration to his comrades and a decisive factor in the defeat of a fanatical enemy.

MEDAL OF HONOR PRESENTATION

General Douglas MacArthur personally awarded the Medal of Honor to Troy McGill's siblings at a ceremony at Fort Sill, Oklahoma.

HONORS

The Military Hall of Fame of Oklahoma at Edmond, Oklahoma, a museum honoring Oklahoma's heroes, inducted Troy McGill into its Hall of Fame in November 2014.

A section of Interstate 40 near Knoxville, Tennessee, is named the Troy McGill Memorial Highway.

The East Tennessee Veterans Memorial, located at the north end of the World's Fair Park in Knoxville, contains the names of 6,222 fallen heroes as well as fourteen Medal of Honor recipients who were from Tennessee. Sergeant McGill's name is among those fourteen Medal of Honor recipients listed.

BURIAL SITE

Troy McGill's remains were reinterred at the Knoxville National Cemetery in Knoxville, Tennessee.

JUNIOR JAMES SPURRIER

BIRTH DATE: December 14, 1922

BIRTH PLACE: Castlewood, Russell County, Virginia

DEATH: February 25, 1984

MEDAL OF HONOR ACTION: Achain, Moselle, France. November 13, 1944.

RANK: Staff Sergeant

UNIT: Company G, 134th Infantry Regiment, 35th Infantry Division

YEARS OF SERVICE: September 1940 - 1951. Also, deployed in Korean War.

AWARDS: Medal of Honor, Distinguished Service Cross, Purple Heart (2), Combat Infantryman Badge.

CCC: F-25, Sugar Grove, Virginia. January - March 1940.

JUNIOR JAMES SPURRIER

James Ira Spurrier (1899-1978) and his wife, Ruby Lucille Nickles, (1901-1989) married in 1919. They had two boys, James and George, and two girls, Hope and Lee. James Senior worked for the railroad. Young James completed fourth grade before dropping out of school. Footloose, he worked at various odd jobs until he joined the Civilian Conservation Corps in 1940. After that short and unhappy experience, his next stop was the US Army.

CCC EXPERIENCE

James Spurrier joined the CCC on January 4, 1940. He served only three months His whole tour of duty was marred by disciplinary problems. His educational adviser said that he had the necessary skills, but his attitude was terrible. He was "pugnacious and argumentative," as well as being unwilling to work. Junior enrolled in two classes: elementary grammar and carpentry but he never attended them. He was also angry because his company commander had docked one day's pay for being AWOL. His main problem, however, stemmed from an Army dress shirt that he had stolen from the supply room. When charged with the theft, Junior admitted to it. In fact, he was wearing the shirt at the time. When asked why he took it, Spurrier said, "I liked it." After a hearing before his company commander, Spurrier was administratively dismissed from the CCC.

MILITARY EXPERIENCE

When James Spurrier enlisted, he listed his first name as Junior. He had filled in the wrong blanks. Since the Army is omniscient, the military recognized him as Junior for the remainder of his career. More significantly, Junior had found a home. Weapons fascinated him, and he quickly became proficient with the rifle, the .45 pistol, and the BAR. Additionally, he had a strong pitching arm, which enabled him to throw a hand grenade twenty yards farther than anyone in his outfit. He was a free spirit who had quickly learned the Army system. Junior knew just how far he could push the envelope without getting snared in the Army's discipline.

When the war broke out, Spurrier had already served in the Pacific. He returned stateside in early 1942 and became part of the 134th Infantry Regiment, 35th Infantry Division. The 35th trained in California and Fort Rucker, Alabama. In early May 1944, the division embarked for England where it arrived two weeks before D-Day. Crossing the Channel on June 7, 1944, the division received its baptism of fire three days later in the hedgerow country of Normandy. By the time St. Lo fell, the division had become an experienced combat unit, and Spurrier had matured into an acknowledged leader. The subsequent breakout from St. Lo opened the road to Paris. By the end of summer, Junior's division had moved deep into France and captured Nancy and Chambrey.

From the Forest to the Battlefield

By September 1944 Spurrier led a platoon of forty combat infantrymen. At Lay St. Christopher, France, he assaulted a heavily fortified German position. Riding a tank destroyer, he used a .50 caliber machine gun to overrun the emplacement. Then Junior, using hand grenades and his rifle, dismounted from the vehicle and destroyed a bunker. During this skirmish, he killed twelve German defenders and captured twenty-two others. For this action Spurrier received the Distinguished Service Cross.

When advancing toward Achain, France, on November 14, 1945, Lt. Colonel Frederick Roecker, a twenty-five-year-old battalion commander, apocryphally ordered, "Attack Achain! G Company from the east! Spurrier from the west!" The next seven hours became legendary. G Company's advance bogged down, unable to move because of heavy fire. But, armed in turn with a BAR, an M1 rifle, a German pistol, numerous hand grenades and two rocket launchers, Spurrier flanked the Germans and advanced fearlessly from the German rear. Under heavy fire he scattered the opposition as he efficiently moved through the village. An officer who knew Spurrier said, "His knowledge of weapons and the capability of each piece made him a highly efficient weapons platform." Afterward Spurrier said, "I didn't know how to aim some of those weapons but I caught on after a while."

Lieutenant Colonel Roecker who witnessed his attack added,

> This was not the move of a dumb, brave soldier; every move he made was carefully figured out. I saw him fire the different weapons, and I've never seen a cooler and smarter soldier under fire. He used one weapon until he ran out of ammo and then picked up another one and fiddled around with it until he started it going. We could have not taken the town that day without him.

Junior Spurrier caused panic among the Germans as he stalked his prey through the village. Many of them rushed into the safety of a barn. Later in the evening when he discovered their hiding place, he poured oil and gasoline at the base of the building and set the barn on fire. He captured four more Germans and shot another who refused to halt.

The successful capture of Achain took less than seven hours. During that time Spurrier killed twenty-five Germans and captured a number of others. In all, Spurrier had destroyed a whole detachment of the German Wehrmacht. One account of this battle credited Sergeant Spurrier of G Company, 2nd Battalion, with the capture of Achain, France. The two captured German officers agreed.

Spurrier's take on that day's event was "I fired a few rounds today. The Germans fired a few rounds at me. It beats me. I was paying no attention to what was coming off in Achain. I was shooting and ducking and I don't remember very much."

Overall, Spurrier's combat experience that day equaled his commanding officer's previous personal evaluation. "Spurrier is the meanest, toughest, and orneriest soldier in the war."

His unit advanced into Belgium in late December 1944 to stop the Germans during the Battle of the Bulge. There a mortar shell exploded nearby, knocking Junior unconscious. His comrades believed that their leader had been killed. A tough man to put down, he was soon leading his platoon back on the point. For this action, he received his second Purple Heart.

By late January 1945, the German offensive had been stopped, allowing his division to move into the Saar Region and toward the Rhine River in March 1945. Spurrier continued to lead numerous attacks, even though he had been recommended for the Medal of Honor. By V-E Day the 35th Infantry Division had fought its way deep into southern Germany.

MEDAL OF HONOR CITATION

For conspicuous gallantry and intrepidity at the risk of his life above and beyond the call of duty in action against the enemy at Achain, France on November 13, 1944. At two PM, Company G attacked the village of Achain from the east. Sergeant Spurrier, armed with a BAR, passed around the village and advanced alone. Attacking from the west, he immediately killed three Germans. He used at different times his BAR and M1 rifle, American and German rocket launchers, a German automatic pistol, and hand grenades, he continued his solitary attack against the enemy regardless of all types of small arms and automatic weapons. As a result of his heroic actions he killed an officer and twenty-four enlisted men and captured two officers and two enlisted men. His valor has shed fresh honor on the U.S. Armed Forces.

MEDAL OF HONOR PRESENTATION

General William Hood Simpson presented the Medal of Honor to Junior Spurrier on March 6, 1945.

JUNIOR SPURRIER'S TURBULENT CIVILIAN LIFE

This highly decorated hero returned to Bluefield, West Virginia, a hero. On July 4, 1945, the community held a huge Hero's Day Celebration that began with a long parade that slowly made its way through the town before twenty thousand people. After speeches had been given and a considerable monetary gift awarded to him, Spurrier rose to speak. He said, "Hello folks. Thanks a lot," and then sat down.

After that his personal life fell apart. This unsophisticated young man was a hero who had killed countless enemy soldiers and was acclaimed by all. It was heady stuff for a kid who loved to drink, fight, and raise hell. His five years in the Army had developed a mean, fighting machine. But by late 1945, however, there was no longer a call for his special talents. His drinking continued. When the North Koreans flooded into South Korea, he deployed to Korea, marking the third-time military duty took him to another continent. That tour, however, was a complete failure. He was no longer a one-man army. In fact, he was no longer in control of himself. When Junior returned stateside, he went AWOL. In the interim he was also arrested for stealing a horse. But because of his hero status, he avoided additional charges. At least he gained an honorable discharge.

SPURRIER'S LEGAL PROBLEMS

Junior went to Baltimore to visit Mrs. Mary Murphy whom he had met previously in West Virginia. By this time she had become frightened of Spurrier because she admitted, "He had smacked me around." Hearing that Junior was in town, she sought refuge at a friend's home. When Junior located her, he charged into the apartment while brandishing a pistol. After mutual recriminations he fired a pistol into the floor. When the police came, he admitted to the shooting but said, "A man who has had as much experience with guns as I have, wouldn't have shot at her that way." Nevertheless, the police charged him with numerous felony counts.

He was jailed and stood trial on the charges.

The media had a field day. One headline read: "Smacked But She Still Loves Her War Hero."

The jury threw out the charges of robbery and intent to kill but found him guilty on a deadly weapon charge. The judge sentenced him to two years in jail. Junior, however, appealed and was freed on bond. Ultimately, he successfully plea bargained. Junior agreed to leave the state immediately and to seek professional help for his alcohol problems.

As a curious sidelight to this sordid situation, Junior and Mrs. Murphy continued to proclaim their love for each other. She said, "I still love him and when I get a divorce, we will be married." Junior told the press, " I love her. She loves me, and we're back together again."

Soon after his appeal was settled, Junior returned to his television repair shop at Bluefield, West Virginia, without Mrs. Murphy.

However, the worst was yet to come.

Junior operated a TV repair business in Bluefield, West Virginia. It was never a sound business. To survive financially, he obtained a loan from a finance company under false pretenses. Subsequently arrested for fraud, he was convicted and sentenced to a West Virginia penitentiary for one to seven years in May 1969. One week before Christmas that same year, West Virginia Governor Arch Moore, issued a clemency order that released the former hero.

When released, he was met by his brother, Joe, who drove him to Limestone, Tennessee, to visit with his daughter, Lily, who was four. After that, he checked in at the Veterans Hospital in Johnson City, Tennessee, for the ravages of alcoholism had taken its toll. He said, "I can whip it so I'm quitting." For the remainder of his life, he was a frequent patient at that facility.

Junior moved to Tennessee where he lived with his daughter, Lily, who had been cared for by her aunt. Junior died in 1984 at age sixty-two.

JUNIOR SPURRIER'S HOMETOWN

Some confusion can surface regarding the hometown of a recipient of the Medal of Honor. For example, New Jersey claimed the birthright of John W. Dutko who actually was a native of Indiana County, Pennsylvania. It took over forty years for the Dutko family to resolve that confusion. So it was with Junior Spurrier. At least four towns in Virginia and Kentucky lay claim to his birth place. The bottom line, however, was that he spent most of his life living in or near Bluefield, West Virginia, thereby giving that town legitimate claim to him.

MEDAL OF HONOR IS FOUND

Somehow, Junior Spurrier's Medal of Honor disappeared. Certainly, that seems logical because of his chaotic life. For over sixty years no one had known its whereabouts. In 2011 Craig Corkrean, Police Chief of Granville, West Virginia, visited his own mother's home in White Sulpher Springs, West Virginia. There he found Spurrier's medals, including a Bronze Star, the Combat Infantryman Badge, and the Medal of Honor locked in his father's safe. It remains a mystery how the medals ended up in the elder Corkrean's possession. Nevertheless, this discovery led to the medals being transferred to the Those Who Served Museum in Mercer County, West Virginia.

Spurrier's sisters, Lee Spurrier Snead and Hope Spurrier Mills, were in attendance for that day when the museum accepted these valuable gifts. Mrs. Mills said that her brother never talked about his war experiences. She did add, however, "He was a brave young man. He knew how to save service men's lives."

Hershel Williams, a Medal of Honor recipient, spoke at the ceremony.

HONORS

Spurrier was one of twelve US Army soldiers awarded the Distinguished Service Cross as well as the Medal of Honor during World War II. He took his place alongside General Douglas MacArthur, General Jonathan Wainwright, and two former CCC men: Herbert H. Burr and James M. Logan.

In March 2012 Governor Steve Beshear unveiled a bronze plaque listing Kentucky's sixty Medal of Honor recipients. Junior Spurrier's name was among them.

Junior Spurrier was honored by Mercer County, West Virginia, as the "Best Fighting Soldier in World War II" during the dedication of a memorial at the Those Who Served Museum. Tony Witlow, director of the museum said, "Spurrier was a super hero whose exploits have no equal." He also added, "Audie Murphy received one more medal than Junior did. We believe it was a Good Conduct Medal."

Spurrier was inducted into the 35th Division's Hall Of Fame in Topeka, Kansas, on September 26, 2009.

It is believed that Junior Spurrier inspired the PFC William G. Kirby character of the long running TV series *Combat* during the mid-1960s. (Kirby's character was that of a quick tempered-argumentative "bad boy" and a fierce fighter who once broke up a French cafe in a brawl over a woman.)

Spurrier was the only former CCC enrollee and Medal of Honor recipient who had played professional baseball. He pitched for the Virginia Leafs of Galax, Virginia, a Class D Blue Ridge League. According to Bob Lemke's blog, "Junior pitched in two games, winning one and losing the other. In his brief baseball career, he gave up seven hits, five runs and five walks."

BURIAL SITE

Junior James Spurrier's remains are interred at the Mountain Home National Cemetery in Johnson City, Tennessee.

 Bill Archer of *the Bluefield Daily Telegraph* best summed up Spurrier's tormented life: "As a soldier, Spurrier did all you could ever ask."

VAN T. BARFOOT

BIRTH DATE: June 15, 1919

BIRTH PLACE: Edinburg, Mississippi

DEATH: March 2, 2012

MEDAL OF HONOR ACTION: Carano, Italy. May 23, 1944.

RANK: Technical Sergeant

UNIT: Company L, 3rd Battalion 157th Infantry Regiment, 45th Infantry Division

YEARS OF SERVICE: March 16, 1940 - 1974

AWARDS: Medal of Honor, Purple Heart (3), Silver Star, Bronze Star, Others

CCC: SCS-3, Lexington, Mississippi. October 1937 - April 1938. P-227, Timber, Oregon. April 1938 - September 1939.

VAN T. BARFOOT

It can be said that Van T. Barfoot defended the Stars and Stripes his entire life. This patriotic man was born Van Thurman Barfoot on June 15, 1919, in Edinburg, Mississippi. Later in life he would change his name to Van Thomas Barfoot. He was the sixth child born to Sim (1883-1969) and Martha Elizabeth Barfoot (1884-1976). Van grew up on a thirty-five acre cotton farm along with five sisters and three brothers. The Barfoot's were hard workers with the children often being dismissed from school at noon to work in the fields.

As a boy Van was one of the best frog hunters in the Pearl River swamps. In a 1944 War Department interview, his father recalled many dinners of frog legs, the product of Van's hunting trips with a carbide lamp and a .22 rifle. He also was a good shot with a twelve gauge shotgun and hunted squirrels and ducks. When not working in the fields or hunting, the young Barfoot enjoyed sandlot baseball. Van attended Edinburg Elementary School and completed eighth grade. Inspired by a devout Christian mother, Van regularly attended the Church of God. His grandmother was Choctaw, but Barfoot himself was not an official member of the Choctaw nation. Although he was eligible, his parents never officially enrolled him.

CCC EXPERIENCE

Barfoot signed on with the CCC at Yazoo City, Mississippi, on October 8, 1937. He was assigned to Camp SCS-3, Company 4426, in Lexington, Mississippi. Van reported that he previously had been a laborer for eight months working on a school building. The twenty-five-dollar allotment was sent to his father, Sim Barfoot, in Carthage, Mississippi. The eighteen-year-old Van was a good sized CCC boy at six foot three inches and weighed in at 166 pounds. With the average enrollee being five foot six inches and weighing approximately 130 pounds, Barfoot towered over his fellow workers! At the time of his enrollment, Van indicated his occupational preferences were general mechanic or stock farmer. At SCS-3, Barfoot received excellent performance ratings in KP and soil conservation work. Barfoot completed his enlistment period on April 11, 1938, and reenrolled for another six months.

This time Van was assigned to Camp Reehers, P-227, Company 5461, in Timber, Oregon. Barfoot spent a week at conditioning camp at Fort McClellan, Alabama, and then spent four days traveling from the 4th Corps area to the 9th Corps area. Camp Reehers was located above the Nehalem river within a forest of huge Douglas fir, cedar, alder, and maple trees. The area would later become the Tillamook State Forest. The CCC men improved roads, built trails, constructed telephone lines, and maintained fire breaks. Van received excellent ratings as a camp utility man from April 1938 through May 1939. Barfoot had found his niche in the CCC and reenrolled on October 1, 1938, and once again on April 1, 1939.

His size and speed were an asset for boxing matches in the CCC and later in the Army. Van was a fire crew leader from May until September 1939 with satisfactory ratings. He was appointed assistant leader on

From the Forest to the Battlefield

July 1, 1939. While at Camp Reehers, Van took classes in arithmetic, grammar, writing, forestry, woodworking, electricity, carpentry, photography, and journalism. He received V.G. (Very Good) grades in every class. His avocational interests were reading, movies, and softball. He told the camp adviser he was anxious to get ahead in life. The adviser reported that Barfoot was honest, dependable, and had very good personal qualities as well as a good interest in the education program. The camp superintendent reported Barfoot was "dependable and a very good worker." Barfoot attempted to reenroll one more time in September of 1939 and was sent to conditioning camp at Fort McClellan, Alabama. However, he was discharged on September 24, 1939, when deemed "ineligible for reenrollment because of length of service." After two years in the Civilian Conservation Corps, it was time to move on.

MILITARY EXPERIENCE

In March 1940 Van T. Barfoot walked to the Leake County courthouse to enlist in the Army. He was assigned to the 1st Infantry Division. After basic training he participated in maneuvers in Louisiana and Puerto Rico. Barfoot was promoted to sergeant and assigned to the newly activated Amphibious Force Atlantic Fleet in Quantico, Virginia. The unit was deactivated in 1943, and Van was then assigned to the 157th Regiment , 45th Infantry Division which shipped out to Europe.

In the final push to defeat the Axis powers of Italy and Germany, the Allied powers invaded Italy in a series of three landings. The Italian Campaign, often called the Road to Rome, turned into a long, brutal slog through treacherous mountain terrain. Technical Sergeant Barfoot earned a Bronze Star for valor during Operation Husky, the amphibious assault of Sicily, in July 1943. Two months later, he participated in Operation Avalanche, the invasion of southern Italy with the landing at Salerno.

Barfoot was awarded the Silver Star for action on December 9 and 10, 1943, near Pozzilli, Italy. While guiding a nighttime reconnaissance party, Barfoot discovered German machine gun nests. He attacked one nest with his Tommy gun and killed two crew members. He silenced another nest with a hand grenade. The next night he led another party into German territory and destroyed another machine gun emplacement. He killed three crew members and captured two German soldiers. Sergeant Barfoot was now well prepared for the last landing in the series, Operation Shingle, the landing at Anzio.

In late January 1944, the 157th landed at Anzio and began moving inland rapidly. The Allied advance was stopped at times by counterattacks by German reinforcements. By May of that year, Barfoot's unit had spent several weeks in a defensive position near the town of Carano. During this time Barfoot conducted patrols day and night where he mentally mapped out the terrain and minefields in front of enemy positions.

Early in the morning of May 23, 1944, Barfoot's unit was ordered to attack. Lead squads approached the German minefields under heavy fire. Technical Sergeant Barfoot requested to lead a squad as he was very familiar with the lanes through the minefields. Advancing on a line through shallow ditches and depressions in the terrain, he destroyed a machine gun with a hand grenade. Then he moved to the next gun emplacement where he killed two soldiers and wounded three others. When Barfoot approached the third machine gun position, the Germans manning the gun surrendered after watching Barfoot's methodical assault.

Later in the day, the Germans, in retaliation, organized a counterattack sending three Mark VI tanks toward his platoon. Standing seventy-five yards in front of the lead tank, Van disabled the tank by destroying the tread with a bazooka grenade launcher. He then killed three of the German tank crew members with a Thompson submachine gun as they attempted to escape. The other two tanks abruptly changed direction having witnessed the destruction. Next Barfoot continued further into enemy territory and destroyed a recently abandoned German fieldpiece with a demolition charge placed in the breech. Sergeant Barfoot ended his day by helping two seriously wounded men from his squad walk nearly a mile to safety. This kid from Mississippi had a full day capturing a total of seventeen enemy soldiers and killing seven.

On June 21, 1944, Barfoot was commissioned a Second Lieutenant. By September his unit had moved from Italy to the French Rhone Valley. There Barfoot was ordered to division headquarters where he was informed he had been awarded the Medal of Honor. Given a choice of returning to the United States for the ceremony or receiving the medal in the field, Van chose the latter so his men could attend. Lieutenant General Alexander Patch awarded him the medal in Epinal, France, on September 28, 1944. Throughout his military career, Barfoot was always considerate and fiercely loyal to his men.

Barfoot remained humble about his World War II heroism throughout his life. "People say I did something miraculous. I don't think so. I don't think I did any more than any good American would do." Barfoot would often be asked how he found the courage to perform such heroic actions on the battlefield. His response was, "Why should I fear when I have the Lord? The Lord will look after me." A man of deep faith, Barfoot carried a pocket Bible from his wife's mother throughout the war. He would read the Bible to his men. At each military post, he taught Sunday School.

MEDAL OF HONOR CITATION

For conspicuous gallantry and intrepidity at the risk of life above and beyond the call of duty on 23 May 1944, near Carano, Italy. With his platoon heavily engaged during an assault against forces well entrenched on commanding ground, 2d Lt. Barfoot (then Tech. Sgt.) moved off alone upon the enemy left flank. He crawled to the proximity of 1 machinegun nest and made a direct hit on it with a hand grenade, killing 2 and wounding 3 Germans. He continued along the German defense line to another machinegun emplacement, and with his Thompson Submachine gun killed 2 and captured 3 soldiers. Members of another enemy machinegun crew then abandoned their position and gave themselves up to Sgt. Barfoot.

Leaving the prisoners for his support squad to pick up, he proceeded to mop up positions in the immediate area, capturing more prisoners and bringing his total count to 17. Later that day, after he had reorganized his men and consolidated the newly captured ground, the enemy launched a fierce armored counterattack directly at his platoon positions. Securing a bazooka, Sgt. Barfoot took up an exposed position directly in front of 3 advancing Mark VI tanks. From a distance of 75 yards his first shot destroyed the track of the leading tank, effectively disabling it, while the other 2 changed direction toward the flank. As the crew of the disabled tank dismounted, Sgt. Barfoot killed 3 of them with his Tommy gun. He continued onward into enemy terrain and destroyed a recently abandoned German fieldpiece with a demolition charge placed in the breech. While returning to his platoon position, Sgt. Barfoot, though greatly fatigued by his Herculean efforts, assisted two of his seriously wounded men 1,700 yards to a position of safety. Sgt. Barfoot's extraordinary heroism, demonstration of magnificent valor, and aggressive determination in the face of pointblank fire were a perpetual inspiration to his fellow soldiers.

LIFE AFTER WORLD WAR II

Lieutenant Barfoot headed home to marry the love of his life, Norma Louise Davis. Norma, a school teacher, frequently wrote letters to Barfoot's parents during the war. They had become engaged while Van was stationed in Virginia but agreed to delay their marriage until after the war. The ceremony took place in Mathews, Virginia, on November 4, 1944.

Having grown up in the segregated South, Barfoot was noted for a comment he made in 1945 regarding Afro-Americans. Theodore G. Bilbo, a staunch segregationist, asked Barfoot if he had much trouble with African American soldiers during the war. To Bilbo's embarrassment Barfoot responded, "I found out after I did some fighting in this war that the colored boys fight just as good as the white boys. I've changed my idea a lot about colored people since I got into this war and so have a lot of other boys from the South."

Van T. Barfoot served in both the Korean and Viet Nam wars. In 1960, at the age of forty, Barfoot completed flight training as a Major and was assigned to the legendary Howze Board. The Board, named after General Hamilton H. Howze, was tasked to review and test integrating helicopters into the Army. Formally known as the Tactical Mobility Requirements Board, this group established the idea of air mobility and modern Army aviation.

During the Viet Nam War, Barfoot again answered the nation's call as Deputy Aviation Officer. During 1967-68, he flew 177 combat hours as a helicopter pilot, earning eleven Air Medals and the Legion of Merit. He was a Senior Army Aviator in both fixed and rotary wing aircraft with fourteen years of aviation service.

From the Forest to the Battlefield

Blake McIlwain, reflected on his time with Barfoot at Fort Hood in 1965. McIlwain was thirty-five years old at the time and Barfoot's Executive Officer. "Physically he is a big man, about 6-foot-7, dark hair when I knew him because he is Choctaw, but he has blue eyes," McIlwain said. "Believe me, he didn't have to tell you to do something twice. He had that look about him and the physical stature to go with it. But usually, he was gentle and soft spoken." Furthermore, McIlwain stated, "Van Barfoot is one of the most spectacular human beings that ever lived. His advice to me was, "Take care of your troops and they will take care of you... He inspired me to go to Viet Nam and be what I can be." Barfoot and McIlwain went their separate ways in Viet Nam with McIlwain piloting helicopter gunships with the 1st Calvary Division and Barfoot commanding an aviation battalion. Barfoot's advice to McIllwain would serve him well for three tours of duty in Viet Nam.

In 1974 Barfoot retired as a Colonel and senior Army Adviser to the Virginia Army National Guard. A highly-decorated soldier, Colonel Barfoot had dedicated thirty-four years of his life to his country.

RETIREMENT LIFE

Van T. Barfoot lived a quiet, rural life with his wife, Norma, on a farm in Amelia County, Virginia. He maintained a vegetable garden, filled bird feeders, and enjoyed catching catfish in his private pond. On March 20, 1992, Barfoot's beloved wife, Norma, passed away. She was sixty-nine years old and they had been married for forty-eight years.

In the summer of 2009, Van moved to the Richmond suburbs to be closer to his daughter, Margaret. Van faithfully awoke each morning at 6:00 A.M. to raise the American flag with a military salute on the lawn of his Henrico, Virginia, townhouse. At dusk, he lowered and folded the flag, hugging the triangular bundle to his chest as he walked back inside.

Barfoot's entire life was rooted in Christian faith. He read the Bible up to three times daily and recalled reading his Bible before and praying through the action that earned him the Medal of Honor. "I always say, 'They held my hand.' That is, my mother and my wife. And anything I accomplished, it was based on Christian love."

In a 1999 *Richmond Times-Dispatch* interview, Barfoot stated his close-knit, churchgoing family was his anchor. "That's the basis of my life as a commander and a civilian. Furthermore, I like to tell about life without war stories. I've always had something more important in my life than war and the military."

Upon his death in 2012, his daughter, Margaret, described her father: "He was a very selfless man, a fiercely independent man. Although the military was a large part of his life, that wasn't him. He was all about family and faith and honor. He believed in serving in the community. He was always out in the community."

HONORS

The Sitter & Barfoot Veterans Care Center is named after Colonel Barfoot and Carl Sitter, both of whom are Medal of Honor recipients. Colonel Sitter, like Colonel Barfoot, served in both World War II and the Korean War. The Center is located on the campus of the McGuire Veterans Medical Center in Richmond, Virginia.

On October 9, 2009, the portion of the Mississippi Highway 16 that runs from Carthage to Barfoot's hometown in Edinburg to the border between Leake and Neshoba counties was named the Van T. Barfoot Medal of Honor Highway. At the time of the highway dedication, Barfoot said, "Don't place me on a pedestal. I am just a country boy who grew up at Rye's Creek and was very fortunate that God has been very good to me."

THE FLAG CONTROVERSY

Van Barfoot made national headlines in 2009 when he erected a twenty-one foot flag pole at his residence without the permission of the Sussex Square Homeowners Association in Henrico County, Virginia. The Association allowed angled poles attached to houses but did not address other flag poles in its bylaws. Van Barfoot was threatened with legal action unless the pole was removed "for aesthetic reasons." After his son-in-law reported the story to a local radio station, the news story was soon picked up by national news networks. "There's never been a day in my life or a place I've lived in my life that you couldn't fly the American flag," Barfoot said in an interview with the *Richmond Times-Dispatch.* The ninety year old veteran contested the order and the ensuing furor drew the support of veterans, two Virginia senators, a former Virginia governor, and White House Press Secretary, Robert Gibbs. The newspaper ran an article about the dispute and asked readers their opinion. There were 147,171 responses with 96 percent in favor of Barfoot being allowed to fly the flag any way he wanted. Consequently, the homeowners association dropped its request on December 8, 2009, and Barfoot continued to fly the American flag.

FINAL SALUTE

Van Thomas Barfoot died on March 2, 2012, at age ninety-two. He tripped near his front door and hit his head on some bricks. A skull fracture led to bleeding of the brain, resulting in his death. Barfoot was survived by his daughter, Margaret, three sons: Jim, Van Jr., and Odell; a sister, Freddie; twelve grandchildren, and six great-grandchildren. Colonel Barfoot is buried at H.C. Smither Memorial Cemetery in Hudgins, Mathews County, Virginia.

In memory and in respect for Barfoot, Governor Robert McDonnell ordered that both the American flag and the flag of the Commonwealth of Virginia be lowered at half mast over the Capitol building at sunrise on March 5, 2012, and remain at half mast until sunset.

Governor McDonnell championed Barfoot's flag dispute back in 2009 when he signed legislation, sponsored by Senator Richard Stuart, that prohibited homeowners associations from banning the proper display of the United States flag. This was a tribute to a patriotic man who said, "In the time I have left, I plan to continue to fly the American flag without interference." He did!

ROY W. HARMON

BIRTH DATE: May 3, 1916

BIRTH PLACE: Talala, Oklahoma

DEATH: July 12, 1944. KIA.

MEDAL OF HONOR ACTION: Casaglia, Italy. July 12, 1944.

RANK: Sergeant

UNIT: 362nd Infantry Regiment, 91st Infantry Division

YEARS OF SERVICE: November 17, 1942 - July 12, 1944

AWARDS: Medal of Honor, Purple Heart, Combat Infantryman Badge, Others

CCC: SCS-2, Stillwater, Oklahoma. April - September 1935. SCS-11, Guthrie, Oklahoma. October 1935 - March 1937.

ROY W. HARMON

Roy E. Harmon and his wife, Rachael, had fourteen children. He had an eighth-grade education and Rachael was a high school graduate. Roy was a blacksmith in Talala, Oklahoma. Theirs was a hardscrabble life. The elder Harmon maintained that his family was part Native American but never pushed the matter because of the stigma attached to having Native American heritage. Rachael died in 1934. Like so many from the Sooner State during the 1930s, Roy E. Harmon moved to California, settling in Pixley, sixty miles south and east of Fresno, the heart of the rich San Joaquin Valley. He died in California, a transplanted Okie. Two of their sons died during World War II: Oliver and Roy.

Roy W. Harmon, called Bill by his family, was born on May 3, 1916, in Talala. He went to Harding Elementary School in Yale, Oklahoma, from 1923 to 1929 before dropping out in the seventh grade. He remained unemployed for almost six years except for a brief stint in which he worked for Paul Howerton, a local dairy owner. Roy never earned more than three dollars a week before his joining the CCC.

CCC EXPERIENCE

In 1935 Harmon enlisted in the CCC. Like most enrollees, he was undernourished, short and skinny. His father received his allotment. From April 1935 until September of that same year, Harmon served at SCS-2 at Stillwater, Oklahoma, as a general laborer. Much of his work there involved building check dams that were necessary to retard soil erosion. When his enrollment expired, he enlisted again. This time Roy and his whole company moved to SCS-11 at Guthrie, Oklahoma, thirty-five miles southwest of Stillwater. There, Harmon planted trees and continued working on other soil erosion projects. At SCS-11, he took a class in agronomy and another in safety. His educational adviser judged him to be a fair student who had little interest in taking classes. His camp supervisor, however, evaluated his work as good throughout his eighteen months at SCS-11. After having completed two years in the CCC, he received an honorable discharge in March 1937.

Returning home from the CCC, Harmon failed to find any employment. At the end of that decade, his father decided to move his family to California. Once there, Roy and his sons worked as farm hands. On November 17, 1942, young Roy was drafted from Pixley, California, into the United States Army.

MILITARY EXPERIENCE

Harmon's first assignment was as a rifleman with the 1st Battalion, 362nd Infantry Regiment of the 91st Division, a newly commissioned unit stationed at Camp White near Medford, Oregon. Because of the division's total inexperience, the entire division underwent a thirty-nine-week training regime ranging from basic military fundamentals to advanced military tactics and maneuvers. Only then did the division engage in War Games in Oregon and Washington. Still considered a training division, the 91st Division shipped out to North Africa for further training. Although one of the division's regimental combat teams saw action on the Italian Gustav Line in late January 1944, it was not until six months later that the entire division entered combat for the first time, south of the Arno River. By this time Harmon had become a sergeant.

As his company approached the small Italian town of Casaglia, it was blocked by heavy machine gun fire coming from three strategically placed haystacks. While most of the company took cover, one platoon that had the point had been trapped and was in danger of being wiped out. Orders came down to Harmon that he and his men were to silence the camouflaged machine gun nests.

As Sergeant James F. Kenny tried to move forward, he found himself in a small draw along with Harmon and one other soldier. He recounted what happened next:

> The machine guns had us covered and the snipers were picking away at us. One was shooting at a man near Sergeant Harmon. Harmon stood up and told the man to be ready to shoot. When the sniper shifted his fire to Sergeant Harmon, the man who had been shot at, picked the sniper off. Then the Sergeant went after the haystacks. When he left us, he said, 'I'm going to see what I can do about this.' He crawled from the little depression that we had found and went straight for the first haystack seventy-five yards away.

Technical Sergeant Fred P. Crane, an eyewitness to Harmon's heroic action, testified

> From our distance of 300 yards, the tracer bullets we fired failed to set fire to the haystacks. I saw the sergeant take his phosphorus grenades and crawl toward the nearest haystack...Dirt was knocked up all around him, and I saw him get hit. He was still for a minute and then he started to crawl again. At twenty-five yards he threw a grenade and it set the haystack afire. He killed some Germans who tried to escape with a submachine gun. He moved on to the second position in the same way and set that stack on fire. When he started for the third, I saw him get hit again. But he went on. He was running to cover the ground faster. As he neared the haystack, he began to crawl the last twenty yards. He rose to his knees and threw his grenade and they shot him. Somehow, he got up and tossed his last grenade before he fell dead.

THE MEDAL OF HONOR CITATION

He was an acting squad leader when heavy machinegun fire from enemy positions, well dug in on commanding ground and camouflaged by haystacks, stopped his company's advance and pinned down 1 platoon where it was exposed to almost certain annihilation. Ordered to rescue the beleaguered platoon by neutralizing the German automatic fire, he led his squad forward along a draw to the right of the trapped unit against 3 key positions which poured murderous fire into his helpless comrades. When within range, his squad fired tracer bullets in an attempt to set fire to the 3 haystacks which were strung out in a loose line directly to the front, 75, 150, and 250 yards away. Realizing that this attack was ineffective, Sgt. Harmon ordered his squad to hold their position and voluntarily began a 1-man assault. Carrying white phosphorus grenades and a submachine gun, he skillfully took advantage of what little cover the terrain afforded and crept to within 25 yards of the first position. He set the haystack afire with a grenade, and when 2 of the enemy attempted to flee from the inferno, he killed them with his submachine gun. Crawling toward the second machine gun emplacement, he attracted fire and was wounded; but he continued to advance and destroyed the position with hand grenades, killing the occupants. He then attacked the third machinegun, running to a small knoll, then crawling over ground which offered no concealment or cover. About halfway to his objective, he was again wounded. But he struggled ahead until within 20 yards of the machinegun nest, where he raised himself to his knees to throw a grenade. He was knocked down by direct enemy fire. With a final, magnificent effort, he again arose, hurled the grenade and fell dead, riddled by bullets. His missile fired the third position, destroying it. Sgt. Harmon's extraordinary heroism, gallantry, and self-sacrifice saved a platoon from being wiped out, and made it possible for his company to advance against powerful enemy resistance.

MEDAL OF HONOR PRESENTATION

President Harry S. Truman awarded Roy W. Harmon's medal posthumously to his father, Roy E. Harmon, on October 21, 1945. Harmon was one of seven Native American men awarded the Medal of Honor during World War II.

HONORS

The city of Pixel, California, named its airport in honor of Harmon.

Two buildings were named for Harmon at the Presidio, 6th Army Headquarters in San Francisco: the Harmon Army Reserve Building and Harmon Hall, USAR Center.

As a class project, the students at the Oologah-Talala High School conducted a study on Roy Harmon. They attempted to locate his family but their search turned up only one sister who lived in California. That inability to locate Harmon's other siblings demonstrates how tenuous family ties are during times of major stress. The students also raised money for a monument in Sergeant Harmon's memory.

The city of Tulsa, Oklahoma, saluted the Oklahoma Medal of Honor recipients on May 8, 2011. Since Tulsa is only thirty-five miles from Talala, the city called Harmon as one of their own.

BURIAL SITE

Roy W. Harmon's remains are interred in the Florence American Cemetery in Florence, Italy.

ANTHONY L. KROTIAK

BIRTH DATE: August 15, 1915

BIRTH PLACE: Chicago, Illinois

DEATH: May 8, 1945. KIA.

MEDAL OF HONOR ACTION: Balete Pass, Luzon, Philippines Islands. May 8, 1945.

RANK: Private First Class

UNIT: Company I, 148th Infantry Regiment, 37th Infantry Division

YEARS OF SERVICE: November 1941 - May 8, 1945

AWARDS: Medal of Honor, Purple Heart, Combat Infantryman Badge

CCC: DG-118, Elko, Nevada. January - June 1939.

ANTHONY L. KROTIAK

Anton Krotjak came to Chicago in 1901 from Czechoslovakia. Although he could not speak English, he was able to find a job easily in the rapidly growing economy of that city. Blessed with a keen mechanical ability, he took employment with a railroad car company where he worked into the 1940s. Carolina Svidon also emigrated from Slovakia. They met in Chicago when she was eighteen and Anton was twenty-one. They married in 1908. From this union came nine children, four boys and five girls. Anthony and John, twin brothers, were born in 1915. The Krotiaks anglicized their Slovakian name and lived in a large house valued at $10,000.00. They even had a radio! Even though Anton and Carolina had no formal education, they valued it a great deal. As a result, the two older sisters, Susan and Anna, graduated from high school and by 1931 were employed as a secretary and stenographer respectively. Ultimately all the children received a sound education. One boy, Rudolph, had some college experience.

Anthony L. Krotiak was a short, stocky, blue-eyed blond young man who grew up on the rough and tumble South LaSalle Street, a major north-south thoroughfare in Chicago. He learned early on to take care of himself. He graduated from high school, Pullman Technical School, where he majored in electricity classes. After knocking around the city streets for a couple of years, he found employment as a tunnel switchman at a local factory. This job lasted for one year. By the beginning of January 1937, he was jobless again and remained so until 1939 when he joined the CCC.

CCC EXPERIENCE

After completing a conditioning camp at Camp Skokie Valley in Illinois, Krotiak was stationed at Camp DG-118 at Elko, Nevada. The camp provided a broad range of work ranging from rodent control to well drilling and from erosion control to road and bridge construction. His record indicates that he was a pick and shovel man. His rating was always satisfactory, and Anthony missed no time because of unauthorized absences. While there, he took a couple of classes and learned how to drive a truck. He received an honorable discharge in early summer of 1939.

MILITARY EXPERIENCE

Two weeks before Pearl Harbor, Anthony joined the United States Army and received basic training at Camp Wheeler, Georgia. After basic training he was assigned to the 148th Infantry Regiment, part of the 37th Infantry Division known as the "Buckeye Division." The entire unit moved north to Indiantown Gap, Pennsylvania, for additional training before receiving its overseas orders.

The next stop was the Fiji Islands. After undergoing amphibious maneuvers, the division moved to Guadalcanal for more training. That summer the division helped secure New Georgia, part of the Western

Province of the Solomon Islands, two hundred miles north and west from Guadalcanal. The march to liberate the Philippines had begun, and Private Krotiak became part of this necessary movement.

After another stop at Guadalcanal, the division moved on to Bougainville. From November 1943 to March 1944, Krotiak's outfit participated in bitter jungle warfare. By early spring 1944, much of Bougainville had been neutralized, thereby allowing his unit to begin training on that same island in preparation for the Invasion on Luzon, the main Island of the Philippines.

In January 1945 troops of the 37rd Division waded ashore at Lingayen Gulf for the final assault to secure Luzon from the Japanese. Within two months, Clark Field, a vital airfield, and Manila had been liberated. After that, the 37rd Division advanced into northwestern Luzon in an effort to capture the retreating, but still very dangerous, Japanese army. At this point Krotiak had successfully slogged through the jungles of New Georgia and Bougainville before his participation in the Philippine Campaign. He had received the Purple Heart and later was promoted to Private First Class. In October 1944 he received the Combat Infantryman Badge, a foot soldier's most treasured award.

KROTIAK'S DEATH

Krotiak's Company I, part of the 148th Infantry Regiment, was assigned to take Hill B at Balete Pass on May 8, 1945. As his company began to advance, it came under heavy offensive fire from the Japanese forces overlooking the Americans. This forced Krotiak's company to hastily build defensive entrenchments. As Acting Squad Leader, he found himself sharing a foxhole with Sergeant Harry Styles of New York, Private First Class Paul C. Joslyn of Missouri, and two other men.

According to Sergeant Styles, "When we were digging in, the Japs on top of Hill B began firing and tossing hand grenades down at us. I jumped into the trench with Private Krotiak."

Private Joslyn said

> Three grenades rolled past us, but the fourth landed in the center of our group. Pushing us aside, Private Krotiak smashed it into the ground with his rifle butt. Then he threw himself over the grenade when it exploded. His body caught all the fragments, shielding us.

MEDAL OF HONOR CITATION

Krotiak was an acting squad leader, directing his men in consolidating a newly won position on Hill B when the enemy concentrated small arms fire and grenades upon him and 4 others, driving them to cover in an abandoned Japanese trench. A grenade thrown from above landed in the center of the group. Instantly pushing his comrades aside and jamming the grenade into the earth with his rifle butt, he threw himself over it, making a shield of his body to protect the other men. The grenade exploded under him, and he died a few minutes later. By his extraordinary heroism in deliberately giving his life to save those of his comrades, Pfc. Krotiak set an inspiring example of utter devotion and self-sacrifice which reflects the highest traditions of the military service.

MEDAL OF HONOR PRESENTATION

On February 13, 1944, Major General Louis A. Craig, Chief of the 6th Service Command, issued the Medal of Honor posthumously to Krotiak's father. At the ceremonies Private Krotiak's mother, Carolina, a sister, Mrs. Mary Ganier, and John, his twin brother, looked on in admiration. Rudolph, the Krotiak's fourth son, a lieutenant in the US Navy, was on active duty in the Pacific at the time.

HONORS

Krotiak is honored by the Polish Legion of American Veterans.

In 2009 the Soldiers of Company B, 1st Battalion, 48th Infantry Regiment, Ohio National Guard established the Soldiers-Krotiak Award.

BURIAL SITE

Anthony L. Krotiak is buried at Holy Sepulcher Cemetery in Alsip, Illinois.

JOSEPH E. MULLER

BIRTH DATE: June 28, 1908

BIRTH PLACE: Holyoke, Massachusetts

DEATH: May 16, 1945. KIA.

MEDAL OF HONOR ACTION: Near Ishimmi, Okinawa Islands. May 16, 1945.

RANK: Sergeant

UNIT: Company B, 3rd Battalion, 305th Infantry Regiment, 77th Infantry Division

YEARS OF SERVICE: March 1942 - May 16, 1945

AWARDS: Medal of Honor, Purple Heart, Combat Infantryman Badge

CCC: Army - 1, Fort Devens, Massachusetts . May 1933 - June 1934.

JOSEPH E. MULLER

Joseph Edward Muller was born on July 28, 1908, in Lowell, Massachusetts, and was the fourth of eleven children. Later, his family moved to Holyoke to the Second Ward, a residential section composed of small apartment buildings adjacent to the town's industrial center. His father, Lewis, a machinist, died during the Great Influenza Epidemic, and later his mother remarried. Joseph went to Holy Rosary Catholic Grammar School. Then he went to Taunton, near Boston, but returned when he was eighteen to work at the local paper company. During that time he enlisted in the Massachusetts National Guard where he served from 1926 to 1927. Later, he became employed as a sign painter. Like so many Americans, he lost his job in 1931 and did not work again until he entered the CCC.

CCC EXPERIENCE

Muller enrolled in the CCC in early May 1933 when the CCC had been operational for only six weeks. He was immediately assigned as a laborer but within weeks, became an office orderly, a post he held until his discharge the following June. Euphemistically, an orderly was called "a dog robber," that is, someone who waits on officers. A carryover from the Great War, a "dog-robber" typically looked after officers, cleaned and pressed their uniforms, brought them their meals, posted their schedules, shined their shoes, and did other odd jobs that made the officers' lives more comfortable. In turn, the officers usually paid their orderlies something extra.

Joseph couldn't type and had only a grammar school education, but he did have something else going for him. Nearly twenty-five years of age, he was more mature than the average fuzzy-cheeked, bewildered enrollee, most of whom were under twenty. Additionally, he had served a full year in the Massachusetts National Guard where he had learned to play the military game, that is, how to survive. When Muller entered the CCC, a quasi-military environment, he was at home in an organization not unlike that of the military; therefore, it is not surprising that he gravitated quickly to one of the best jobs in a CCC company. Throughout his CCC career, his evaluations were always excellent. Occasionally, he was on TDY, temporary duty, and was assigned briefly to other camps. This certainly was testament to his thoroughness. He received his honorable discharge in June 1934.

After his CCC enlistment, he worked at various jobs, all unskilled. He was employed by a local paper mill and also worked as a painter and a construction worker. Later, he moved to New York City where he found employment as a sign painter.

MILITARY EXPERIENCE

Joseph Muller was drafted on December 19, 1942, entering the service in the US Army at Camp Upton, Yaphank, Long Island, New York. He became part of the 77th Infantry Division. He received his basic

From the Forest to the Battlefield

training at Fort Jackson, South Carolina, where he was part of Company B of the 305th Infantry Regiment.

He had an interesting Army record. Rising in rank quickly, Muller acquired his first stripe in only six months. A year later (October 1943), he became a corporal. While stationed in Hawaii, he made sergeant. Later, during the Leyte Campaign, he was "busted" to private (October 1944), not really an unusual occurrence for men who were in combat. Disobeying a direct order, brawling, and drunkenness were the usual causes of rate reduction. They were serious charges, but all were solved at the company level. However, Muller's experience and leadership qualities were invaluable. He regained his first stripe in less than sixty days, and by the end of February 1945 (four months later), he had regained his sergeant's stripes.

From 1942 to 1944, Muller's regiment, the 305th, remained stateside, as if searching for an identity. It participated in the Louisiana War Games in early 1942 and then embarked to Arizona and California for desert training. Certain that that they were headed for Africa, the men of the 305th were surprised when their next station was Indiantown Gap, Pennsylvania, with a brief foray to Camp A.P. Hill in Virginia. The next stop was Beckley, West Virginia, where the regiment took part in mountain training. From there the 305th shipped to the Virginia coast, practicing amphibious training at two different stations near Norfolk.

Finally, in early 1944, the outfit shipped from California to Hawaii. After additional training there, the regiment became part of the invasion force that recaptured Guam in 1944. From there the unit moved to Luzon where it saw almost daily combat with a stubborn and determined Japanese Army. Eventually, the 305th was pulled out of Luzon for the impending invasion of the Ryukyus Islands. From March to early May 1945, the regiment fought and secured Ie Shima, a small island of that island chain. In early May, the 305th pushed on to Okinawa.

By this time Muller led an infantry squad from Company B, Third Battalion, 305th Infantry Regiment. They landed at Okinawa on May 7, 1945, where the fighting had been raging since early April. They then moved inland by trucks to an assembly area within the central part of the island.

The Japanese had been fortifying Okinawa because they knew the strategic importance of the Island. They used the terrain to their best advantage interconnecting caves, tombs, and pillboxes. Still another tactic was to employ a reverse slope tactic; that is, while the US troops fought up one hill, the Japanese used the other side of the slope to marshal and to disperse troops to their advantage. This necessitated the US artillery to bombard the forward areas with absolute precision being careful not to drop short rounds. Gully by gully, cave by cave, hill by hill, pillbox by pillbox, the Americans troops had to repeat the same tactic over and over. Frequently, success was measured by a two-hundred-foot advance.

The battlefield became a sea of mud caused by frequent torrential rain storms. At times it resembled trench warfare of World War I. Sherman tanks became stuck in the quagmire and became easy prey for tank killer teams who used satchel charges to blow up the tank. Pervading the battle sites was an overwhelming stench as frequently the Marines dug foxholes where the Japanese had previously buried their dead. The nights were marked by mortar and artillery barrages as well as Japanese infiltration. At the same time, the Japanese unleashed a new, heavy mortar weapon (320mm) that GIs called the "the flying jeep." It made a distinctive sound when fired and had a deadly explosive force.

SECOND TO NONE: A HISTORY OF THE 305th INFANTRY REGIMENT:

> At 0900, May 15, following an intense artillery barrage thrown up to us by the Japs, Companies A and C supported by M4 Sherman tanks attacked from their previous occupied position. Company C moved through the draw using flame throwers, satchel charges, and bazookas to destroy the many caves abundant in the area and whatever else they might encounter. At the elimination of the strongly defended draw, Company B (Muller's company) was able to position a small knob of land that lay to the front...but heavy mortar fire began to fall on that unit. So to better secure the line for the night, it was withdrawn to a position with better defense.

During that same day, Sergeant Muller had difficulty moving his squad forward, for they were pinned down by intense and accurate artillery fire from the ridge above him. He positioned his men for covering fire and then crawled through heavy fire and attacked the enemy with grenades. This spontaneous attack forced the enemy into the open where Muller's squad cut them down. When he saw enemy soldiers trying to man a machine gun, he charged again, this time killing four more of the enemy. The following morning, the enemy launched a counterattack on Muller's position. Armed with hand grenades and a rifle, he charged forward and turned back the attack. Later, he returned to his foxhole with two buddies. A Japanese grenade rolled in, and he covered it with his body.

MEDAL OF HONOR CITATION

He displayed conspicuous gallantry and intrepidity above and beyond the call of duty. When his platoon was stopped by deadly fire from a strongly defended ridge, he directed men to points where they could cover his attack. Then through the vicious machinegun and automatic fire, crawling forward alone, he suddenly jumped up, hurled his grenades, charged the enemy, and drove them into the open where his squad shot them down. Seeing enemy survivors about to man a machinegun, He fired his rifle at point-blank range, hurled himself upon them, and killed the remaining 4. Before dawn the next day, the enemy counterattacked fiercely to retake the position. Sgt. Muller crawled forward through the flying bullets and explosives, then leaping to his feet, hurling grenades and firing his rifle, he charged the Japs and routed them. As he moved into his foxhole shared with 2 other men, a lone enemy, who had been feigning death, threw a grenade. Quickly seeing the danger to his companions, Sgt. Muller threw himself over it and smothered the blast with his body. Heroically sacrificing his life to save his comrades, he upheld the highest traditions of the military service.

From the Forest to the Battlefield

MEDAL OF HONOR PRESENTATION

Joseph E. Muller was awarded the Medal of Honor posthumously on August 18, 1946, in a ceremony at his mother's house. Mary St. Germaine, Muller's mother, accepted the medal, while his stepfather, Joseph St. Germaine, looked on. Joseph's oldest brother, Wilfred, also attended as did a nephew and a few friends.

HONORS

The Joseph E. Muller Bridge is a 1444-foot span over the Connecticut River in Western Massachusetts that connects the towns of Holyoke and South Hadley. Well-marked on both sides of the river, the bridge carries thousands of commuters daily.

Joseph E. Muller's portrait hangs in the War Memorial Building in Holyoke. His Medal of Honor, donated by his nephew Norman, is on permanent display along with the Medals of Honor of Raymond Beaudoin and John S. Mackenzie, Holyoke's two other Medal of Honor recipients.

The US Army named an Army Reserve Center in the Bronx, New York City, in Mueller's honor.

The USNS Sgt. Joseph E. Muller(T-AG-171), a naval vessel, was transferred to the US Army and rechristened USAT Sgt. Joseph E. Muller.

PLAYGROUND ERECTED IN WARD TWO, HOLYOKE

On September 5, 1947, Holyoke, Massachusetts, honored their fallen heroes of Ward Two by erecting a children's playground. Although the ceremony commemorated twenty-nine other men from the same ward who had sacrificed their lives in their country's service, Sergeant Joseph Muller and Sergeant Raymond Beaudoin, Medal of Honor recipients, commanded the most attention.

The similarities between the two men were eerie. Both men had lived in Ward Two in Holyoke, Massachusetts. Each exercised a command position while serving in the US Infantry. Both men died in the closing days of the war--Beaudoin in April 1945 during the final push to Berlin and Muller a month later in the Pacific. To further raise these comparisons to a *Twilight Zone* level- both men had lived on the same street. Although Muller was ten years older, they had played on the same streets, had used the same local pool, had played baseball in the Ward Two playground, and had attended the same school. Completing these coincidences, their families were friends. Now their names are engraved on the same bronze plaque in the playground.

At least five thousand people attended the parade and subsequent dedication that "old timers" called, "One of the best midsummer parades ever held in Holyoke." The occasion honored the thirty-one Gold Star mothers led by Mrs. Beaudoin and Mrs. Mary St. Germaine. As those two women walked to the podium, the Westover Field soldiers stood at attention.

From the Forest to the Battlefield

According to the *Transcript-Telegram*, a Holyoke newspaper, "State and nation, city and ward had their spokesmen during the ceremonies of dedication. Military leaders, political leaders, civic leaders, and religious leaders had their places in paying tribute."

The thirty-one Gold star mothers each received a fifty-dollar war bond. Brigadier General Thomas M. Lowe, commander of Westover Field and Colonel Harold C. Vandermeer, Chief of the First Service Command, gave the mothers of the Medal of Honor recipients their bonds. Mayor Toepfert made the bond presentations to the other Gold Star mothers.

BURIAL SITE

Sergeant Joseph E. Muller is buried at the National Memorial Cemetery of the Pacific located in Honolulu, Hawaii.

WALTER C. WETZEL

BIRTH DATE: 1919

BIRTH PLACE: Huntington, West Virginia

DEATH: April 3, 1945. KIA.

MEDAL OF HONOR ACTION: Birken, Germany. April 3, 1945.

RANK: Private First Class

UNIT: 13th Infantry Regiment, 8th Infantry Division

YEARS OF SERVICE: July 9, 1941 - April 3, 1945

AWARDS: Medal of Honor, Purple Heart

CCC: SP-23, Utica, Illinois. July - December 1939.

WALTER C. WETZEL

Walter C. Wetzel was born to Walter and Alice (Anderson) Wetzel in Huntington, West Virginia, in 1919. He had a brother, Harry (1921) and a sister, Elmajean (1923).

West Virginia was hit hard by the Great Depression. Like so many people from Appalachia, Walter Wetzel Sr. looked elsewhere for employment. The auto industry in Detroit offered hope. He uprooted his family and moved to Roseville, near Detroit.

Young Walter went to Bellevue Elementary School but dropped out at the age of sixteen in 1935. He worked sporadically for the next few years, first at a catering company and later as a truck driver. By 1939 he enlisted in the Civilian Conservation Corps.

His hitch was the standard CCC enlistment of six months, July to December 1939. His duty station was SP-23, Camp Starved Rock, near Utica, Illinois, a reforestation camp specializing in tree planting, building of trails, and conducting stream improvement projects. Wetzel drove trucks. His CCC career was not noteworthy. The camp supervisor rated his work as satisfactory. While the camp educational adviser judged Wetzel's physical health and attitude as good, he downgraded his personality qualities as being only fair. Wetzel was honorably discharged two days before Christmas in 1939.

Returning to the private sector, he worked at an auto manufacturing plant. With war clouds hovering over the country, Wetzel, like many young Americans, decided to enlist.

MILITARY EXPERIENCE

Walter C. Wetzel was a wiry young man who weighed 150 pounds and was nearly six feet tall. Before he was twenty, he drove truck in Detroit, a tough job in a very tough city. Sergeant Leo Bolick, Wetzel's platoon sergeant from 1943 to 1945, recalled Wetzel's physical strength. "He had powerful stomach and great upper body muscles that had been acquired by his mounting tires in an auto assembly plant." Bolick recounted that Wetzel, "Would dare anyone in the company to hit him in the stomach as hard as they could. No one ever hurt him."

Wetzel's army career from 1941-43 was checkered. After completing basic training at Camp Walters in Texas, he joined an anti-tank company attached to the 13th Infantry Regiment, part of the 8th Infantry Division stationed at Fort Jackson, South Carolina. While undergoing intensive training at Fort Jackson, he went AWOL.

He returned home to Dorothy Caffke, his fiancé, who lived in Roseville. Michigan. While there, Sal and Eugene Caffke, Dorothy's brothers, urged him to surrender to the authorities. He turned himself into the

From the Forest to the Battlefield

Detroit police. Shortly thereafter, he returned to base under military police escort. He spent time in the stockade prior to being returned to active duty.

He rejoined his unit in time to begin six months of desert training in California. After that, the division shipped out to Northern Ireland in late December 1943. Preparations for the assault on Hitler's Fortress Europe were in full swing. Nearly a million American soldiers crowded into England.

There again, Wetzel went AWOL. This time, according to Sergeant Leo Bolick, his platoon sergeant, he crossed over into the Republic of Ireland, raising the possibility of a diplomatic problem. Undeterred, Wetzel returned to his company voluntarily and again was confined in the post lock-up. As a private, he could not be reduced in rate, but he suffered a significant pay loss because of fines.

A narrow line exists between the charges of AWOL and desertion. Desertion comes about with a possibility of a lengthy prison sentence or an outside chance of it becoming a capital offense. Somehow, Wetzel traversed that personal mine field without being sentenced to Leavenworth.

The 8th Division left Ireland and landed at Omaha Beach, Normandy, on July 4, 1944. Three days later, the unit was engaged in vicious fighting through the hedgerows of Normandy. After Brest had been secured, the division moved eastward, fighting daily, racing through Northern France and Luxembourg. Finally, it slowed down as late fall approached because the Army had outrun its supply lines. Additionally, the Allies march to Berlin was stymied in a fifty-square mile area called the Battle of Hurtgen Forest.

It began in September and ultimately involved 120,000 Allied troops, including the 8th Division. Strategically important, the Hurtgen Forest was the gateway to the industrial Ruhr and the Rhineland areas. The 8th Division engaged the Germans during November 1944. The overall battle, however, continued until December. Eventually, the Germans withdrew from the Hurtgen Forest when the huge losses at the Battle of the Bulge became untenable. Nevertheless, the Allies suffered 25 percent cent losses. Historians called Hurtgen Forest, "An Allied defeat of the first magnitude."

By mid-January 1945, the Allies began their push into Germany. The 8th Division was a part of this offense and slowly pushed back a determined German defense until the Rhine was crossed in March 1945. With crumbling German defenses, the division dashed into the heart of the industrial Ruhr Valley. It was during this time that Walter Wetzel was killed, thirty days before the German surrender on May 7, 1945. He was the last member of his platoon to be KIA.

SHORTLY AFTER MIDNIGHT APRIL 3, 1945

According to an official Army Press Release:

PFC Walter Wetzel's platoon had been assigned to defend their regiment's left flank at Birkin, Germany. After establishing a command post in a battered, unoccupied building, Sergeant Bolick led a patrol through Birkin's narrow streets. Wetzel, on guard duty, remained outside the CP, alert for any approaching German soldiers. A radio operator, Technician First Class John Chassin and PFC Henry C. Pippen, a jeep driver, remained inside the CP on the first floor. At about two AM, Pippen heard Wetzel shout, "Halt!" Then he heard Wetzel open fire on Germans moving toward the CP. In the meantime, Bolick's patrol had been spotted by the Germans who opened up with automatic weapons. Out-gunned, the patrol pulled back toward the CP, some taking position in the adjacent buildings. Bolick made it to the CP, and he and Wetzel moved to an open window and began to fire toward the advancing hostile troops. However, in the darkness, the Germans were able to get close enough to throw at least two grenades at the outpost. Someone shouted, "Grenades" and Wetzel threw himself on them, absorbing the impact while simultaneously saving the men inside. Inexplicably, Germans stopped their attack and withdrew. Wetzel was not killed immediately. According to Bolick, Wetzel alternately prayed and swore. The last thing he said before dying was, "Sarge, I think the god-damn sons of bitches have killed me."

Wetzel left behind his wife, Dorothy, whom he had married just before his outfit shipped overseas.

MEDAL OF HONOR CITATION

Pfc. Wetzel, an acting squad leader with the Antitank Company of the 13th Infantry, was guarding his platoon's command post in a house at Birken, Germany, during the early morning hours of 3 April 1945, when he detected strong enemy forces moving in to attack. He ran into the house, alerted the occupants and immediately began defending the post against heavy automatic weapons fire coming from the hostile troops. Under cover of darkness the Germans forced their way close to the building where they hurled grenades, 2 of which landed in the room where Pfc. Wetzel and the others had taken up firing positions. Shouting a warning to his fellow soldiers, Pfc. Wetzel threw himself on the grenades and, as they exploded, absorbed their entire blast, suffering wounds from which he died. The supreme gallantry of Pfc. Wetzel saved his comrades from death or serious injury and made it possible for them to continue the defense of the command post and break the power of a dangerous local counterthrust by the enemy. His unhesitating sacrifice of his life was in keeping with the U.S. Army's highest traditions of bravery and heroism.

MEDAL OF HONOR PRESENTATION

At the Federal Building in Detroit, Michigan, Colonel William H. McCarthy of Michigan's 6th Service Command presented Walter Wetzel's Medal of Honor posthumously to his wife, Mrs. Dorothy Wetzel, on February 26, 1946.

HONORS

In his honor the US Army named an elementary school for US military and civilian personnel in Baumholder, Germany.

The Wetzel State Recreation Area in Macomb County, Michigan, was dedicated on August 2, 1997. This war memorial is one of thirteen recreational areas scattered throughout Michigan that honor Michigan Medal Of Honor recipients.

On May 15, 1999, the new Administration Building of Macomb County, Michigan, was dedicated to Walter C. Wetzel. In the lobby of that building is a twenty-one-inch bronze bust of Wetzel.

On April 4, 2008, veterans' groups gathered at downtown Mount Clemens, Michigan, to mark the sixty-third anniversary of the death of Walter Wetzel, Macomb County's only recipient of the Medal of Honor. The ceremonies rededicated the memorial to Wetzel in the County Administration Building.

Walter C. Wetzel was enshrined at the Michigan's Military and Space Heroes Museum at Frankenmuth, Michigan. Frank Wetzel donated his brother's Medal of Honor to the museum.

A street In Roseville, Michigan, is named after Wetzel as well as an Army barracks in South Carolina.

NEVER TO BE FORGOTTEN

Sergeant Leo Bolick, along with his son, Tom, returned to Birken, Germany, in 1990. They hoped to find the house where Wetzel had saved Bolick's life. Unable to do so, they traveled to the American War Cemetery at Margraten, Netherlands, to visit Wetzel's grave site. As they stood there in contemplation, Tom Bolick said, "That was the only time I saw my father cry."

In 1997 Tom Bolick and his daughter returned to the cemetery to visit Wetzel's grave. He wanted her to remember her grandfather. Tom Bolick said, "I have been told this story all my life...never to forget what we owe Wetzel. I have my father's copy of the Blue Book, the Regimental History. His picture is in there with the Anti-Tank Company."

BURIAL SITE

Wetzel is buried at the American War Cemetery at Margraten, Netherlands, along with 8,300 other young Americans. The stones have the same blue markings except for six stones lettered in gold. Those stones commemorate the six recipients of the Medal of Honor buried there.

A GREATER TRANSPARENCY FOR MINORITIES

Even though over one million black men served in the armed services during World War II, not one received the Medal of Honor. That shocking statistic remained true for over fifty years after the end of the war. As the recollection of the war receded into the nation's memory, this injustice continued to highlight the obvious racial intolerance that was rampant then and still exists in subtle ways to the present.

In the Viet Nam War, the recipients of the Medal of Honor totaled 239. Of those, only twenty black men were singled out for the award. Only two black men were medal recipients out of 131 medals awarded during the Korean War. World War I saw one black man awarded the medal (awarded posthumously under the George H. W. Bush administration in 1989).

It can be argued that in World War II a sizeable percentage of black men never reached the front lines because of Jim Crow mentality. The nation was segregated and so was the military. Therefore, the second-class citizenship of the black civilian naturally carried over into the military. Most command officers such as General George Patton did not hide their prejudices regarding the black man's inferiority. However, as the war took its awful toll, black soldiers were needed for replacements. Even Patton became more realistic.

Sadly, the urgency of war did not improve the negative perceptions of the black man. The Army awarded ten black men the Distinguished Service Cross, second only to the Medal of Honor. Research showed that line officers did recommend at least four black men for the Medal of Honor, but as often happens in a bureaucracy, the recommendations somehow became "lost" in transit.

In 1947 President Harry Truman desegregated the armed forces. It was a bold, principled move, seven years ahead of *Brown v The Board of Education.* Truman's edict, though unpopular at the time, precipitated a seismic shift in the military. However, old habits changed very slowly. As a result, those injustices regarding the Medal of Honor oversights remained. It wasn't until the Clinton presidency that the government finally reexamined those oversights. In 1993 the Army contacted Shaw University, a predominately black school from Raleigh, North Carolina, to determine whether there was a racial disparity in the way the Medal of Honor recipients were selected. Doctor Daniel Gibran chaired the study that included prominent civilians and military personnel.

Fifteen months later, the committee produced a 272 page document that showed, "There is very strong evidence that racism played a role in the Medal of Honor selection process... and that...Racism was alive and it was there." The report did not find any "smoking gun," that is, anyone who specifically blocked recommendations for the medal.

As a result, the study found that ten black men who received the Distinguished Service Cross in World War II had also met the rigid requirements for the Medal of Honor. Therefore, they should become

234

recipients of the Medal of Honor. After further review, however, the Pentagon recommended that only seven of those cited should receive the medal. These men were

Lieutenant Vernon Baker

Lieutenant Charles Thomas

Private George Watson

S/Sergeant Edward Carter Jr.

S/Sergeant Ruben Rivers

Lieutenant John Fox

Private Willy James

Of those recipients, all were awarded posthumously except Vernon Baker who was living and present. Of the posthumous recipients, S/Sergeant Ruben Rivers was a former CCC enrollee killed in action in France.

The Shaw Report set a precedent by which Congress could bypass the statute of limitations and reopen examinations of service records of individuals regarding their eligibility for the Medal of Honor. Senator Daniel K. Akaka, US Senator from Hawaii, continued this push for transparency by sponsoring a bill that authorized the US Army to review the records of 104 decorated servicemen of Asian background. He argued that while over forty thousand Asian Americans had fought in World War II only two Asian Americans received the Medal of Honor. Because of that act, the Army reexamined the records of the 104 Asian American soldiers who had received the Distinguished Service Cross. Senator Akaka's actions bore fruit when on June 21, 2000, President Clinton bestowed the Medal of Honor on twenty-two servicemen of Asian descent whose accomplishments met the medal's requirements. One of the recipients was Rudolph B. Davila, a former CCC man, who was awarded the Medal of Honor posthumously fifty-six years after his extraordinary act of valor in the Italian campaign in 1944.

Through the Defense Authorization Act, the Pentagon called for a review of Jewish-American and Hispanic-American veterans' war records of World War II. The study entailed six thousand men who had received the Distinguished Service Cross. Eventually the list was winnowed to six hundred men. Finally, twenty-four men made the cut: seven warriors from World War II, nine heroes from the Korean War, and eight valiant soldiers from the Viet Nam War.

In a ceremony at the Pentagon in 2014, the Valor 24, as they were dubbed, received their Medals of Honor from President Barrack Obama. The family of Manual V. Mendoza, a CCC man, was present to accept his medal posthumously. Secretary of the Army John McHugh phrased it well:

From the Forest to the Battlefield

Their stories are as diverse as their service. They valiantly and defiantly, in German forests, Korean hilltops, and in the Viet Nam countryside, fought against a tremendous and fierce enemy and equally tremendous odds. Each of their stories, when taken alone, is truly breathtaking. But when taken together, they really form an incredible volume of history.

RUDOLPH B. DAVILA

BIRTH DATE: April 27, 1916

BIRTH PLACE: El Paso, Texas

DEATH: January 26, 2002

MEDAL OF HONOR ACTION: Artena, Italy. May 28, 1944.

RANK: Staff Sergeant

UNIT: Company H, 7th Infantry Regiment, 3rd Infantry Division

YEARS OF SERVICE: March 6, 1941 - 1950

AWARDS: Medal of Honor, Distinguished Service Cross, Purple Heart

CCC: SP-29, Lompoc, California. May - November 1935.

RUDOLPH B. DAVILA

Maria Agar married Nicholas Davila. The couple had four children, three boys and a girl. Nicholas, the eldest, was born in Gomez Palacio, State of Durango, Mexico. His sister, Candelaria, and brother, Umberto, were also born in Mexico. The family moved to the Watts section in Los Angeles, California, when Rudy was very young. There Rudy received his elementary and high school education, graduating in 1933. He was unemployed until 1935 when he enrolled in the CCC.

CCC EXPERIENCE

Rudy served at SP-29 at Lompoc, California, from May to November 1935. Initially, he helped construct wood and lattice work for local vintners. Then the company moved to Mission La Purisima, a Spanish mission dating to 1787. The CCC restored the mission, a massive project that only the CCC had the manpower to accomplish. Here Rudy's carpentry skills were challenged to the utmost. He helped rebuild and restore interiors of the buildings. His work was judged as excellent for his entire tour of duty. He was discharged honorably and returned home with a salable skill.

MILITARY EXPERIENCE

On March 6, 1941, Rudy was inducted into the Army where he served with Company H, 7th Infantry Regiment, 3rd Infantry Division. He participated in two amphibious invasions: Anzio and Southern France.

When the Anzio breakout occurred, Sergeant Davila was leading a rifle company near Artena, Italy, on May 28, 1944. As the company moved up a hill, it was ambushed. He yelled to bring the machine guns up front. Frozen in fear, no one moved. Davila then crawled back to retrieve a machine gun and dragged it close to the enemy line. There he reassembled it and fired more than 750 rounds before routing the Germans. Then, Davila called for backup. When a platoon leader moved in to fill his position, Davila dashed ahead, directing fire upon the enemy. He spotted a damaged American tank where he hoped to find another machine gun. Dodging a hail of bullets, he reached the tank only to find that its machine gun was missing. Then he directed his company to fire toward the tree line that hid enemy snipers. As the snipers fell, Rudy raced another one hundred yards to a burned-out house and killed five more Germans. Then he raced upstairs and continued to direct fire on the retreating Germans.

Afterward his company commander told him that he was submitting his name for a Medal of Honor. The captain reasoned, "If you hadn't done this, I think we all would have been slaughtered." Davila did receive the Distinguished Service Cross for valor, but nothing more was ever said about the Medal of Honor.

Davila did receive a battlefield commission for his exploits on that day. He remembered General Daniels placing the bars on his shoulders:

> After the battle I was ordered to leave the front and was taken to the hospital by Jeep. There the entire staff of the hospital was assembled and General Daniels gave a speech. I thought he was going to give me a medal. The general asked if anyone had second lieutenant bars. No one did. He then asked a nurse to bring him a tape and scissors. He himself took the tape and cut it into little pieces He put one on my collar and the other on my helmet. General Daniels then said, "You are now an officer and a gentleman."

Later Davila's unit was pulled out of Europe to prepare for the invasion of the French Rivera on August 14, 1944. Davila continued to lead with distinction until late that year when he was seriously wounded. A tank round had hit a tree and its fragments tore into his chest and right arm. His combat days were over, and he faced nearly five years of rehabilitation.

RECOGNITION DECADES LATER

President Clinton presented twenty-two Medals of Honor on June 21, 2000, at the South Lawn Pavilion. Of the twenty-two recipients of the Medal of Honor on that sunny Washington day, all but one man had Asian surnames. That man was Rudolph Davila. The fact that Davila was listed as an Asian American surprised many, particularly within the Davila family. Jeffery Davila, Rudy's son, explained his father's Filipino heritage:

> It turns out that the government made this discovery while reviewing Distinguished Service Cross recipients looking for people of Asian descent. How they figured out that my father's mom was Filipino was news to the entire family. The logic follows the notion that grandfather came from Spain and fought in the Philippines. He fell in love with a Filipino woman, our grandmother, and married her after the conflict. Spaniards not being popular in the Philippines, they moved to Mexico where three of Rudy's siblings were born. When the Revolution broke out our grandfather, who was a wealthy land owner, was shot to death on a trip to town. My grandmother, who was pregnant with Rudy, fled to Texas. He was born on April 27, 1916, in El Paso. Apparently, there was some legal issue with grandfather being a Filipino so she never mentioned anything else except about her Mexican descent.

> This has not been a popular revelation with some members of the family. All of Dad's siblings have died and his second brother's wife, Carmen, takes issue. She met her future husband, Umberto, and our father when they were 19 and 16 respectively. She says she has seen photographs of grandmother growing up in Mexico with her siblings. My personal feeling is the Filipino logic makes more sense. Irrespective, Dad has always been aware of Spanish and of Mexican descent in our family, and he himself was surprised, amused, and unconcerned about this discovery.

MEDAL OF HONOR CITATION

Staff Sergeant Rudolph B. Davila distinguished himself by extraordinary heroism in action on 28 May 1944, near Artena, Italy. During the offensive which broke through the German mountain strongholds surrounding the Anzio beachhead, Staff Sergeant Davila risked death to provide heavy weapons support for a beleaguered rifle company. Caught on an exposed hillside by heavy, grazing fire from a well-entrenched German force, his machine gunners were reluctant to risk putting their guns into action. Crawling fifty yards to the nearest machine gun, Staff Sergeant Davila set it up alone and opened fire on the enemy. In order to observe the effect of his fire, Sergeant Davila fired from the kneeling position, ignoring the enemy fire that struck the tripod and passed between his legs. Ordering a gunner to take over, he crawled forward to a vantage point and directed the firefight with hand and arm signals until both hostile machine guns were silenced. Bringing his three remaining machine guns into action, he drove the enemy to a reserve position two hundred yards to the rear. When he received a painful wound in the leg, he dashed to a burned tank and, despite the crash of bullets on the hull, engaged a second enemy force from the tank's turret. Dismounting, he advanced 130 yards in short rushes, crawled 20 yards and charged into an enemy-held house to eliminate the defending force of five with a hand grenade and rifle fire. Climbing to the attic, he straddled a large shell hole in the wall and opened fire on the enemy. Although the walls of the house were crumbling, he continued to fire until he had destroyed two more machine guns. His intrepid actions brought desperately needed heavy weapons support to a hard-pressed rifle company and silenced four machine gunners, which forced the enemy to abandon their prepared positions. Staff Sergeant Davila's extraordinary heroism and devotion to duty are in keeping with the highest traditions of military service and reflect great credit on him, his unit, and the United States Army.

LIFE AFTER WORLD WAR II

Rudy went to a military hospital in Modesto, California, where he had thirteen surgeries on his right arm. During one operation a nerve in his right arm was severed, causing paralysis. While there, however, he met his future wife, Harriet. "Walking down the hospital hallway, I grabbed a nurse's arm without saying a word. Three months later we were married."

In 1944 Congress had passed the Servicemen's Readjustment Bill (G.I. Bill of Rights) which President Franklin Roosevelt signed into law. The bill was predicated on the simple fear that by the war's end, sixteen million veterans would flood the job market, triggering an economic depression even greater than the downturn in the 1930s. Nearly eight million veterans took advantage of some form of advanced education.

When Rudy left the service, he wanted to have a better life than he had experienced as a youngster. Before the war any chance of college for a kid from Watts was a total dream, absolutely unobtainable. The G.I. Bill, however, provided how he could advance himself. After his marriage he enrolled at the University of Southern California and received his Bachelor and Master's Degree in Sociology. In 1953 he completed his university work and was hired by the Los Angeles Unified School District, teaching history at Gardena High School. A few years later, Rudy transferred to Peary Junior High School. By 1968 he had become a counselor at Banning High School. There he began several career training programs, including vocational nursing and telephone repair. Recognizing a need for strengthening student discipline, he also instituted a Junior Naval Reserve Officer training program. In all, he spent twenty-five years working with young people. It was a rewarding career for someone born in political exile.

Although hampered by his inability to use his right arm, Rudy never considered it a handicap. His carpentry skills honed in the CCC carried over into the post-war years. At his first home in Harbor City, not too far from where he grew up in Watts, he landscaped and terraced his back yard. When he retired, he moved to Vista, California, twenty five miles south of Harbor City, and built his second home. Rudy also loved to cook and frequently relieved his wife of that chore. His friends looked forward to an invitation to his house where they enjoyed Rudy's culinary talents.

Rudy and Harriet had five children: three sons, Greg, Jeffery, and Roland, and two daughters, Tana and Jill. Rudy spoke little of his wartime experiences, but Harriet lobbied considerably for the Army to reconsider his apparent snub for the Medal of Honor. In addition to telephoning Army officials, she researched military records and wrote a stream of letters to the Pentagon. Sadly, she never once received a response. Ironically, Mrs. Davila died six months prior to President Clinton's placing the blue ribbon around her husband's neck. Rudy's comment about her missing the Medal of Honor ceremony was, "She would have been thrilled."

SIGNIFICANT QUOTES FROM RUDOLPH DAVILA

Rudy Davila tried to live his life based on his personal philosophy, "You are no better than anyone else, *but no one else is better than you.*"

In a YouTube video, Rudy talked briefly about his transition from a civilian to a soldier. "When I went into the service I was a civilian. For a long time, I was a civilian in uniform. When I saw the war and the killing, I became a different person and I became a soldier. We were fighting for the freedom of the world and that was my motivation."

Regarding the incident where his rifle company was trapped by overwhelming fire at Artena on May 28, 1944, Davila said, " I had no time to think of anything but how all those Americans were going to be killed."

Two years before receiving the Medal of Honor Rudy said, "To this day I can't tell you I killed. I don't want to think that I killed. I like to think I scared them away."

In 2001 Davila said, I didn't want to think that my country would deny me something because I am not an Anglo... In my case, the conscience of America went to sleep for fifty-six years."

From the Forest to the Battlefield

Rudy Davila told a *North Country Times* reporter, "I don't remember being afraid or timid. It just happened. I wasn't that kind of person. I wasn't violent. in fact I was kind of a passive guy. I just wanted to be a good soldier."

After saving his entire company from destruction, Rudy said, "It was all automatic. I just thought that this is what I have to do as a soldier, and I am doing it."

When he was eighty-three years old, a reporter asked Rudy why he opened up on the Germans when it meant certain death. He replied, "I knew what I was fighting for and most of the kids didn't. I had a fervor about the defense of freedom, even though I couldn't define freedom. I just knew that we were not going to be enslaved to Hitler."

His description of being wounded in the chest and shoulder while fighting in the Vosges Mountains was, "It felt as if someone had taken a baseball bat and hit me on the chest with all their might."

When asked about losing the use of his right arm, he said, "You'd go crazy about what could have been. You just do the best you can."

HONORS

The westbound portion of Route 91 (Gardenia Freeway) between Central Avenue and Figueroa in the city of Carson, California, was renamed the Rudolph B. Davila Memorial Freeway.

Rudy was the guest speaker at the VFW Memorial Day Commemoration in Vista, California, in 2001.

In 2001 Davila was inducted into the Pentagon's Hall of Heroes.

In 2015 the Army War College at Carlisle Barracks recognized the twenty-two Asian Americans for their heroics during World War II.

DAVILA'S DEATH

On January 26, 2002, Rudolph B. Davila, passed away after a lengthy battle with cancer. According to his son, Roland Davila, "He was a strong believer in God and was very active in his church for many years...He's always been an exemplary individual as far as being trustworthy, hardworking, faithful to his wife, and supportive to his children."

BURIAL SITE

Rudolph B. Davila was cremated. His remains were buried with full military honors in Section 67, Grave 3458, Arlington National Cemetery, Arlington, Virginia.

MANUAL V. MENDOZA

BIRTH DATE: June 15, 1922

BIRTH PLACE: Miami, Arizona

DEATH: December 12, 2001

MEDAL OF HONOR ACTION: Mt. Battaglia, Italy. October 4, 1944.

RANK: Staff Sergeant

UNIT: Company B, 350th Infantry Regiment, 88th Infantry Division

YEARS OF SERVICE: November 21, 1942 - 1945 (World War II). 1949 - 1953 (Korea).

AWARDS: Medal of Honor, Distinguished Service Cross, Bronze Star, Purple Heart (2), Combat Infantry Badge, Others

CCC: F-35A, Camp Verde, Arizona. May - June 1940.

MANUEL V. MENDOZA

Manuel Mendoza's could trace his roots from Mexico and to the then lush Arizona citrus groves. Julio Mendoza (1897-1965) and his wife Guadalupe Verdugo (1903-1993) were of meager means. Both were born in Mexico. Julio and his wife had no formal education. After their marriage, they moved to the United States to find employment. Soon after the move to the United States, the children were born. By 1940 the couple had ten children, six girls and four boys. All were born in Arizona. The 1940 US Census listed Julio's wages at $160.00 for the entire year. Most of his wages came from working in citrus orchards.

Manuel, the eldest, was born in the small mining town of Miami in Gila County in 1922. His family moved to Mesa soon afterward. He attended grade school in Mesa but only completed fifth grade before dropping out to support the growing family. A stocky kid, Manuel weighed 130 pounds. Standing at five foot six inches tall, he was a tough but able young man, capable of doing of a man's work. He worked sporadically at Sam Ankel's ranch from 1936-1939. During the last year, 1939, he made $40.00 for eight weeks of employment. In May 1940 Manuel struck out for a new experience: the CCC.

It was an unhappy choice.

Manual was stationed at Camp F-35A at Camp Verde, Arizona. His job was road construction. Although his first month's evaluation was satisfactory, Manuel walked away from camp, causing the officials to give him a dishonorable discharge. As with many of the young enrollees, he could not cope with his homesickness.

In August 1940 he married Alice Gaona. The couple eventually had four children, two boys, Ben and Manuel Jr., and two girls, Sylvia and Barbara. Mendoza continued his work in agriculture, mostly driving a tractor. This met the farm's seasonal needs.

On November 21, 1942, Mendoza entered the Army. He served in the US Army until 1945, reaching the rank of staff sergeant. Upon returning home, he joined the Arizona National Guard and later reenlisted during the Korean War.

MENDOZA'S COMBAT RECORD IN WORLD WAR II

Mendoza was part of Company B, the 350th Infantry Regiment, 88th Infantry Division. The regiment's first foreign posting was in Northern Africa in December 1943. There his company underwent intensive training near Casablanca for six weeks before shipping out to Naples, Italy, where it moved immediately to the Gustav Line anchored by Monte Cassino. For the next four months, Company B slugged it out with the Germans until the Allied breakthrough in May 1944. By the end of that month, the division hooked up with parts of the American 3rd Division as they streaked toward Rome. On June 4, 1944, elements of the 88th Division became the first Allied troops to enter the Eternal City. After the liberation of Rome, the unit moved northward toward the Gothic Line, the last major line of defense that stretched 150 miles from Pisa on the Ligurian Sea, to Riamini on the Adriatic Sea. That line was anchored by the Northern Apennines, terrain as formidable as the mountains surrounding Monte Cassino to the south. In late fall a major battle centered on Mount Battaglia, a key German stronghold. After its conclusion, the Italian winter set in and the division hunkered down in a defensive position. However, by late January 1945, the final push began. Retreating toward the Alps, the Germans fought doggedly, inflicting heavy losses. It was not until April 1945 that the 88th Division crossed the Alps into Innsbruck, Austria, where it joined with the 103rd Infantry Division. Within days the hostilities ceased. But victory came at a high cost. The 88th Division had seen 344 combat days since debarking at Naples in 1943, and it had sustained nearly 15,000 casualties.

THE ARIZONA KID RIDES AGAIN

Staff Sergeant Manuel Mendoza rode into the annals of American military lore when on the afternoon of October 4, 1944, on Mount Battaglia, he single-handedly broke up a German company sized counterattack. Initially the Germans pounded the American position atop a hill with heavy mortars, wounding many American GIs including Mendoza. When the barrage lifted, Mendoza left his position and raced to the edge of the hill and saw two hundred Germans advancing up the hill toward his position. He grabbed a Thompson submachine gun, and blasted away. When he ran out of ammunition Mendoza continued the attack using his rifle. Then he shot an enemy soldier, who carried a flame-thrower, almost at a point-blank range. Still moving offensively, Mendoza jumped into an abandoned German machine gun position, picked up the weapon, and fired it from his hip and laid down a withering fusillade. When the gun jammed, he hurled hand grenades. Always in motion, Sergeant Mendoza raced along the edge of the hill and captured some enemy weapons as well as at least one German soldier. He then returned to the safety of his own line. His comrades marveled at his exploits and christened him the "Arizona Kid," an appellation that carried over into the Korean War.

LIFE AFTER WORLD WAR II

In 1949, after the North Koreans invaded South Korea, Manuel rejoined the Army and served his country until his discharge in May 1954. During his deployment in Korea, he saw much combat, having participated in five of the thirteen UN Campaigns in Korea. When discharged in 1953, Master Sergeant Manuel V. Mendoza had gained another Combat Infantryman Badge and his second Purple Heart. During his seven plus years in the military, he had experienced an inordinate amount of combat time- at least three full years. A much-decorated veteran, he acquired twenty-five medals and service ribbons. Manuel Mendoza served his country long and well. He was, indeed, a credit to the American soldier.

From the Forest to the Battlefield

After his discharge in 1954, Mendoza moved to California where he lived for about one year. There he worked in agriculture, driving tractors necessary on large farms. Upon returning to Arizona he found sporadic employment in agriculture and in a local copper mine. Later he went to school to study auto mechanics.

According to his daughter, Sylvia Nandin, Manuel was a "problem solver" who possessed a highly intuitive mind. "He could identify a problem and fix it easily," she said. "Dad was excellent at plumbing, electrical work, motorcycle and auto mechanics, and construction work." The latter ability led to his becoming a construction foreman at the Palo Verde Nuclear Station at Tonopah, Arizona, forty-five miles west of Phoenix. He worked there for almost a decade before suffering a stroke that led to his early retirement.

RECOGNITION DECADES LATER

In the East Room of the White House on March 18, 2014, the Medal of Honor ceremony for the Valor 24 was conducted. Twenty-one of the twenty-four men honored received their medals posthumously. In his opening address, President Obama remarked, "Although no nation is perfect, here in America we confront our imperfections and face a somewhat painful past, including the truth that some of our heroes fought and died for a country that did not always see them as equal."

The news of Manuel Mendoza's upgrading to the Medal of Honor came as a complete surprise to the entire Mendoza family. In May 2013 a family member answered the phone and said, "'It's the President. He wants to talk with you." Alice Mendoza, Manuel's wife, was very surprised to hear the President's voice on the phone. She later reported, "I almost fainted! I was so nervous that I said, 'Thank you, Mr. Obama' instead of 'Thank you, Mr. President.'" Sylvia Nandin, Mendoza's daughter, reported that the family was very honored to receive the award on behalf of her father. The news, however, was to remain secret until the White House Press officially announced the news. The Mendoza family was sworn to secrecy until February 2014.

During the Medal of Honor proceedings, Alice Mendoza wiped tears from her eyes as an Army representative read her husband's citation. She and the POTUS stood side-by-side on a small podium, making for an interesting contrast: small in stature, but strong at heart, she stood proudly next to President Obama who towered over her. At that moment, this beautiful, ninety-year -old, silver-haired lady stole everyone's heart including the President's. When he bent over to hug the diminutive nonagenarian, it was the emotional highlight of an already highly charged ceremony.

Regarding her mother, daughter Sylvia reported, "The President helped my extremely nervous mother navigate through the sea of reporters and the banks of the cameras. And she even received a couple of pecks on the cheek from the President. She came through it like a trouper."

Nandin also stated that the Medal of Honor ceremony as well as the Hall of Heroes event the following day was cathartic. "No one in the room harbored anger...The tone was more celebratory...It was long overdue, but it was a positive experience," she said.

MEDAL OF HONOR CITATION

The President of the United States, in the name of Congress, takes pride in presenting the Medal of Honor (posthumously) to Staff Sergeant Manuel Verdugo Mendoza, United States Army, for acts of gallantry and intrepidity, above and beyond the call of duty, while serving as a Platoon Sergeant with Company B, 350th Infantry Regiment, 88th Infantry Division during combat operations against an armed enemy at Mt. Battaglia, Italy on 4 October 1944. That afternoon the enemy launched a violent counterattack preceded by a heavy mortar barrage. Staff Sergeant Mendoza, already wounded in the arm and leg, grabbed a Thompson sub-machine gun and ran to the crest of the hill where he saw approximately 200 enemy troops charging up the slopes employing flame-throwers, machine pistols, rifles and hand grenades. Staff Sergeant Mendoza immediately began to engage the enemy, firing five clips, killing ten enemy soldiers. After exhausting his ammunition, he picked up a carbine and emptied its magazine at the enemy. By this time an enemy soldier with a flame-thrower had almost reached the crest, but was quickly eliminated as Staff Sergeant Mendoza drew his pistol and fired. Seeing the enemy continue to advance, Staff Sergeant Mendoza jumped into a machine gun emplacement that had been abandoned and opened fire. Unable to engage the entire enemy force from that position, he picked up the machine gun and moved forward, firing from his hip and spraying a withering hail of bullets into the oncoming enemy, causing them to break into confusion. He then set the machine gun on the ground and continued firing until the gun jammed. Without hesitating, Staff Sergeant Mendoza began throwing hand grenades at the enemy, causing them to flee. After the enemy had withdrawn, he advanced down the forward slope of the hill and retrieved numerous enemy weapons scattered in the area, captured a wounded enemy soldier, and returned to consolidate friendly positions with all available men. Staff Sergeant Mendoza's gallant stand resulted in thirty German soldiers killed and a successful defense of the hill. Staff Sergeant Mendoza's extraordinary heroism and selflessness above and beyond the call of duty are in keeping with the highest traditions of military service and reflect great credit upon himself, his unit, and the United States Army.

HONORS

Mendoza became the third Latino in Arizona to receive the Medal of Honor on March 18, 2014.

Mendoza was inducted into the Arizona Army Hall of Fame on March 19, 2014, in a formal ceremony at the Pentagon.

The Arizona Historical Society of Tempe, Arizona, hosted the Mendoza family at the May 2014 opening of the *Above and Beyond: Arizona and the Medal of Honor Exhibit*, which displayed Mendoza's Medal of Honor.

Mendoza was memorialized as a Medal of Honor recipient on Memorial Day 2014 at his birthplace of Miami, Arizona. A kiosk was unveiled displaying his image and his Medal of Honor citation at the Town Square Veterans Memorial. In addition, two highway signs were posted along the main highway indicating Miami as his hometown.

The United States Post Office at Miami, Arizona, was renamed in his honor on June 19, 2015.

On October 25, 2014, Mendoza was awarded the Ambassador of Peace medal by the Korea Ministry of Patriots and Veteran Affairs for his service during the Korean War.

BURIAL SITE

After his stroke Mendoza's physical and mental health slowly deteriorated. He developed Alzheimer's disease and died in December 2001 at age seventy-nine. He was buried at Mountain View Cemetery, Mesa County, Maricopa, Arizona. A ceremony was held in November 2014 to unveil a new grave marker honoring Mendoza as a Medal of Honor recipient.

A QUIET HERO

Like countless contemporary veterans, Manuel Mendoza spoke little about his war time exploits. He came home, resumed his family life, and went about making a living for himself and his family. His heroics only became known when he was nominated for the Medal of Honor in 2014. A modest man, he had lived a dangerous and harsh life in the military. This was a side of Manuel Mendoza that he chose not to share with anyone. Those battles were a long time ago and required a different mindset. It was necessary to forget them. Manuel Mendoza, the Arizona Kid, was not the same as Manuel Mendoza, husband and devoted father. Perhaps that was how he coped with those awful years. He wanted to shield his family from what he had seen. Additionally, his strong family ties served as a bulwark against the past.

DAUGHTER SYLVIA NANDIN REMEMBERS HER FATHER

> I learned about my Dad's experiences when I read a book on Hispanic soldiers who had served during World War II. There I learned how he had acquired the Distinguished Service Cross. It opened up the door to questioning on my part...That's when I learned how extensive my father's military career was and how highly decorated he was...I never knew because he had tucked away his medals and ribbons in a drawer for no one to see.

Manuel Mendoza's entire family is extremely proud of his newly recognized fame. Sylvia bubbles with pride about her father. His posthumous fame resulted in numerous invitations to state and local recognition ceremonies. His family is proud to represent Master Sergeant Manuel V. Mendoza at those functions. He has created an honorable legacy for future generations to come. Their memories of him, however, are not the war years. Instead, his family remembers him for the many loving years he was with them at home.

A SON'S QUESTION

Mendoza's son, Manuel Jr., once asked his father why he served so many years in the Army during dangerous times. He replied, "So you don't have to."

RUBEN RIVERS

BIRTH DATE: October 30, 1919

BIRTH PLACE: Tecumseh, Oklahoma

DEATH: November 19, 1944. KIA.

MEDAL OF HONOR ACTION: Guebling, France. November 19, 1944.

RANK: Staff Sergeant

UNIT: 761st Tank Battalion, 26th Infantry Division

YEARS OF SERVICE: January 16, 1944 - November 19, 1944

AWARDS: Medal of Honor, Purple Heart, Silver Star, Others

CCC: SCS-29, Kanawa, Oklahoma. July 1938 - June 1940.

RUBEN RIVERS

Ruben Rivers's parents were William Rivers, a black American, and Lillian Rivers, a Cherokee Native American. Will was born in Arkansas, and Lillian was born in Alabama. Their respective families moved to Oklahoma. Will had a sixth-grade education while his wife had completed nine years of school. They lived on a farm that Will Rivers owned. According to the US Census of 1940, Will placed a value on his farm and house at $1000.00. His income for that year was only $160.00 even though he worked fifty-two weeks. The family lived in a small, shabby house with a fence around it to keep out the cattle. It was a hard life, made even worse since their farm was located on the eastern edge of the Dust Bowl. Subsequently, the couple had eleven children. Poor but proud, Will and Lillian instilled into their children the love of the land and respect for their heritage, traits that Ruben carried the rest of his life.

Ruben had been born in Tecumseh, Oklahoma, on October 30, 1919. He was a conscientious student who exhibited a natural curiosity about things around him. He dropped out of school in tenth grade at Dunbar High School in Shawnee, Oklahoma, to supplement the family's meager income. He was tall, almost six feet, but weighed only 150 pounds. Used to arduous work, he worked on his father's farm but eventually got a job with J.R. Nash of Tecumseh who had a trucking business. Ruben worked there for almost a year before being laid off. He joined the CCC on July 7, 1938.

His hitch in the CCC was exemplary. He made the very most out of what the CCC could offer. In addition, his monthly allotment of twenty-five dollars was a godsend to his family.

The CCC was racially segregated. In some states, like Georgia, the first black CCC camps were located on federal land, as the local communities were powerfully opposed to having a black CCC camp near them. It wasn't until a few years into the CCC program that localities saw the economic benefit of having a CCC camp *of any color* in their vicinity, as each camp represented $5000 infused into local communities each month. Eventually, the color of green (money) trumped over their aversion to the color black.

The racial realities of the 1930s were harsh. Segregation was insidiously embedded in all phases of life nationwide, but it was most obvious in the South. Many southern states opposed the black man's entry into the CCC. On the other hand, the federal government tacitly threatened to pull out all CCC support in those states that prohibited black CCC enrollment. Eventually an agreement was reached whereby 10 percent of the total CCC enrollment had to be black; that percentage also represented the total black population of the country. This figure was strongly opposed by many, but Roosevelt stood firm. The hard-core segregationist states like Georgia and Mississippi grudgingly complied.

It was in the organization of the CCC camps where segregation became blatantly obvious. All officers were white, as were all the camp's overhead personnel, such as the foreman, sub- foremen, and the camp supervisor and his staff. Prevailing wisdom was that no black man was capable of running a CCC camp. It wasn't until 1936 that the black camps could have black chaplains!

Entrance into a black segregated community had to have been a cultural shock for Ruben Rivers, as it raised racism to a level he had never experienced. Tecumseh, Oklahoma, had a far greater Native American population than black Americans; therefore, having biracial parents in Tecumseh was not unusual. Trumping racism was poverty, an even more powerful condition than skin color.

It is remarkable and a huge testament to Ruben Rivers that during his term in the CCC he could rise above the bigotry, and enjoyed a productive time. Significantly, the CCC's paramilitary life toughened him mentally for the even more extreme prejudice facing him in the military during World War II.

CCC EXPERIENCE

Rivers served his entire tour of duty at SCS Camp-29, a soil conservation camp, located near Kanawa, Oklahoma, only thirty miles from Tecumseh. His first year, Ruben worked as a laborer, but in his final year, he was promoted to assistant leader. Personally, the promotion doubled his pay from five dollars to ten dollars a month, a princely income.

Rivers absences from camp were all AWP (Absent With Permission). He enjoyed two traditional leaves, each one for six days. In addition, he took three emergency leaves of absence. Since he was only thirty miles from home, he also enjoyed a few weekend passes.

Ruben was a poster boy for the CCC educational program. He excelled in the academic classes of spelling, algebra, religious education, and surveying. From a technical aspect relative to his job, he received certificates in safety and forest fire management. He attended vocational classes including auto welding and auto mechanics. Besides all that, Rivers had enough time to study transportation, general agriculture, and one course in pre-engineering. When Rivers returned from his CCC service, he was considerably richer in education.

WORLD WAR II

When Pearl Harbor occurred, it was obvious that Ruben would soon enter the service because he felt this war was his fight as well as any white man's war. He went into the Army in early 1942. After basic training he became part of the 761st Tank Battalion, a black unit. The Army was as segregated as were the states where he served: Texas, Louisiana, and Kentucky. While training for almost two years, individuals in his unit suffered beatings and deaths, particularly by white citizens in Louisiana.

By this time Rivers had seen and heard it all regarding the inferiority of the black troops. General Patton thought that the black soldier was unreliable at best and doubted if they could think fast enough to operate in an armored unit. Colonel James Moss, Commander of the 367th Infantry Division, said, "Negro troops must be rated second class troops due to their inferior intelligence and their lack of mental and moral qualities."

But the war wore on, and the American losses in men and material became staggering. The need for more soldiers overcame the extreme racial bias. The Black Panthers, as they were called, landed at Normandy in the late fall of 1944, the first black armored unit to enter France. Commanded by Lieutenant Colonel Paul Bates, a white man, the unit was at full strength with six white officers, thirty black officers, and 676 black enlisted men.

The Germans were poised for their major counter offensive in the Ardennes. At the same time, Patton was in desperate need of more tankers. When told that the only outfit left was a black unit, Patton reportedly said, "Who the ... asked for color? I asked for tankers." The 761st battalion was ready for combat.

As the unit readied for its baptism of fire, General Patton visited them. He addressed the Black Panthers in this famous speech:

> Men, you are the first Negro tankers to ever fight in the US Army. I have nothing of the best in my Army. I don't care what color you are as long as you go up there and kill the Kraut sons of bitches. Everyone has their eyes on you and is expecting great things from you. Most of all your race is looking forward to your success. Don't let them down and God damn you, don't let me down. They say it is patriotic to die for your country. Well let's see how many patriots we can make out of those German sons of bitches...You may thank God that thirty years from now when you are sitting with your grandson on your knee and he asks, "Grandfather, what did you do in the war?" You don't have to say, "I shoveled shit in Mississippi."

Thus began 183 straight days of combat in which the 761st Battalion fought in four major campaigns in six different countries and inflicted more than 100,000 enemy casualties. Some historians argue that the unit was frequently thrown into impossible military situations where the outcome was bleak. If that were the case, the 761st certainly proved them wrong as the unit fought brilliantly. Within a short time, three of the Black Panthers assumed legendary status: Sergeant Samuel Turley, Sergeant Warren G. H. Crecy, and Sergeant Ruben Rivers.

Rivers was extremely aggressive and his ability with the .50 caliber machine gun made all soldiers recognize him. He was without fear. Captain David Williams, his white company commander, admired Rivers greatly. He said, "Rivers was a cut above and destined to be killed. I told him, you don't mess with the Germans like that." In one attack, an American officer called to tell him not to advance into a particular village. "It's too hot," the officer said. Rivers radioed back, "Sorry, sir, I am already through that town."

General Patton selected the 761st Tank Battalion to lead the Third Army into the Saar Region of Germany.

From the Forest to the Battlefield

This required the breaching of the Siegfried Line, a series of pillboxes, tank traps, and strong points on the entire eastern border of Germany. In early November Patton made his move. On November 8, 1944, Able Company, Ruben's company, was attached to an infantry unit whose objective was Vic-sur Seille in northeastern France. En route the Americans hit heavy resistance from the Germans. Rivers was in the lead tank. His citation for the Silver Star, the Army's third highest award for valor, told the story for that day:

> Upon hitting a road block that held up the advance...Staff Sergeant Rivers courageously dismounted from his tank in the face of directed enemy small arms fire, attached a cable to the road block and moved it off the road thus allowing the combat team to proceed. His prompt action thus prevented a serious delay in the offensive action and was instrumental in the successful assault and capture of the town.

A few days later, Able Company was moving toward Guebling, France, with Rivers's tank in the lead position. His tank hit a mine, tearing off its right tread. Rivers was severely wounded. His left leg had been cut to the bone, an injury that would have merited Rivers a trip home. He ignored any offer of pain medication and Captain David Williams's order to withdraw to an aid station. He then assumed command of another tank and proceeded into action. The attack on Guebling was successful, but that afternoon the medics detected that gangrene had set in on his leg. Once again he refused to pull himself out of combat. On the dawn of November 19, 1944, his tanks were forced to stop because of heavy concentration of fire from enemy tanks and a well-positioned anti-tank gun. With two of the M-4s already hit, Rivers was ordered, "Pull back Panthers! Pull Back!"

His response was, "I see them. We fight them."

Rivers covered the safe withdrawal of the remaining tanks by charging straight ahead along with another Sherman M-4 at his side. The attack led to the destruction of three enemy tanks while successfully allowing the remaining American tanks to escape. His tank, however, was struck twice, killing Ruben and his gunner and injuring the remaining crew members.

Trezzvant Anderson, a black journalist embedded with the 761st Battalion, described this last battle:

> From a comparatively short distance of 200 yards the Germans threw two HE (high explosive) shots that scored. The first shot hit the front of the tank and penetrated with ricocheting fragments confined inside the steel walls. The second shot scored inside the tank. The first shot blew his brains against the back of the tank and the second went through his head emerging from the rear. And the intrepid leader, the fearless, daring fighter was no more.

Captain Williams recommended Rivers for the Medal of Honor. A week later he requested the status of his recommendation. He was told it was lost.

254

From the Forest to the Battlefield

By 1952 the cut-off date for Congress to consider any recommendations for the Medal of Honor had passed. Undeterred, Williams continued his quest. He said, "Rivers was a Negro. He was humiliated and I was humiliated with him... With the Germans, I knew the enemy. But racism was hard to beat."

In 1993 the US Army commissioned an independent study by Shaw University to reexamine whether there had been any racial disparity regarding recommendations for the Medal of Honor. Because of this study, seven Black Americans from World War II received the Medal of Honor from President Bill Clinton in January 1997.

Among the attendees at the Medal of Honor presentation were Grace Rivers Woodfork and May Rivers Hill, both sisters of Ruben. Captain David Williams was also in attendance.

Former Captain David Williams deserved much credit for the nomination as he worked tirelessly for nearly fifty years for the recognition of Ruben Rivers. Williams had been working with Congressman Jim Inhofe of Oklahoma in an attempt to get Congress to reopen the case. Williams had already acquired the necessary information from eyewitnesses. Therefore, when the Officers Review Board was created, Ruben's materials were immediately submitted for consideration.

MEDAL OF HONOR CITATION

For extraordinary heroism in action during the 15-19 November 1944, toward Guebling, France. Though severely wounded in the leg, Sergeant Rivers refused medical treatment and evacuation, took command of another tank, and advanced with his company in Guebling the next day. Repeatedly refusing evacuation, Sergeant Rivers continued to direct his tank's fire at enemy positions through the morning of 19 November 1944. At dawn, Company A's tanks began to advance towards Bougaktroff, but were stopped by enemy fire. Sergeant Rivers, joined by another tank, opened fire on the enemy tanks, covering company A as they withdrew. While doing so, Sergeant River's tank was hit, killing him and wounding the crew. His fighting spirit and daring leadership were an inspiration to his unit and exemplify the highest traditions of military service.

HONORS

Rivers is honored on the Tecumseh, Oklahoma, Veterans Memorial.

On October 12, 2012, Mayor Sylvain Hinschberger of Bourgaltraff, France, paid homage to Ruben Rivers by visiting a memorial for Rivers in Tecumseh, Oklahoma. The Mayor also laid a wreath at the Oklahoma City National Memorial where Rivers is also honored. Hinschberger said, "This is a big thanks for the US Army and all the soldiers who died for my freedom and the freedom of my country."

The Ruben Rivers Highway traverses Tecumseh, Oklahoma.

From the Forest to the Battlefield

A video, *Honor Deferred*, produced for the History Channel, told the stories of seven black Americans who had received the Medal of Honor from President Clinton on January 13, 1997.

The US Army Air Defenders of the 10th US Army Air and Missile Defenders honored Rivers at his burial site, the Lorraine American Cemetery at Saint-Avold, France, on February 27, 2014.

Rivers was an inductee into the Oklahoma History Center.

The US Army Central (Patton's 3rd Army in World War II) honored Rivers with a cake-cutting ceremony on January 15, 2011. In this ceremony, Rivers joined Patton's Hall of Heroes.

Rivers's name was included at the African-American Medal of Honor Recipients Memorial in Brandywine Park, Wilmington, Delaware, in 1997.

The city of El Paso established a Staff Sergeant Rivers Court in his honor.

On August 24, 2012, a barracks was named for Rivers at Fort Benning, Georgia.

On February 13, 1997, the US Armor School at Fort Knox, Kentucky, dedicated the Gaffey II Auditorium of Gaffey Hall in the memory of Ruben Rivers.

BURIAL SITE

Sergeant Rivers's grave is at the Lorraine American Cemetery, Saint-Avold, Moselle, France.

BIBLIOGRAPHY

LUCIAN ADAMS

"Adams, Lucian." Texas State Historical Association. www.tshaonline.org

Ancestry. Com. www.ancestry.com

CCC Record. National Archives. St. Louis, Missouri.

Goldstein, Richard. "Lucian Adams, 80, Is Dead." *The New York Times*. April 4, 2003.

King, Kevin. "Port Arthur Hero, Veterans To Be Honored At Luther Theater." *The Examiner*. October 18, 2013.

"Lucian Adams." World Public Library. www.worldlibrary.org

"Lucian Adams In Memorium." *San Diego Union-Tribune*. April 5, 2003.

"Notable People: Lucian Adams." Museum Of The Gulf Coast. www.museumofthegulfcoast.org

Oliver, Myrna. "Lucian Adams, 80, Cited For World War II Bravery." *Los Angeles Times*. April 7, 2003.

US Army Press Release.

US Census Records. 1940.

YouTube. Lucian Adams, Medal Of Honor, World War II. www.youtube.com

Wikipedia. www.wikipedia.org

RICHARD B. ANDERSON

Ancestry.Com. www.ancestry.com

CCC Record. National Archives. St. Louis, Missouri.

Denfeld, Duane C., Ph.D. "Richard B. Anderson Receives Medal Of Honor." May 5, 2015. www.historylink.org

Gottlieb, Paul. "TRIBUTE: Medal Of Honor Heroes of The North Olympic Peninsula." *Peninsula Daily News*. October 10, 2000.

Gottlieb, Paul. "Port Angeles Federal Building Gets A Hero's Name." *Peninsula Daily News*. September 2, 2008.

"Learn and Talk About Richard B. Anderson." March 4, 2014. www.digplanet.com

"Namur: Penetrating The Outer Ring." The Fighting Fourth: Division History. *www.fightingfourth.com*

"Pfc. Richard Beatty Anderson." Together We Served. https://marines.togetherweserved.com

"Port Angeles Federal Building Named The Richard B. Anderson." *Seattle-Post Intelligencer*. Digitalreporter. September 3, 2003.

"Port Angeles Memorial Salutes Marine Hero Of World War II Combat." *Seattle-Intelligencer*. Associated Press. May 27, 2001.

"Richard B. Anderson." The Marine Corps Medal Of Honor Recipients. www.marinemedals.com

"Richard B. Anderson." *Naval History And Command*. September 29, 2005.

Schwartz, Jeremy. "Terry Roth, Veterans Advocate, Former Marine, Dies In Port Angeles At 72." *Peninsula Daily News.* March 5, 2014.

US Census Records. 1940.

Wikipedia. www.wikipedia.org

THOMAS A. BAKER

Ancestry.com. www.ancestry.com

"Banzai At Battle Of Saipan." www.spotlight.fold.3

Block, Gordon. "Fort Drum Buildings Renamed." *Watertown Times*. September 23, 2014.

Crowe, Kenneth II. "New Honors For War Heroes." *Times Union,* Albany, New York. November 6, 2009.

CCC Record. National Archives. St. Louis, Missouri.

Chaisson, Patrick. Major, New York National Guard. "Obie's Last Stand: A Study Of Leadership Under Fire."

"Ten Astounding Actions Winning The Medal Of Honor." www.listverse.com. February 19, 2010.

US Census Records. 1940.

US Army Enlistment Record.

US Army Press Release.

Wikipedia. www.wikipedia.org

VAN T. BARFOOT

Ancestry. Com. www.ancestry.com

CCC Record. National Archives.St. Louis, Missouri.

"Col. Van Barfoot Medal of Honor Recipient Dies At 92." *Medal of Honor News.* March 5, 2012.

Elkins, Chris. "Fight For Old Glory Brings Memories For Miss Veteran." *Northeast MS Daily Journal,* Tupelo, Mississippi. December 11, 2009.

Goldstein, Richard. "Van T. Barfoot, Medal of Honor Recipient, Dies At 92." The *New York Times.* March 4, 2012.

Mooradanian, Helen. "Heroes In Our Midst: Col. Van T. Barfoot." *The Valley Patriot,* North Andover, Massachusetts. August 2011.

Robertson, Ellen. "Col. Van Barfoot, Medal Of Honor Recipient, Dies at 92." *Richmond Times Dispatch.* March 3, 2012.

Shapiro, T. Rees. "Van T. Barfoot, Va. Medal Of Honor Recipient Who Won Fight To Fly Flag In Front Yard Dies At 92." *The Washington Post.* March 5, 2012.

US Army Press Release. 1944.

WDAM, Moselle, Mississippi. "Van T. Barfoot Medal of Honor Highway Named." December 9, 2009.

Wikipedia. www.wikipedia.org

CARLTON BARRETT

Ambrose, Stephen E. *D-Day, June 6, 1944: The Climatic Battle Of World War II.* Simon & Schuster. 1994.

Ancestry.Com. www.ancestry.com

CCC Record. National Archives. St. Louis, Missouri.

Fuller, Samuel. *The Big Red One.* Bantam Press. 1980.

"Hell Is A Very Small Place." Lost In America blog. June 6, 2014. www.lostinamericablogspot.com

McManus, John C. *The Dead And Those About To Die: D-Day: The Big Red One At Omaha Beach.* Penguin Publishing Group. Reprint 2015.

US Army Press Release.

US Census Records. 1920. 1930. 1940.

Wikipedia. www.wikipedia.org

STANLEY BENDER

Ancestry.Com. www.ancestry.com

Ball, Harry. *The Cumberland News.* "W.Va Opens Second Link of Turnpike." November 9, 1954.

Brown, Judith. "Sgt. Stanley Bender." *The Frontline.* August 20, 2009.

CCC Record. National Archives. St. Louis, Missouri.

Donnelly, Shirley. "Stanley Bender's Medal of Honor Award." *Beckley Post-Herald.* December 24, 1962.

Knight, Wallace. *Charleston Daily Mail.* "Dedication Of West Virginia Turnpike." November 9, 1954.

Leonard, Dick. "War Shaped Fate Of State Heroes." *The Gazette Mall.* December 3, 1961.

Porterfield, Mannix. "Death of a Hero." *The Register Herald.* June 24, 1994.

 Beckley Post-Herald. "Ten To Retire From VA Staff." October 30, 1969.

The Raleigh Register. "Stanley Bender To Retire." October 30, 1969.

Tribe, Henry Franklin. "Stanley Bender." *The West Virginia Encyclopedia.* April 23, 2013. www.wvaencyclopedia.org

US Army Press Release.

US Census Records. 1920. 1930. 1940.

Wikipedia. www.wikipedia.org

ORVILLE E. BLOCH

Ancestry.Com. www.ancestry.com

Beverly M. Asplund Bloch (1921 - 2014) Obituary. www.findagrave.com

CCC Record. National Archives. St. Louis, Missouri.

Denfeld, Duane C., PhD. "Orville Bloch Receives Medal of Honor On February 6, 1945." October 21, 2014. www.historylink.org

Eriksmoen, Curt. "Medal of Honor Winner From ND." *Bismarck Tribune.* February 24, 2013.

"Evergreen Washelli Remembers Colonel Orville Emil Bloch." Evergreen Washelli Funeral Services. May 30, 1983.

"Ex-Streeter Resident To Be Honored At NDSU Ceremony." *Fargo Forum.* October 10, 1965.

"Medal of Honor Society Elects Officers." *New York Times.* October 28, 1962.
"Streeter Man Is Lone Medal of Honor Winner In The Last War." *Bismarck Tribune.* November 1, 1948.
US Army Enlistment Record.
US Census Records. 1920. 1930. 1940.
Wikipedia. www.wikipedia.org

HERBERT H. BURR
Ancestry.Com. www.ancestry.com
CCC Record. National Archives. St. Louis, Missouri.
Reichley, John. "Herbert Hoover Burr, Hero." *Leavenworth Times.* February 18, 1990.
Slater, Frederick. "Why Not Honor A Medal of Honor Veteran?" *Saint Joseph News-Press.* January 25, 1990.
"The 41st Tank Battalion History. 11th Armored Division." www.11tharmoreddivision.com/history/41st_Tank_History.html
US Army Press Release.
US Census Records. 1930. 1940.
Wikipedia. www.wikipedia.org

DARRELL S. COLE
Ancestry.Com. www.ancestry.com
CCC Record. National Archives. St. Louis, Missouri.
"Sergeant Darrell Cole, USMCR (1920 -1945)." Naval History and Heritage Command. www.history.navy.mil
Stark, Al. "A Young Man From Missouri Passed Our Way." *Detroit News.* July 1995.
Stars and Stripes Museum/Library. Bloomfield, Missouri. Unpublished materials.
Trokey, Travis. Librarian, Farmington Public Library, Farmington, Missouri. Unpublished materials.
Vachon, Duane A., PhD. "Bugler To Batteler: The Fighting Field Musician." *Hawaii Reporter.* February 23, 2013.
Wikipedia. www.wikipedia.org

WILLIAM CRAWFORD
Ancestry.Com. www.ancestry.com
CCC Record. National Archives. St. Louis, Missouri.
Interview with Doug Turner, Webmaster. Home Of Heroes. June 2015.
"Medal of Honor Recipient William Crawford Dies At 81." *The Pueblo Chieftain.* March 16, 2000.
Moschgat, James. "Leadership And The Janitor." *On Patrol.* Fall 2010.
"Pueblo War Hero Dies." *Rocky Mountain News.* March 17, 2000.
"Retired Master Sergeant William Crawford Dead." *Colorado Springs Gazette.* March 19, 2000.
"The President And The Janitor." Home of Heroes. www.homeofheroes.com
US Army Press Release.
US Census Records. 1920. 1930. 1940.
Wikipedia. www.wikipedia.org

RUDOLPH B. DAVILA
Ancestry.Com. www.ancestry.com
CCC Record. National Archives. St. Louis, Missouri.
California Legislative Information. Senate Concurrent Resolution #107. September 7, 2002.
Freudensprung, Amanda. "Medal of Honor: Rudolph Davila." *Waco Tribune.* March 25, 2012. www.wacotrib.com
Goldstein, Richard. "Rudolph Davila, 85, Recipient of Highest Award For Valor." *The New York Times.* February 11, 2002.
McLellan, Dennis. "Rudolph B. Davila, 85, Given Medal of Honor 56 Years After Feat." *Los Angeles Times.* February 7, 2002.
Patterson, Robert. "Rudolph Davila, Second Lieutenant, US Army." February 22, 2002. www.arlingtoncemetery.net
"Rudolph B. Davila: Vista, California." Gen Forum and Family History Search. March 7, 2002. www.geneology.com
Stout, David. "21 Asian-Americans Receive The Medal of Honor." *The New York Times.* March 14, 2000.
White House Press Release. Medal of Honor Recipients. June 21, 2000.
Wikipedia. www.wikipedia.org
YouTube. Rudolph Davila, Medal of Honor, World War II. www.youtube.com

RUSSELL E. DUNHAM
CCC Record. National Archives. St. Louis, Missouri.
Ellebracht, Mark. "Highways To Be Renamed For Dunham." *Alton Daily News.* June 6, 2012.
Holly , Joe. "Russell Dunham, 89, Awarded Medal Of Honor In World War II." Obituary. *The Washington Post.* April 8, 2009.
Illinois GenWeb. Russell Dunham, World War II, Medal Of Honor Winner. www.illinoisgenweb.org
Leighty, George. *Alton Evening Telegraph.* May 23, 1959.
Trap Shooting Forum. www.trapshooters.com
Wikipedia. www.wikipedia.org
Wilson, D. Ray. *Episode on Hill 616.* Crossroads Communications, Inc. 1981.
YouTube. Russell Dunham, Medal of Honor, World War II. www.youtube.com

JOHN W. DUTKO
Ancestry.Com. www.ancestry.com
Articles from *Indiana Evening Gazette.* 1935 - 2000.
Breuer, William Jr. *Agony At Anzio.* Zeus Publishing Company. 1990.
CCC Record. National Archives. St. Louis, Missouri.
Interviews with Wallace McGaughey and Wallace McGaughey Jr., brother-in-law and nephew respectively of John W. Dutko by
        Michael Schultz. October 25, 2014.
Mary Leidel. "Letter To Editor." *Lima Daily News.* November 11, 2007.
Newspaper articles. Riverside Public Library. Riverside, New Jersey.
O'Pake, Michael J. "Congressional Medal Of Honor." Unpublished paper. September 1995.
"What Price Freedom?" Unpublished article from the Dutko family.
US Army Press Release.
"War Hero Buried In New Jersey." *Warren Times Mirror.* August 14, 1948.
Wikipedia. www.wikipedia.org

GERALD L. ENDL
Ancestry.Com. www.ancestry.com
Anna Marie Kirchif Obituary. Schneider Funeral Home. Janesville, Wisconsin. July 28, 2007.
CCC Record. National Archives. St. Louis, Missouri.
"Medal of Honor Day Observed." VFW Wisconsin.
Statz, Lydia. "Endl's Medal of Honor Part of Museum Exhibit." *Daily Jefferson County Union.* November 14, 2013.
"Wisconsin Hero Honored." *Ironwood Daily Globe.* March 28, 1945.
US Army Press Release.
US Census Records. 1920. 1930. 1940.
Wikipedia. www.wikipedia.org

HAROLD A.GARMAN
Ancestry.Com. www.ancestry.com
CCC Records. National Archives. St. Louis, Missouri.
Interview of Steve Garman, Harold Garman's son, by Edward Slagle. July 2015.
New York Times. "Saved Four Wounded in Boat." April 7, 1945.
The Daily Chronicle. "Army Parade Is Tomorrow." April 5, 1946.
The Pentagraph. "Congressional Medal Winner Tells Story." October 23, 1945.
The Pentagraph. "President's Guest." April 4, 1946.
US Army Press Release.
US Census Records. 1920. 1930. 1940.
Wikipedia. www.wikipedia.org.

From the Forest to the Battlefield

HENRY GURKE
CCC Record. National Archives. St. Louis, Missouri.
Horgan, Purdy. "Henry Gorki." *The Cavalier Chronicle.* 2002.
Mulcher, T. "The CCC In Grand Forks County." Unpublished seminar paper.
Robinson, Nate. "Sioux City Veterans Honor Those Who Made Ultimate Sacrifice." *Sioux City Journal.* May 28, 2012.
"Sacrifice Of Life For A Pal Wins Congressional Medal Of Honor." *Stars and Stripes.* May 23, 1944.
US Census Records. 1940.
US Marine Corps Records.
Welcome To The USS Gurke DD-783. www.ussgurke.org
Wikipedia. www.wikipedia.org

OWEN F. P. HAMMERBERG
Ancestry. Com. www.ancestry.com
Berto, Roy, Commander of VFW Post #5966. "Veterans News." *Menominee County Journal.* April 8, 2004.
Camp Skokie Valley. https://skokielagoons.omeka.net
CCC Record. National Archives. St. Louis, Missouri.
Cornebise, Alfred Emile. *CCC Chronicles: Camp Newspapers of the Civilian Conservation Corps, 1933 - 1942.* McFarland. 2004.
Ebsch, Larry. "Former Resident Received Medal of Honor." *Bye Lines.* April 26, 2004.
Salmond, John. *The Civilian Conservation Corps, 1933 - 1942. A New Deal Case Study,.* Duke University Press. 1967.
Wikipedia. www.wikipedia.org

ROY W. HARMON
Ancestry.Com. www.ancestry.com
CCC Record. National Archives. St. Louis, Missouri.
"Sergeant Roy W. Harmon." Their Finest Hour Blog & Show. July 12, 2014. www.theirfinesthour.net
Scott, Richard and Scott Thompson. "Students Honoring War Hero." December 4, 2014.
US Army Press Release.
US Census Records. 1930. 1940.
Wikipedia. www.wikipedia.org

JAMES L. HARRIS
Ancestry.Com. www.ancestry.com
CCC Record. National Archives. St. Louis, Missouri.
Barrett, Michael L. "Medal Of Honor: James Harris." *Waco Tribune.* August 28, 2011.
Barrett, Roy Lee. "The Story Of James L. Harris." Unpublished paper. 1970.
"James Harris: Military History." Heart of Texas Tales. www.heartoftexastales.com.
"James Harris." Texas State Historical Association. www.tshaonline.org
Taggart, Donald. Editor. *The History Of The 756th Tank Battalion.* Battery Press. 1987.
US Army Press Release.
US Census Records. 1920. 1930. 1940.
Wikipedia. www.wikipedia.org

LEROY JOHNSON
Ancestry.Com. www.ancestry.com
CCC Records. National Archives. St. Louis, Missouri.
Iles, Curt and Dede. "A Memorial Day For The Ages: 24,055 Extra Days Of Life." *Creekbank Stories.* May 27, 2012. www.creekbank.net
US Army Press Release.
US Draft Registration Card.
Unpublished materials from Edward Slagle. February 26, 2015.
Wikipedia. www.wikipedia.org

From the Forest to the Battlefield

GEORGE D. KEATHLEY

Ancestry.Com. www.ancestry.com
CCC Record. National Archives. St. Louis, Missouri.
Cameron University Press Release. "Cameron University Department Of Military Science Named For Medal Of Honor Winner."
    March 25, 2010. www.army.mil
"Custer Division. The 85th Infantry Division In World War II." user.pa.net/-cjheiser
Department of Agriculture Records.
Dethloff, Henry C. and Adams, John A. *Texas Aggies Go To War: In The Service Of Their Country.* Texas A & M University Press.
    2006.
Dictionary of American Naval Fighting Ships. DANFS Online. www.hazegray.org
S/Sgt George D. Keathley. Class of 1937. www.myaggienation.com
S/Sgt. George D. Keathley. Together We Served. https://army.togetherweserved.com
Tribe, Henry Franklin. "Keathley, George Dennis." Texas State Historical Association. www.tshaonline.org
US Army Press Release.
Wikipedia. www.wikipedia.org
Woodall, James R. *Texas Aggie Medals Of Honor.* Texas A & M University Press. 2010.
www.wikipedia.org

ANTHONY L. KROTIAK

Ancestry.Com. www.ancestry.com
CCC Record. National Archives. St. Louis, Missouri.
"Parents Gets Hero's Honor Medal." *Chicago Tribune.* February 22, 1946.
US Army Enlistment Record.
US Army Press Release.
US Headstones Application.
Wikipedia. www.wikipedia.org

JAMES M. LOGAN

Ancestry.Com. www.ancestry.com
Buckman, Robert. "Modest Rancher Remembers." *Houston Post.* September 9, 1993.
Buckman, Robert. "MOH Recipient Recalls The Battle of Salerno." *War Dispatch* " Spring 1994.
CCC Record. National Archives. St. Louis, Missouri.
Goldstein, Richard. "James Logan Dead At 78." The *New York Times.* October 14, 1999.
Lynch, Clint and John Walker. "Logan, James Marion (1920-1999)." Texas State Historical Association. www.tshaonline.org
Ramey, Michael. "A Quiet Hero." *Longview News-Journal.* September 9, 1993.
Scribner, John C. L. "James M. Logan." Texas Military Forces Museum. www.texasmilitaryforcesmuseum.org
US Census Records. 1920. 1930.
US War Department. "Medal Of Honor Awarded Infantryman." July 14, 1944.
Wikipedia. www.wikipedia.org

THOMAS E. McCALL

Ancestry.Com. www.ancestry.com
CCC Record. National Archives. St. Louis, Missouri.
"Biography of Robert L. Call, Camp Tecumseh, Lafayette, Indiana." James F. Justin Museum.
    www.justinmuseum.com/oralbio/callrbio.html
"Heroic Soldier Dies In River." *Bridgeport Post.* September 21, 1965.
Kriebel, Bob. "Medal Of Honor Recipient A Hero To The End." *Journal and Courier.* August 4, 2004.
Wikipedia. www.wikipedia.org

LLOYD G. McCARTER

Ancestry.Com. www.ancestry.com

CCC Record. National Archives. St. Louis, Missouri.

Calhoun, Bill. The 503rd P.R.C.T. Heritage Battalion Online. "The Best Warrior I Ever Knew."
        http://corregidor.org/heritage_battalion/moh/mccarter_calhoun.html

Telephone interview with Priscilla Berry of St. Maries, Idaho, by Michael Schultz. June 2015.

Telephone interview with Jack Botts of St. Maries, Idaho, by Michael Schultz. June 2015.

Telephone interview with Ida McCarter of St. Maries, Idaho, by Michael Schultz. June 2015.

Telephone interview with Jack Shuman of St. Maries, Idaho, by Michael Schultz. June 2015.

US Army Press Release.

US Census Records. 1920. 1930. 1940.

Wikipedia. www.wikipedia.org

VERNON McGARITY

Ancestry.Com. www.ancestry.com

Branston, John. "Taps For A Memphian Awarded The Medal Of Honor." *The Memphis Flyer.* May 26, 2013.

CCC Record. National Archives. St. Louis, Missouri.

Freudensprung, Amanda. "Medal Of Honor: Vernon McGarity." *Waco Tribune.* June 28, 2013.

Martin, Douglas S. "Vernon McGarity, War Hero, Dies." The *New York Times.* May 23, 2013.

"Sgt. McGarity Missing." *Stewart County Times. January 25, 1945.*

"Sgt. McGarity A War Prisoner." *Stewart County Times.* April 12, 1945.

"Sgt. McGarity Is Liberated." *Stewart County Times.* June 6, 1945.

"Two Of Last Living Medal Of Honor Recipients." *Scripps Howard News Service.* July 9, 2014.

US Army Press Release.

Wikipedia. www.wikipedia.org

TROY A. McGILL

Ancestry.Com. www.ancestry.com

CCC Record. National Archives. St. Louis, Missouri.

Shearer John. "Local Film Producer's Show Airs Saturday, Sunday." The Tennesseans: A Voluntary Legacy.
        News Sentinel, Knoxville, Tennessee. July 2, 2015.

US Army Press Release.

US Army Enlistment Record.

US Census Records. 1920. 1930. 1940.

WBIR. Television Station, Knoxville, Tennessee. Profiles In Courage: Troy McGill. September 2014. www.wbir.com

Wikipedia. www.wikipedia.org

MANUEL V. MENDOZA

Ancestry.Com. www.ancestry.com

"Arizona Veteran Among 24 To Receive Medal Of Honor." *The Arizona Republic.* February 21, 2014.

Fletcher, Howard, Capital Media Services. *East Valley Tribune.* "Family Of Mesa Veteran Receives Belated Medal Of Honor
        During White House Ceremony." March 23, 2014.

Gross, L. C. "Arizona Kid From Miami To Receive Medal Of Honor, March 18th." *Globe Miami Times.* March 9, 2014.

Telephone Interview with Sylvia Nandin, Manual Mendoza's daughter, by Michael Schultz. June 2015.

Jeong, Yihyun."World War II Vet 'Arizona Kid' Posthumously Awarded The Medal Of Honor." *The Arizona Republic.*
        March 19, 2014.

Lake, Ted. "Mendoza's Wife To Accept Medal Of Honor From President Obama." *Arizona Silver Belt.* March 10, 2014.

"Soldier Spotlight: Master Sergeant Manuel V. Mendoza." *The Stafford Voice.* March 9, 2014.

US Army Press Release.

US Census Records. 1930. 1940.

US Senate Press Release. Senator John McClain.

Wikipedia. www.wikipedia.org

JOSEPH E. MULLER

Ancestry. Com. www.ancestry.com

Burke, Mike. "Medal Gets Place Of Honor." The *Republican.* November 20, 1999.

CCC Record. National Archives. St. Louis, Missouri.

"Impressive Program." Holyoke Transcript-Telegram. July 7, 1947.

Jackowski, Jim. "Inside The Rail." *Holyoke Daily Sun.* November 21, 1999.

Ours To Hold It High: The History of the 77th Infantry Division in World War II By Men Who Were There. Infantry Journal Press. 1947.

Passa, Meridith. "The Hero Behind The Muller Bridge." *Holyoke Daily Sun.* February 8, 1996.

Pudio, Janet E. "A New Bridge". *Holyoke Transcript -Telegram.* November 16, 1955.

Scholfield, Lois. "People." *Holyoke Transcript-Telegram.* July 28, 1965.

Sgt . Joseph E. Muller. Naval History And Heritage Command. www.history.navy.mil

Statement Of Military Service. Joseph E. Muller. September 26, 1956.

US Army Records.

West, Charles O., et al. *Second To None! The Story of the 305th Infantry Division in World War II.* Infantry Journal Press. 1949.

Wikipedia. www.wikipedia.org

RUBEN RIVERS

Ancestry.Com. www.ancestry.com

"Black History Month: Ruben Rivers." *Global Domination Through Applied Inactivity.* 2011. www.mojosteve.blogspot.com

CCC Record. National Archives. St. Louis, Missouri.

Galloway, Joseph, et al. "50 Years Late For Seven Black Heroes." *U.S. News.* May 6, 1996.

Haskew, Michael E. " The World War II: July 1997 From The Editor." August 19, 1997. www.historynet.com

Jagord, Steven. "All Black Unit To Be Featured." *Clarence Bee.* February 18, 2015.

McDonald, Leon L. Jr. "Ruben Rivers." USGenNet. www.usgennet.org

Metcalf, Darryl. "Above And Beyond." Air Force Libraries. www.myairforcelife.com

Neville, John. "761st Tank Battalion." *The Turret.* 2007.

Sasser, Charles W. " 761st Tank Battalion: Patton's Panthers Would Not Quit." *The History Reader.* July 12, 2011.

US Census Records. 1930.

Wikipedia. www.wikipedia.org

Williams, Rudi. "Overdue Honors." *Soldiers.* March 1997.

www.wikipedia.org

WILLIAM R. SHOCKLEY

Ancestry.Com. www.ancestry.com

CCC Record. National Archives. St. Louis, Missouri.

"Congressional Medal Of Honor To Be Presented To Mother Of Pfc. W. R. Shockley Today." *The Selma Irrigator.* November 1, 1945.

"Death Of Two Selma Soldiers On Luzon Told." *The Selma Irrigator.* April 26, 1945.

Derks, Tracy L. "The U.S. 32nd Division Battle To Control The Villa Verde Trail." July 12, 2006. www.historynet.com.

US Army Press Release.

US Census Records. 1930.

Wikipedia. www.wikipedia.org

LUTHER SKAGGS JR.

CCC Record. National Archives. St. Louis, Missouri.

Coleman, Poucher. "'Tough Little Guy' Lost Leg But Fought On." *The Courier- Journal.* June 26, 1945.

Cornebise, Alfred Emile. *CCC Chronicles: Camp Newsletters of the Civilian Conservation Corps, 1933 - 1942.* McFarland. 2004.

John F. Kennedy Presidential Library and Museum. www.jfklibrary.org

"Luther Skaggs Jr." Congressional Medal Of Honor Society. www.cmhs.org

O'Brien, Cyril J. *Liberation: Marines In The Recapture Of Guam.* Marine Corps Historical Center pamphlet. 1994.

Stinnett, Chuck. "Medal Of Honor Recipients Honored With Highway Designation." *The Courier-Journal.* August 6, 2014.

From the Forest to the Battlefield

Telephone interview with Jean Skaggs of Utica, Kentucky, by Martha Smith. April, 12, 2016.
Telephone interview with Julie Skaggs by Martha Smith. April 19, 2016.
The Henderson War Memorial Foundation. www.hendersonwarmemorial.org
Vachon, Duane A., PhD. "'Tough Little Guy' - Cpl Luther Skaggs Jr., USMCR (1923-1976)." *Hawaii Reporter.* March 21, 2011.
Wikipedia. www.wikipedia.org

JUNIOR JAMES SPURRIER
Ancestry.Com. www.ancestry.com
Archer, Bill. "Museum Retrieving Heroic Legacy From Shadows Of Soldier's Post-War Turmoil." *Bluefield Daily Telegraph.*
    June 25, 2006.
Archer, Bill. "Museum Immortalizes Service Of Staff Sgt. Junior Spurrier." *Bluefield Daily Telegraph.* July 3, 2006.
Archer, Bill. "As A Soldier Spurrier Did All That Was Asked." *Bluefield Daily Telegraph.* April 24, 2011.
Archer, Bill. "Staff Sgt. Spurrier's Medal Of Honor Returning To Mercer." *Bluefield Daily Telegraph.* November 27, 2011.
"Attack! The Story Of The 35th Infantry Division." *Stars and Stripes.* Paris. 1944 - 1945. www.lonesentry.com
Baltimore News. "Smacked But She Still Loves Him" December 13, 1955.
"Beshear Unveils Medal Of Honor Plaque." *Kentucky New Era,* Hopkinsville, Kentucky. March 15, 2012.
CCC Record. National Archives. St. Louis, Missouri.
Cannon, Jimmy. "Achain Produces A Hero." *Stars and Stripes.* December 12, 1944.
"James I. (Junior) Spurrier, Jr., CMOH, Staff Sergeant, Company G, 134th Infantry Regiment." Wehrmacht Awards.
    www.wehrmacht-awards.com
LaPann, Paul. "Vienna Woman Attends Brother's Medal Of Honor Ceremony." *News and Sentinel,* Parkersburg, West Virginia.
    December 8, 2011.
Lemke, Bob. "Minor Leaguer Spurrier Won Medal Of Honor." Bob Lemke blog. April 12, 2014. www.boblemkeblogspot.com
Miami News. "One Man Army Sentenced To Jail." December 6, 1961.
New York Times. "Freed Medal of Honor Winner Leaves Prison." December 26, 1969.
Record Argus. Greenville, Pennsylvania. "Jail Time Faced By Medal of Honor Winner." December 9, 1955.
US Army Press Release.
US Census Records. 1920. 1930. 1940.
Wikipedia. www.wikipedia.org

TONY STEIN
Ancestry.Com. wwwancestry.com
CCC Record. National Archives. St. Louis, Missouri.
Facebook. Rosehill Rangers Post. February 11, 2017.
Holman, Jake Jr. "A Bullet Chewing Frankenstein Of A Medal Of Honor Recipient." Dieselpunks. June 15, 2011.
    www.dieselpunks.com
Huffman, Dale. "Kiser Honors Its Own." *Dayton Daily News.* April 7, 2009.
Huffman, Dale. "Old North Dayton Festival Honors World War II Hero." *Dayton Daily News.* July 5, 2009.
Matthews, Alan R. "Iwo Jima." *Mission: History.* February 5, 2001. www.navalorder.org
Page, Doug. "Six Inducted Into Walk Of Fame." *Dayton Daily News.* July 11, 2011.
Terrance, Kyle. "Tony Stein And The Stinger." *Leatherneck.* March 6, 2007.
"The Stein Workout." *Military Times.* November 15, 2009.
"Tony Stein And The Stinger." The *Drawn Cutlass* blog. October 14, 2008. www.thedrawncutlassblogspot.com
Vachon, Duane A., PhD. "A Creative Marine." *Hawaii Reporter.* February 3, 2013.
Wikipedia. wikipedia.org

WILSON D. WATSON
Ancestry.Com. www.ancestry.com
CCC Record. National Archives. St. Louis, Missouri.
"Deployments. 2nd. Battalion. 9th Marine Regiment." www.2ndbattalion9thmarines.org
Hallas, James. *Uncommon Valor At Iwo Jima.* Stackpole Books. July 2016.
Hicks, Linda. "Veterans Honored At Hall Of Fame Ceremony." November 11, 2011. www.thecabin.net

Johnson County Graphic. Clarksville, Arkansas. "Wilson Watson Obituary." December 21, 1994.
Milwaukee Journal. "Medal Of Honor Holder Charged With Desertion." February 14. 1963.
Randall, Mark. "Farm Boy From Earle." *Evening Times.* Marion, Arkansas. November 11, 2011.
Remarks at the presentation of the Medal of Honor. Harry S. Truman Presidential Library. October 1945.
St. Petersburg Times. "Hometown Hero In Jail." February 14. 1963.
The Hero Among Us." *World War II* magazine. May 2005.
Tonawanda News. "Medal Of Honor Hero Charged With Desertion." February 15, 1963."
US Census Records. 1930.
US Marine Corps Enlistment Records.
Wikipedia. www.wikipedia.org

WALTER C. WETZEL

Ancestry.Com. www.ancestry.com
Bozich, Stanley. *Michigan's Own: The Medal Of Honor, Civil War To Vietnam.* Polar Bear Publishing Company. 1987.
CCC Record. National Archives. St. Louis, Missouri.
Cousins, Fred. "Hero's Wife Gets Top Award." *Detroit Free Press.* February 27, 1945.
Jackson, Lisa. "Macomb Honors War Hero." *Detroit News.* February 27, 1945.
Schabath, Gene. "Macomb To Salute County's Only Medal Of Honor Winner." *Detroit News.* November 11, 1998.
Schabath, Gene. "New Monument To Honor Macomb County War Hero." *Detroit News.* May 13, 1999.
US Army Press Release.
Wikipedia. www.wikipedia.org

HERSHEL W. WILLIAMS

Ancestry.Com. www.ancestry.com
Arrington, Shane. "Medal Of Honor Wall Of Memory Unveiled At VAMC." *Times Herald-Dispatch.* November 13, 2014.
Bartel, Bill. "Aboard The Iwo Jima, Hero Recalls Epic Battle." *The Virginian Pilot.* February 24, 2011.
Berbera, Marie. "Iwo Jima Survivors Share Legacy." United States Army website. February 20, 2014. www.army.mil
Belisle, Richard. "W. Va. Medal Of Honor Recipient Visits Martinsburg, VA." *Herald -Mail.* January 30, 2014.
Burke, Matthew M. "Marines Old And New Return To Iwo Jima." *Stars and Stripes.* March 22, 2015.
CCC Record. National Archives. St. Louis, Missouri.
Duran, Dee and Tess Maune. "Last Living Medal Of Honor Recipient From Iwo Jima Honored In Tulsa." News 9. April 27, 2013.
        www.news9.com
Gallagher, Emily. "Navy Ship To Be Named After Woody Williams." *Times West Virginian.* October 20, 2015.
Gamble, Oscar. "Medal Of Honor Recipients Gather At Plymouth Diner To Tout Fundraiser." *The Times Herald.* April 14, 2015.
Gromelski, Joe. "Medal Of Honor Recipients Goal: Tribute To Gold Star Families In All 50 States." *Stars and Stripes.*
        September 19, 2014.
Interview of Hershel WIlliams by Richard Bailey. January 2014.
Interviews of Hershel Williams. C-SPAN. November 16, 2006. October 1, 2014. www.C-SPAN.org
Karnath, Melissa, Sergeant. "Humble Farmer Now Legendary Marine." United States Marine Corps website. February 23, 2015.
        www.marines.mil
Kearne, Mindy. "Military Gold Star Families Honored." *Daily Sentinel.* November 3, 2014.
Mays, Mackenzie. "Woody Williams Celebrates His 90th, Launches Foundation To Support Gold Star Families."
        Charleston Gazette- Mail. October 1, 2013.
Medal of Honor Recipient Hershel "Woody" Williams interview. Pritzker Military Museum & Library. Podcast. January 24, 2008.
Petersen, Hans. "A Veteran Who Was On Iwo Jima 70 Years Ago Today." Veterans Health Administration. February 23, 2015.
www.va.gov/HEALTH
Smith, Charlotte Ferrell. "Ona Medal Of Honor Recipient Woody Williams Honored On Stamp." *Charleston Gazette- Mail.*
        November 10, 2013.
Talmadge, Eric. "US Veterans Return To Iwo Jima For 70th Anniversary." March 21, 2015. www.CNSNews.com
US Census Records. 1930. 1940.
Wikipedia. www.wikipedia.org

ALFRED L. WILSON

Ancestry.Com. www.ancestry.com
CCC Record. National Archives. St. Louis, Missouri.
McKinney, Carolyn. "Personal Memories of My Uncle, Alfred Wilson." 2015.
McKinney, Carolyn. *The Gentle Giant Of The 26th Division.* Headline Books, Inc. 1994.
US Census Records. 1930. 1940.
Wikipedia. www.wikipedia.org

HOMER L. WISE

Ancestry.Com. www.ancestry.com
CCC Record. National Archives. St. Louis, Missouri.
Carella, Angela. "Homer Wise Honored Governor Rell of Connecticut." *The Stamford Advocate.* May 1, 2008.
King, Kate. "World War II Hero To Be Honored At Stamford Memorial Day Event." *The Stamford Advocate.* May 23, 2013.
Morganteen, Jeff. "Homer Wise Honored Rell of Connecticut." *The Stamford Advocate.* November 17, 2009.
Russell, Don. "Homer Lee Wise: Truly A Man Of Honor." *The Stamford Advocate.* September 21, 2008.
The Homer L. Wise Memorial Committee. www.sgthomerlwisememorial.org
US Census Records. 1930.
US Army Press Release. November 1944.
Wikipedia. www.wikipedia.org

FRANK P. WITEK

Ancestry.Com. www.ancestry.com
CCC Record. National Archives. St. Louis, Missouri.
"Frank Witek." *Semper Fi.* January 24, 2012.
"Local TV Program Honors Frank Witek." September 19, 2013.
"Marines Name Ball Field For Chicago Hero." *Chicago Tribune.* December 24, 1944.
US Census Records. 1920. 1920. 1940.
"US Marine And Medal Of Honor Recipient's Plaques Worth $10,000 Stolen." *Medal Of Honor News.* November 10, 2011.
Wikipedia. www.wikipedia.org

Made in the USA
Middletown, DE
08 July 2017